The Mantle of Maturity

SUNY Series in Medical Anthropology
Setha M. Low, Editor

The Mantle of Maturity

A History of Ideas
About Character Development

Christie W. Kiefer

State University of New York Press

Credits

PAGES 96-97   *From Primitive Man as Philosopher* by Paul Radin,
               © copyright Dover Publications. Reprinted by
               permission of the publisher.

PAGES 163-164 From *Harmonium* by Wallace Stevens, © copyright
               1923, 1951 by Wallace Stevens. Reprinted by
               permission of Alfred A. Knopf, Inc.

Published by
State University of New York Press, Albany

© 1988   State University of New York

For information, address State University of New York Press, State
University Plaza, Albany, N.Y., 12246

Library of Congress Cataloging-in-Publication Data

Kiefer, Christie W.
    The mantle of maturity.

    (SUNY series in medical anthropology)
    Bibliography: p.
    Includes index.
    1. Maturation (Psychology)—Philosophy—History.
2. Character—History. 3. Developmental psychology.
I. Title. II. Series.
BF710.K53 1988   155.2'5   87-33602
ISBN 0-88706-821-9
ISBN 0-88706-822-7 (pbk.)

10 9 8 7 6 5 4 3 2 1

For Else

Contents

PART III: STUDIES IN SELF-CONSCIOUS PSYCHOLOGY

Foreword

Ideas about maturity touch upon a wide range of human interests, including religion, art, and psychotherapy. I hope what I have to say about the subject will interest many people whose work has little to do with academic psychology. It should, because this book is meant to serve as a general introduction to the discipline of human development and, therefore, to make sense to readers with little experience in the field.

A problem one faces in studying the development of character is the great range and volume of writing, ancient and modern, that is relevant. To become proficient, one needs to specialize in some part of this study; but one must do so without losing sight of the relation of that part to the field as a whole.

For many years I have taught introductory courses in this field in the graduate program in Human Development and Aging at the University of California, San Francisco. I have tried teaching it by following the usual list of topics one finds in general textbooks; that is, according to theoretical schools (structuralism, psychoanalysis, learning theory, humanistic perspectives) or problem areas (biological development, cognition and memory, social behavior, emotions, mental health) or life stages (childhood, adolescence, young adulthood, middle and old age); and I have tried teaching it as it is presented here, from a sociology-of-knowledge perspective. The latter has some benefits. If one wants a clear idea of a forest, there are advantages to looking at it from a distance, as well as to walking among the trees. The views from history and philosophy show

how ideas stand in relation to one another, and what their limits are. Further, knowledge is *for* something, and it is not always easy to tell by looking at a theory, particularly a psychological theory, what that something is. The uses of ideas are easier to see when one looks at the roles they have played in society—what the aims were of the people who proposed them, and how the ideas in turn affected institutions.

Given the size of the subject, a difficulty in presenting an overview is to select a sample of material that is at once coherent and diverse. I have tried to do this by following two principles: First, I have limited my discussion mostly to issues that are well known and widely debated among developmental psychologists. Occasionally I mention bodies of literature or philosophic viewpoints that are scarcely known in this field, but only to let their exclusion more clearly indicate the boundaries of the terrain I have elected to cover. For example, I have excluded works, even by well-known Western writers, whose roots lie deeply in Asian philosophy. The works of Carl Jung, for example, are scarcely mentioned. I have also tried to keep the discussion only on writers and works whose ideas I think have been seminal, not merely interesting. I am sure personal taste has played a part in such choice, but I hope not with the effect of serious historical distortion.

Second, I have outspokenly presented this history through the lens of a personal viewpoint, which I set forth in the first and last chapters. It is not an original view, but it is one that holds a minority position in academic psychology I believe. I hope this strategy will help to strengthen for readers their own philosophic leanings, pro or con. I would like this book to be taken not as an unbiased "definitive work," but as a polemic—as an example of how a student of human development can come to grips with the major ideas in the field, by way of his or her own beliefs, in a way that lends coherence to both the field and the beliefs. Of course I am neither a philosopher nor a historian. I believe the value of eclecticism and wide synthesis is great enough, and the task it sets is difficult enough, that any serious student of man should be willing to take moderate risks with history, rather than remain blind to the relevance of his or her own work to the big questions of life. I am confident others will correct my mistakes.

The structure of the book is largely dictated by its function as a teaching tool. Moral concepts of maturity are rarely discussed in courses on developmental psychology, but they are crucial for a broad understanding of the usual subject matter—theories of natural developmental process. I have therefore devoted part 1 to the history of moral ideas, and reserved the discussion of process for part 2. In part 3, there are four chapters that illustrate ways in which a historical view of development can be applied to the practice of developmental studies. I hope other students of the field are stimulated to apply this perspective to other problems.

The writing of this book required the collaboration of many. I would

xii   THE MANTLE OF MATURITY

especially like to thank Rosalie Robertston at The State University of New York Press, and the editors and reviewers who worked with her. Thanks also to Elise Boulding, John Ingham, Setha Low, Roger Walsh, and Bob Rubinstein for their encouragement, and to Brother William Short, S.T.D., and Father Paul Philibert, O.P. for their valuable help.

1. Introduction:
Maturity, Culture, and History

The Promise of a Science of Maturity

The sciences of man in the twentieth century have been derelict in the study of their own philosophic origins. A number of excellent books and essays have been written on the history of modern social and psychological observation and theory, and many contemporary scholars have warned us that there ought to be more such works. However, few social science students are systematically exposed to the philosophic origins of the ideas they are asked to learn. Today, the words Norbert Elias wrote fifty years ago still hold true: "In the present structure of scholarly research a sharp dividing line is generally drawn between the work of the historian and of the psychologist. Only Western people living at present appear in need of or accessible to psychological investigation" (Elias, [1939] 1982:282).

In order to advance our understanding of ourselves as human beings, it is vital that we make use of the long and worthy history of man's serious self-reflection; this book seeks to make a contribution to that end. My goal is to reconstruct the development of the idea of maturity in the Western world from preliterate times to the present, looking at the concept first as a moral ideal, then as a natural process. In this way I hope to show how extensively our modern concepts of maturity are rooted in past cultures, and how a knowledge of their roots helps us, both as social scientists and as moral individuals, to think clearly about it. This exercise can make our thinking about maturity and maturation more satisfying and beautiful in itself, and it can lead to better practical applications of that thinking.

The beauty of ideas is something that defies complete analysis, but there is no doubt that the aesthetics of science centers on the way in which the parts of our knowledge fit together to form large harmonious wholes (Heisenberg 1955). To know the origins of our ideas is both to enlarge the wholes of which they are parts, and to be able to shape them so they articulate better within the general frame of human knowledge. If I know how the invention of agriculture affected ideas of maturity, for example, I can see more clearly many points of articulation among important ideas whose relationship was formerly obscure to me. I can see how cities, occupational specialization, writing, and warfare entered into our thought about human nature and still play a role in our moral attitudes. The result of such discovery is a more satisfying understanding of any given set of ideas about maturity, because I can see that set as it nests among many other facets of my culture. I can also see more clearly the aesthetic results of any attempt to change the ideas.

With the help of historical consciousness, it is also easier to see similarities and differences among the many shifting viewpoints held by one's acquaintances. Historical study forces us to look for the roots of things, and in doing so we must distill the essential ideas from the ephemeral language in which they happen to be expressed. Plato's ideas on maturity contained certain distinct themes, such as respect for emotional understanding, that distinguish them from Aristotle's; this distinction is repeated again and again in the history of ethics. Knowledge of such things allows us to see more clearly the fundamental contradictions in our own science. The more thoroughly immersed we are in the details of the human sciences, the more difficult it is for us to see the basic structure of ideas and their historical interconnectedness. Useful as historicism is likely to be for the layman, the professional thinker needs it even more—and the veteran professional more than the novice.

Moving the question of *practicality*, we can see that this too is served by the wider integration of ideas that historical consciousness provides. Many of the problems of modern life result from the speed of technological and social change, and the resulting tension between beliefs and attitudes on one hand, and practical realities on the other. Historicism helps in several ways. By clarifying the basic structure and origins of our beliefs and attitudes, it allows us to view them more objectively. By showing the embeddedness of ideas and ideals in technology and social organization, it suggests some of the consequences that might follow contemplated changes.

Perhaps most important, history gives us a sounder basis upon which to judge the relative merit of practical ideas and ideals. As Allan Bloom (1987) has so vividly shown, the radical relativism of American ethical edution has left recent generations with something far worse than mere ignorance of our traditions—we have become almost unable to distinguish between moral shallowness and profundity, and almost indifferent to the distinction.

Critique in Philosophy and Social Science

Any modern attempt at a history of ideas owes much to post-Kantian philosophy, and especially to the Frankfurt and French schools since the 1960s. Two hundred years ago, Kant established what Foucault (1984:38) has called the "attitude of modernity" in philosophy. He sought to exclude absolute certainty from the limits of rationality, and he suggested that maturity consists in taking responsibility for one's own decisions; a responsibility that rests on an awareness of the uses and misuses of rationality itself; and the self discipline to act rationally when it is possible to do so. With these projects, Kant helped to move philosophy out of the naïve positivism of the Enlightenment, to establish the dependency of knowledge on its historical context, and to lay the groundwork for relativistic ethics.

Since that time, the humanities have always had to take into account Kant's charge; the result has been a literature, a historiography, an anthropology, and a philosophy that are more and more aware of their own temporal and cultural limits. These branches of human knowledge have increasingly challenged the natural sciences, and that variety of social science that imitates the natural sciences in method, to follow suit. Jurgen Habermas in Frankfurt, and Michel Foucault in Paris, building on a tradition that had already established an honored place in philosophy, have stated the case most forcefully: The purpose of social science is to interpret ourselves to ourselves as products of culture and history. Only then can we see clearly where our responsibility lies.

> The critical ontology of ourselves has to be considered not, certainly, as a theory, a doctrine, nor even as a permanent body of knowledge that is accumulating; it has to be conceived as an attitude, an ethos, a philosophical life in which the critique of what we are is at one and the same time the historical analysis of the limits that are imposed on us and an experiment with the possibility of going beyond them. (Foucault, 1984:50)

But academic psychology has had difficulties absorbing post-Kantian philosophy. Rather than a steady progression toward historical self-consciousness, there we have seen a division between styles that are for the most part mutually hostile: a scientistic style based on naïve empiricist methods, and a humanistic style that is relativistic. The former is the style that one finds expressed in most of the major psychology journals, in which an attempt is made to isolate a small set of variables and test their interconnectedness, using quasiexperimental methods. In academia at least, this is by far the larger style of study.

As a serious outlook on scholarship that requires a fundamental change in attitude, historically conscious psychology occupies the only position it can in academic psychology, without transforming the science. It is the same position occupied by other large, unassimilable truths in other sciences—for example, the study of nutrition in medicine—recognized as important by most people, but studied by only a few, and largely ignored when its relevance is pointed out by those who understand it.

This situation will surely continue at least as long as most research in psychology is financially supported by government agencies and private foundations that embody the pre-Kantian worldview. As I will argue throughout this book, one of the best ways to preserve an idea is to found a set of large social institutions on it; conversely, innovation is easiest when it involves the fewest vested powers. One reason the humanities have been able to absorb relativistic ideas with comparative ease is that their brand of scholarship is seen as largely irrelevant by most of the important economic bodies in our society. A historically conscious psychology could thrive, it seems, only if there were sweeping changes in modern Western culture.

Critique and Human Development

What I am proposing in this book, however, is not so much a social revolution (although that might be worthwhile on several counts), but a modest reform of the science of human development, by way of incorporating historical critique. How would developmental studies be different if such a suggestion were followed systematically? I would like to suggest four ways. First, the history of psychology demonstrates the culture-boundness of all knowledge, and therefore the limitations of maturation models based on any given cultural tradition. A critical science of development would keep the central values and ideas of its own cultural matrix in view, and at the same time clarify those ideas that seem most compatible with man's deepest intuitions concerning truth and virtue.

Second, history demonstrates the interdependence of knowledge and power; a critical scholarship would be suspicious of ideas that have the support of great constituencies.

Third, the past reveals that certain intellectual problems will not yield to certain methods—a good example being the intractability of moral truth to scientific demonstration. A critical scholarship would confront such problems. It would avoid the attempts to combine ethics and positivism that have led either to corruption of method, or to trivialization of ethics.

Fourth, we learn from history that we human beings are endlessly credulous—that we apparently hunger so keenly for secure knowledge that we are capable of believing fanatically in almost anything, without any more reason for believing it than our desire to believe. As Nietzsche said, "Esteeming itself is of all esteemed things the most estimable treasure" (Nietzsche 1891). Belief is only loosely related to intelligence or experience or behavior. It tends to be internally inconsistent and to change unpredictably, showing that a true science of mental life must be much more complex than we might suppose if we did not have the benefit of historical vision. We must not be discouraged by this complexity from the attempt to understand ourselves; but neither should we be seduced by oversimplifications masquerading as insights.

There are several examples in this book of the culture-boundness of contemporary developmental ideas. Perhaps the best example is the dependency of Piagetian cognitive development, and the moral conclusions drawn from it by Kohlberg, on an aesthetics that places the generality and consistency of beliefs at a higher level than ad hoc judgement. The scholar who can liberate himself from such notions is able, for example, to recognize other useful forms of maturity, and might be moved to inquire how these other forms develop.

The historical lessons concerning power I consider even more important. The collapse of the Athenian state in 404 B.C. led to a power vacuum that in turn helped to overturn the orthodoxy of state religion, and to usher in the most remarkable revolution in philosophy the West has ever seen. The decay of papal power in the Renaissance also led to dramatic new forms of knowledge about human nature. Today we see an orthodoxy of method in psychology, closely linked to the power of an immense science bureaucracy. We see that this orthodoxy tends to reproduce a highly ethnocentric, class-bound, and gender-centric view of human nature, society and health. The historically conscious person will be at least sceptical of this orthodoxy, if only because he knows there are other useful methods than the ones on which the powerful institutions insist.

There are certain linkages between methods and results that can be understood only if one takes a long view of scholarship. It is still fashionable in academic psychology to blame the triviality of most academic work on the youthfulness of the science, but history shows that another millenium of positivist psychology, armed with the latest computers, will not contribute much to the improvement of society. Computers cannot predict the moral effects of complex decisions involving humans.

In fact, computers usually cannot even help us distinguish between a morally good effect and a bad one, because the qualitative nature of human well-being is so hard to quantify. Such a perspective can be added to the suspicion of power as a prescription for avoiding undue slavery to natural science methods.

Finally, there is the lesson of human credulity. Historically blind psychology, unaware of its limits, is capable of self-hypnotic certainty—a conviction devoid of humor and compassion, which the relativistic view simply cannot share. Philosophic history is, among other things, an endless march of earnest absurdities. Familiarity with it generally nurtures irony, the ability to laugh at, and to forgive, the human in oneself and in others. A science of human development based upon such an attitude will have less trouble recognizing and accommodating the paradoxes in the most mature character: the coexistence of weakness and strength, the holding of self-contradictory views, the inconsistency of belief and behavior.

These last advantages of historicism are essential if we are to restore to psychology its main function as a tool for self understanding. The path toward insight is slippery and steep. It discourages us if we expect too much of ourselves. For encouragement, we need the evidence of history to demonstrate that even the best of us often fail, as well as the evidence that there is real progress to be made.

The Application of Developmental Knowledge

So far I have spoken mainly of the intellectual gains offered to the study of human development by historical critique. The greatest gains of this approach, however, are practical. It offers a method whereby the behavioral sciences can make themselves far more understandable and useful to society. An accelerating rate of social change lies at the heart of much confusion and suffering today, as expectations and realities lose synchrony. The history of ideas is *about* social change; it bears the same general relationship to society that psychodynamic life history bears to the individual: It locates experience in an interpretable stream of events.

As the twentieth century draws to a close in America, for example, we find ourselves facing some unprecedented challenges as social beings. Many of us will spend a quarter or a third of our lives in retirement from active work. How are we to keep our self esteem in a society where work is the measure of a person's worth? Also central to our self esteem is our sense of independence, the conviction that we control our own fate through our own abilities. Yet as our economic and legal institutions have become larger, more complex, and more centralized, all of us depend for our daily survival on institutions that are remote and inscrutable, and we are affected deeply by decisions over which we have no control. Even that keystone of self-respect, "reputation," threatens to slip from our control as the last vestiges of community are eroded by the mobility and compart-mentalization of life. The American view of maturity is based, too, on a belief that opportunity for wealth and power is almost unlimited for the self-disciplined and able, a belief that was always a bit optimistic, but that is rapidly becoming even less true.

Social science can and should help us find our individual solutions to such problems. As C. Wright Mills once wrote, the purpose of social science is the "union of history and biography" (Mills 1959). The cultural climate in which we live today is the growing tip of a historical process; the problems we confront in the management of our outward relations and our socially conditioned inner feelings are likewise products of that process. To the extent that we see before us both the larger historical and the smaller biographical processes, we are self-aware and our choices are reasoned.

In this view, social science is by definition moral activity. It shows individuals as purposeful and free, and its function is to interpret free human beings to one another and to themselves, not to predict or control. The branch of social science that guides this book—human develop-ment—is the branch that performs this function by focusing on the way people grow and change throughout life. Human development sets individual change in the context of human biology, of social process, and of history. It encourages us to see in our own biographies—in that process of overcoming what we have been—the implacable organic forces of our species, the effects of our dependencies and the expectations of our consociates, and beyond these to the historical process of which these effects are the distillations. These explanations should enrich us even where they affect our choices not at all. They should clarify our longings, our confusion and our pain; they should connect us with the struggles and overcomings of generations.

The field of human development is really a set of ideas that have evolved (this book is about their evolution) to answer a few basic questions about who we are. It is a discipline that seeks to: (1) describe and account for similarities of behavior on the basis of developmental regularities; (2) describe and account for differences of behavior on the basis of developmental differences; (3) describe and account for regulari-ties in the way people change over time; and (4) account for exceptional behavior and exceptional suffering.

The personal relevance of each of these questions becomes clear once we reflect on them. In order to know the extent to which my behavior, and that of those around me, is "free," I must know what accounts for our similarities and our differences. In order to understand the failures of communication and the causes of the conflict from which we all suffer, I must know how and why people diverge in their behavior. In order to understand myself as an integrated person, and to anticipate my future, I must know the regularities of change that affect me. The ordinary, moreover, is often both explained with greatest clarity and overcome with greatest effect by the extraordinary; one must know that, too.

The Idea of Maturity

Many of our hopes and frustrations as social beings are brought into focus by the concept of maturity—one of the key concepts, in fact *the* key concept, of the discipline of human development. The idea of development implies an end state toward which change in human life is directed. "Piaget," Carol Gilligan reminds us, "challenging the common impression that a developmental theory is built like a pyramid from its base in infancy, points out that a conception of development instead hangs from its vertex of maturity, the point toward which progress is traced. Thus, a change in the definition of maturity does not simply alter the description of the highest stage but recasts the understanding of development, changing the entire account" (Gilligan 1982:18-19). We will have many opportunities to see this principle at work as we examine different accounts of what maturity is, and how it is achieved.

Maturity is fundamentally a social idea, and it differs from place to place and era to era. In our own society, it takes on many meanings in different situations, some of them very complex. For example, the word *mature* in American society means much more than just functionally grown up. Most Americans spend their adolescent years worrying about when, or whether, they are really going to grow up. Many continue to worry about it throughout their twenties and thirties, even after they have launched promising careers, established families, and dedicated themselves to the solvency of a dozen creditors. It seems completely natural for us to feel that one must acquire certain personal qualities of character before one is "really" mature. As a culture we have, it would seem, an unquestioned and largely unconscious model of personal development that includes some interesting ideas. For example, we believe that development is somewhat independent of social role, age, and even stage of life. We believe, apparently, that moral maturity is very difficult to attain, and that few people in fact attain it. Those who do are unusually self-reliant, altruistic, poised, and inwardly at peace. Hence the irony of such phrases as "for mature audiences," as applied to television programming. Once the full idea of maturity enters our mind, we at once sense that the form of entertainment we are about to see is really for the masses and hardly likely to appeal to fully mature people at all.

These ideas are, of course, historical products. In order to understand them, we must know what the great thinkers down through the ages left us in the way of instruction on moral maturity. The example just given, of the ironic conflict between mature meaning "adult," and mature meaning "morally superior," actually results from the coexistence of primitive and literate views of maturity that have both been passed down to us through history. Moreover, if beliefs about maturity are like other moral ideas, we should be able to see a correspondence between such beliefs and other features of the ways of life that produced them, including—and this is the real point—the relations of our own views, both popular and scientific, to our own way of life. I make no pretense of understanding fully the relationship between the history of ideas and their functions, which is a complex relationship indeed. But I will try now to set forth clearly how I do see them related.

A Historical View of Ideas

To begin by putting my view of history as simply as possible, I think ideas and values are partly determined by the economic, technical, political, and social conditions of the societies that share them, and are partly independent of these conditions. Their dependence derives from their usefulness in the socialization of the young to a way of life, and in extending the power of societies and social classes. I will try to show, for example, how classical Greek notions of maturity—notions that we have inherited to a great extent—developed out of the economic conditions and institutions of Hellenic life, especially the institutions of slavery and land tenure, and the economic condition of agricultural surplus.

I believe there is a discernable evolutionary sequence in the way human societies developed in the Western world too, and that ideas correspondingly followed this sequence in certain ways. When I say the way societies in the Western world *did* develop, I want to exclude the notion that all societies necessarily follow a fixed evolutionary sequence. Technology, social organization, and ideas just seem to have progressed in an orderly way at certain points. I will say more about this later.

The independence of ideas from their cultural and ecological matrices derives from two related facts about them. First, important ideas bind anxiety and reduce the uncertainty let loose in the human world by the presence of language and the premonition of a future. Because language vastly increases the possible ways humans can understand and react to their sensory experience, the species is susceptible to "supermarket trauma" in trying to sort out and respond to experience. People desperately need important ideas to make decisions, and those intellectual constructions of their culture that have survived the winds of change and gained wide currency naturally command attention and respect. We can see this clearly in the phrase *time honored,* and in the survival into modern times of ideas like astrology and creationism—ideas that conflict sharply with the dominant institutions and ideals of their believers' culture but at the same time help them find meaning where other beliefs fail.

Second, ideas *generate* social institutions, and these institutions protect and foster their ideological bases in the face of serious functional problems. This can be seen in each of the many ideological wars, inquisitions, and purges that have marked human history through the ages.

Shortly we will be looking at concepts of maturity in their cultural and historical settings with the aim of showing how our own ideas evolved. Necessarily this will involve such judgements as which ideas are most relevant and which must be left out for the sake of brevity. I have included ideas that seemed to be widely characteristic of a historical era or of cultures at a given level of social and technological development, and have created the impression that those eras and cultural types are more homogeneous and simple-minded in their beliefs than they in fact are. No individual, let alone society, believes steadfastly and unambiguously anything simply stated about a topic as complex and important as maturity. Social traditions contain mixtures of mutually incompatible ideas, and the beliefs of individuals vary according to the roles they occupy, the company in which they find themselves, and the developing states of their knowledge.

And yet we can identify important trends in belief that unite some societies and distinguish them from others; I am convinced that these trends actually influence individual lives in a powerful way. The things people strive to achieve, the ways they go about it, the characteristic emotions with which they view life—all these and more are influenced by widely held beliefs. I once took part in a study of elderly Japanese Americans and Mexican Americans in San Francisco. I was struck by the similarity of many conditions of life in the two cultures, and equally by the great differences in perceptions and goals. With their deep Catholic tradition, the Mexican Americans viewed life as a lonely spiritual struggle in which the individual fought to remain aloof and dignified among the corrupting and stifling influences of society. The Japanese, on the other hand, saw life as a precious gift bestowed by their ancestors upon themselves, and by themselves upon their progeny. The mature person was a grateful person, regardless of life's circumstances, a "smooth stone," who fit snugly into every social situation.

This is not to say that individual desires usually correspond with cultural ideals. The opposite is the case for primitives and moderns alike. Rather, the cultural ideals pose *problems* that each individual must somehow solve if one is to get the things one does want in life. Ideals are part of the environment, an intimately felt presence to which we must adapt, much as we must adapt to our relatives. Whether we like it or not, we are members of families whose composition and character affect our lives. The same is true of culture at large.

I have taken other liberties with history as well. First, I have treated modern nonliterate societies as representatives of a hypothetical preliterate period in our own ancestry. I had to decide whether to consider the ethnographic present relevant at all, and chose to include it. I did this because I found this choice interesting. It helps explain what seem to be essentially preliterate ideas that survive in modern Western societies. Second, I have taken modern, mainstream, positivist developmental psychology as my starting and ending point. Other books could be written about the influence on our culture of non-Western ideas of maturity, and about the influence of the less mainstream, nonpositivist psychologies, such as those of the Jungians, the phenomenologists, the existentialists, the Christian mystics, and the hermeneuticists. I have chosen this limitation not only because I know this topic best, but because it is the topic of greatest relevance to most students.

Academic developmental psychology itself is, of course, as much a product of history as is the rest of our culture. It is not common to treat it critically as such, even in the occasional scholarly search for the origins of its key ideas. From within the discipline, ideas are scrutinized according to accepted tests of their empirical validity and internal consistency, rarely according to the long-term economic, cultural, and intellectual currents that constrain their main direction. But values and beliefs are the subject matter of the social scientist. He cannot take the habits of his culture or of his trade for granted in his work without forfeiting too much of his integrity. It is, after all, his critical self awareness that distinguishes the scientist from the dilettante.

Nor is this issue an insignificant one when it comes to fulfilling the promise of social science as a moral activity. As I shall show in part 3, academic developmental psychology *does* address some of the urgent moral issues of our time, and it does so in such a way that it unwittingly distorts certain ancient and valuable ideas. This distortion might actually be a major cause for the weak relevance of psychology to the moral life of modern man.

Continuity and Discontinuity in History

In the history of any set of ideas, one probably encounters periods of rapid change in some details, as well as astounding persistence in others. Most of the history of ideas about maturity can be broken up into small steps that are easy to follow, steps like a shift in emphasis from one kind of moral activity to another, or the combination of previously unrelated ideas to form a new one. But it is not all like that. Some large principles of continuity and discontinuity must be grasped at the beginning before one can make sense out of the history we are about to pursue.

One such principle is that complex and socially important concepts like maturity affect a number of disparate and loosely related intellectual traditions, and these traditions often diverge, producing odd inconsistencies in the history of the concept of interest. Moral ideas about the qualities of the mature person on one hand, and practical ideas about how one achieves maturity on the other hand, belong to such divergent traditions. They develop somewhat independently of each other, and they occupy different places in the moral and intellectual life of society. I have therefore assigned concepts of moral maturity to part 1 of this book, and concepts of the maturation process to part 2. In part 3 I will reconsider the matter of their relationship.

Second, the history of ideas occasionally undergoes cataclysmic transformations brought about by shifts in thinking on such fundamental issues as the nature of knowledge and the mind—shifts that Foucault calls "crises of modernity." I will deal mainly with two such shifts, from nonliterate to literate views of the man/cosmos relationship, and from the literate metaphysical to the empiricist views of that relationship.

Yet a third principle has to do with continuity in the face of change. Most crises of modernity actually seem to be gradual, often spanning several centuries, and they are never complete, in the sense that they transform the whole mental life of a society; rather, they always seem to result in the *addition* of a new viewpoint to the old ones, so that several layers, however contradictory, co-exist within the same society and some-times within the same individual at different times. Preliterate and meta-physical ideas about maturity still thrive in the popular thinking of modern urban cultures. Moreover, there are certain persistent *structures* that seem to underlie Western man's thought about maturity, so that as the specific contents and even epistemological bases of the concept evolve, some central features of it remain fixed, such as the great dualisms—emotion/reason and nature/nurture—and the four stage theory of develop-ment, which I will introduce shortly.

This recognition of the role of crises in historical change, together with this perception that the resulting transformations are partial and additive rather than complete and substitutive, leads one to agree simul-taneously with two kinds of historians whose views might seem at first to be incompatible. There are those "great event" theorists, like Foucault, who emphasize the critical points when something new emerges, and there are those "gradualists," like Elias, who downplay the role of individual minds and events and emphasize instead the gradual ebb and flow of economic and social forces. Throughout this book, both kinds of change are described.

The Crises of Modernity

The first intellectual cataclysm of interest here corresponded with the introduction of writing and monumental architecture in human civilization. This was a shift, among intellectuals, from the assumption that *all knowledge is of the same order,* which I call the *Conscious, Anthropo-morphic Universe,* to the assumption that the universe includes conscious-nesses that transcend the human, which I call the *Conscious, Transcendent Universe.* How this transformation affected ideas of maturity is a topic that will be taken up in detail in the chapters that follow. Here I want only to explain what it was, and how I think it happened.

As we will see when we look at ideas of maturity in nonliterate societies, cultural beliefs in such societies generally view knowledge of the sort that humans have as a uniform commodity of enormous value that pervades the animate and inanimate universe, much like our modern notion of matter, except that knowledge is more useful than mere matter, and it also pervades incorporeal objects like spirits. According to this theory, knowledge is equally accessible to every normal adult in the society who knows how to get it. However, it is the secret of power and social success, and every individual jealously guards his knowledge, sharing it only with those he loves and trusts—typically, members of his family. Animals, plants, spirits, and all kinds of natural phenomena have consciousness of the same order as humans, meaning that they each have their own knowledge contents, which they also guard jealously against prying ears and eyes. A truly clever person is one who knows how to coax information from his environment, information that will give him and his allies power. A well-educated person is one who has been taught these skills. The skills themselves consist of the use of charms and magic, and the attainment of nonordinary states of consciousness wherein the individual can see, hear, and understand things (for example, the conversations of spirits or animals) that give him important information (for example, a clear view of the future, or the cause of an illness he wishes to inflict or cure).

This view of knowledge is probably the most natural one in societies that lack writing, because everything that is known in such societies is known by living beings with their limited perceptual and mnemonic powers; it is natural to assume that everything that *can be* known is known the same way. Since there are no written records, the details of history fade rapidly, and "what we now know or can find out" is taken to circumscribe the domain of knowledge.

This situation is changed gradually by the introduction of writing and literate classes, monumental architecture, and trade over long distances. Through these innovations, mainly, the past and the unfamiliar begin to accumulate in the here and now. Knowledge is no longer restricted merely by the jealousy of its possessors, but by its location in time and space as well. Major gaps develop between the knowledge of the nonliterate and the literate, the traveller and the garden plot slave. From this situation it is a short step to the assumption that someone, somewhere, must know everything, but that this consciousness cannot possibly be human—the world view I call the *Conscious, Transcendent Universe*. At this point, the quest for knowledge shifts from the "clever person" strategy of the anthropomorphic universe to a "devotee" strategy in a transcendent universe. At the same time, the definition of maturity ceases to coincide with normal adulthood, and comes to include the hierarchical idea of degrees of enlightenment or divine favor. In our own history, this is the transformation that distinguishes the preliterate period from the monotheistic Hebrews and the polytheistic Greeks.

The second crisis of modernity took root in the thirteenth century, and came to flower in the Enlightenment of the sixteenth and seventeenth centuries. This was the idea, spawned by a growing confidence in the power of the human intellect, that knowledge consisted not in consciousness itself, but in nonconscious *order*; that it was discoverable by an order-finding machine called the mind. We need not go into the causes and consequences of this cataclysm now, but need notice only that its effect on normative ideas of maturity was a radical shift of direction. Where classical and medieval cultures had sought a balance between hot passion and cool contemplation, the new maturity insisted upon the absolute dominance of sober, controlled reason. Knowledge, after all, consisted in cold facts. Like the earlier transformation to the transcendent universe of literate society, the birth of this *Nonconscious, Lawful Universe* did not sweep away its predecessors. It evoked a radical reaction, and sparked a host of debates that still rage in Western intellectual circles. The history upon which we are about to embark should help us to understand these debates, and their effects on everyday life.

It is often said by modern philosophers that another crisis of modernity occurred with the work of Kant, namely the shift to historical self-consciousness. According to Foucault, Kant's modernity consisted in his realization that his own thinking "arises out of and is an attempt to respond to his historical situation" (Dreyfus and Rabinow 1986:111). Although it might be true that Kant's essay on Enlightenment, in 1784, contains the first explicit recognition of this principle, I am sceptical of the implication that earlier philosophers had not thought about it. Both Buddhism and Taoism, founded in the first millenium B.C., recognize the historical relativity of ideas. Plato, according to Jaeger (1943), deliberately seized the crisis of Athens's defeat in the fifth century B.C. to promulgate a radical new philosophy. Aquinas also made an apparently conscious decision to revise many medieval scholastic ideas. Even granted that these works accepted the existence of a transcendent, timeless consciousness, is it likely that their authors failed to see the historical dependence of their own thought?

For now, this is a minor question. The fact is, Western philosophy is now fully aware of its own cultural and historical embeddedness; that fact has come to the center of educated discussion on the fundamental questions to which we shall soon turn—questions of man's nature and purpose.

Persisting Themes

In a society with a long literate history, it is not surprising to find that certain ideas survive great changes in technology and values; an important function of writing, after all, is to preserve useful thoughts for posterity. Neither is it puzzling to find that the specific links whereby durable ideas come down to us often get lost. To the extent that a thought is repeated by many thinkers, the chain of communication, if not the origin itself, will tend to grow diffuse and vague.

Of the many persisting themes in the history of ideas about character development, three are central enough that they lend substantial structure to this book: The emotion/reason dichotomy, the nature/nurture dichotomy, and the idea of four moral stages. We can no longer be certain where these themes originated, nor can we precisely reconstruct their genealogy. Here I simply want to add coherence to the history that follows by anticipating their major role.

The idea that emotion and reason are separate psychic functions, and that they can lead in different moral directions, is well developed in the works of Plato and Aristotle. In fact, as we shall see in chapters 3 and 7, the two philosophers disagree in their emphasis upon one function or the other as a guide to wise conduct; Plato emphasizes emotion, Aristotle emphasizes reason. The controversy is continued by the Stoics, who influenced the early Christian fathers with their Aristotelian emphasis on emotional self-control, which was somehow blended with Christ's essentially Platonic teaching on the subject. The controversy becomes explicit again in the late Middle Ages, when pagan learning begins to invade scholarly thought. We will see that Peter Abelard, the Franciscans—Saint Bonaventure, Dante Alighieri, and Saint Francis himself—and the Cistercians—Saint Bernard—were drawn to the Platonic position, while Aquinas and his followers followed Aristotle. In the early Renaissance, Erasmus advanced the cause of the emotions, but by the seventeenth century the Aristotelian emphasis held sway in Enlightenment England, with vast consequences for the whole of philosophy and science. The Platonic emphasis contintued to influence the romantic movement, especially in Germany and France in the eighteenth and nineteenth centuries.

This problem is very much alive in developmental psychology today. In chapter 11, I review it as the "path of love" and the "path of reason," and show how it has influenced some modern writers—especially Carol Gilligan and Lawrence Kohlberg.

The idea that there are four distinct natural stages of moral development—materialism, eros, honor, and wisdom, in that order—is also fully developed in Plato's *Symposium* (chapters 3 and 7). It recurs in the medieval Platonists, especially Dante and Saint Bernard, and then seems to disappear in the West (emphatically not in Asia, but that is another book), only to resurface with new vigor in the work of such seminal modern thinkers as Erik Erikson, Abraham Maslow, and Charlotte Buhler. In chapter 13 I suggest that this model is a powerful unconscious ideal in our society, a kind of cultural engram, and that we can use it to help understand the obstacles to maturity posed by our present historical condition.

The nature/nurture controversy really developed as an important theme after the thirteenth century. Before that, the prevailing view of the cosmos held that virtue, and hence maturity, was a gift of a conscious, purposeful universe or god or society of gods. The distinction between biology and experience seems to have been secondary to the question of how one cultivated the gift. Aristotle, Plato and the Stoics held that virtue is acquired through instruction and practice. Aquinas distinguished between acquired and "infused," or God-given virtues, and in this he was followed by William of Ockham and Duns Scotus. But the problem moved to the center of developmental theory only after the science of biology began to develop in the seventeenth century. It has played such an important role in psychology ever since that I have devoted the whole of chapter 10 to it.

Ideas like these take root in a culture and develop an authority based on their durability and pervasiveness. How well they serve us as intellectual tools, however, depends on how well they answer the questions put to us by our own evolving culture and natural environment. To know their history is not to reject them, but to be clearer about their uses.

PART I

Maturity and Morals

2. Maturity Without History

The word for "maturity," in whatever language one finds it, refers to a complex abstraction. Its precise meaning is elusive, and it is difficult to translate or define, because it conveys customary beliefs about good and evil, about nature and the cosmos. Such beliefs nearly always differ from culture to culture and from era to era. If we want to understand fully the meaning of the word in any culture, then, we must try to make clear not only the range of thoughts and feelings that are evoked by it, but also the way the culture *structures* experience—we must seek the nature of what Clifford Geertz calls the "webs of meaning" of which culture consists— since it is only by knowing these structures that we can interpret the complex abstractions people share as members of society. These structures of meaning evolve slowly, and we can learn a great deal about them by studying their evolution. The main purpose of this book is to clarify the concept of maturity as it is used in Western society, by studying the history of that complex web of beliefs of which it is a central strand. The belief complex surrounding maturity in our culture includes our basic ideas about the nature of man and his place in the universe.

All human beings seem to have some concept of maturity, and we can guess that the idea probably developed fairly early in our history as language-using creatures. If we started using language about forty thousand years ago, as the linguists guess we might have (Washburn 1971), this means we must have brooded about maturity without the help of writing for about thirty-four thousand years. This probably left an impression on humanity's literati, and it would be nice to know what sort of impression it was. If the conditions of nonliterate societies around the world today seem to produce characteristic ways of looking at maturity, whether people hunt walruses or plant manioc, and whether they speak Algonquin or Urdu, perhaps we can infer that our cultural ancestors — proto-Greeks, proto-Hebrews, and others—also shared some of these characteristic ideas.

Primitive Selfhood

Early accounts of nonliterate people that come from the missionaries and naturalists of the nineteenth century resound with emotion, most of it in the spectra of amazement and disgust. The customs of nonliterate people were so different from those of the middle-class Victorian Europeans and Americans who studied them that the scholars could scarcely believe what they saw. Thus Lord Avebury could write in *The Origin of Civilization and the Primitive Condition of Man* (1870) that savages often have "absurd reasons for what they do and believe," and that "the mind of the savage then appears to rock to and fro out of mere weakness, and he tells lies and talks nonsense" (quoted in Langness 1974:31). Primitives must be of a fundamentally imitative and unoriginal mentality, the early scholars concluded, in order to slavishly follow such patently irrational customs. The nonliterate peoples' own accounts of why they split their young men's penises or burned huge heaps of valuable goods did little to improve their image. "It is the most important in life," they were likely to say. "Without it, we would not be human." This way of speaking set off a debate about nonliterate views of the self that still boils in the ethnological literature, and it is instructive to look at certain developments in that debate over the decades.

In 1926, Bronislaw Malinowski wrote:

> Take the real savage, keen on evading his duties, swaggering and boastful when he has fulfilled them, and compare him with the anthropologist's dummy who slavishly follows custom and automatically obeys every regulation. There is not the remotest resemblance between the teachings of anthropology on this subject and the reality of native life. (1926:26)

A brilliant eccentric who had spent two years among the Trobriand Islanders of Melanesia between 1915 and 1918, Malinowski was probably the most influential anthropologist of his time. A Polish national, he had been virtually trapped in the South Pacific by the outbreak of World War I. As a result, he had revised the way anthropologists study cultures, pitching his tent in a native village, becoming fluent in the language, observing first-hand the entire yearly round of work, ritual, love, death, and frivolity.

But the issue of understanding nonliterate man's selfhood was far from settled by Malinowski's authoritative reports. Thirty-three years later, in fact, Mercia Eliade could write that the meaning and value of human acts in primitive society "derive from their property of reproducing a primordial act, of repeating a mythic example" (1959:4). "The man of traditional culture," said Eliade, "sees himself as real only to the extent that he ceases to be himself, and imitates or repeats an archetype" (p. 34).

What a discrepancy! We can detect in Malinowski's words a certain lack of respect for his subjects—perhaps he was talking about their *failure* to live up to their own ideals; whereas Eliade was talking about nonliterate man's ideals themselves. But there are other voices in the debate, like that of Paul Radin. A passionate advocate of the wisdom and dignity of nonliterate peoples, and a tireless student of their subtlest self expressions, Radin was a contemporary of Malinowski's who agreed with his views of primitive individualism, but with different aims.

> I have dwelt upon the desire for glory and prestige hunting at such
> length because we encounter it so obtrusively in aboriginal tribes,
> and because its abuses are so patent and lead to so much conflict. If
> these abuses are more rampant and if they are treated more leniently
> there than among us, this is due to the insistence [of primitives] on
> unhampered self expression. Every man and woman seeks
> individuation—outer and inner individuation—and this is the
> psychological basis for their otherwise bewildering and unintelligible
> tolerance of the fullest expression of personality. (Radin, 1927:34)

Malinowski and Radin seem to imply that all nonliterates are basically competitive and individualistic. Eliade implies the opposite. Perhaps both views are a bit overgeneral. Yet another anthropologist, also a contemporary of Malinowski and Radin, taught two generations of Americans that nonliterate cultures differ fundamentally in their ideas about virtue and individuality. Ruth Benedict's *Patterns of Culture* was a literary jewel and a bold intellectual adventure that found its way into more undergraduates' libraries than perhaps any other treatise ever written on primitive man. There Benedict proposed that societies can be ranked on a scale, with passion, conflict and competitiveness highly valued at one end (for which she borrowed Nietzche's term *dionysian*, drawn from the orgiastic rites of the ancient Greek wine cult), and the opposite qualities of harmony, sobriety, and cooperation at the other end (called *appolonian*, after the divine symbol of the Golden Mean). Benedict's work later drew severe criticism for oversimplifying the nonliterate picture, but her point about the diversity of primitive views of the ideal person stands.

Benedict's work stimulated many attempts to relate the morals of societies to more "fundamental" aspects of their way of life—aspects such as levels and kinds of technology. Among the more interesting of these for our purposes was a study by Barry, Child, and Bacon published in 1959. The three anthropologists surveyed 104 societies (most of them nonliterate) to see if they could detect any influence of economic practices on such moral traits as individualism and conformity. Ethnographic descriptions of these societies were studied in an effort to measure the extent to which obedience, self reliance, responsibility, nurturance, and general independence seemed to be emphasized in the upbringing of children. The societies were also rated according to their degree of economic dependence on agriculture, herding, and hunting. In herding societies, the authors reasoned,

> future food supply seems to be best assured by faithful adherence to routines designed to maintain the good health of the herd. (Barry, Child, and Bacon 1959:52)

In agricultural societies likewise,

> social rules prescribe the best known way to bring the growing plants to successful harvest, and to protect the stored produce for gradual consumption until the next harvest. . . . Under these conditions, there might be a premium on obedience to the older and wiser, and on responsibility in faithful performance of the routine laid down by custom for one's economic role. (ibid.)

But hunting societies ought to have different moral rules:

> At an opposite extreme is subsistence primarily through hunting or fishing, with no means for extended storing of the catch. Here individual initiative and development of high individual skill seem to be at a premium. (ibid.)

The resulting analysis seemed to suggest a loose but significant relationship between economy and morality. Societies that depended heavily upon agriculture or animal husbandry seemed to "pressure their children toward compliance." Hunters, on the other hand, tended to exert an opposite kind of pressure—toward autonomy and assertiveness.

This would seem to be the germ, at least, of an evolutionary theory of maturity. But more recent work with large numbers of ethnographic descriptions drawn from around the world shows that many agricultural societies seethe with repressed envy and overt malicious gossip, and some, like the Alorese of Indonesia and the Pacific Island Marquesans, stimulate and value levels of aggression and competition most hunting peoples would consider downright crazy if they could conceive of it at all (Cohen 1961).

Must we despair, then, of finding anything invariant in the views of self and maturity presented to us by nonliterate people? I think not. Our confusion arises, I believe, from a habit of our own that is very typical of urban industrial people: We are almost continuously self conscious. We view our own acts as performances, distinct from and often in conflict with our inner thoughts and feelings. The close observation of nonliterate people tells us that this way of thinking is a rare exception among them. While acting idiosyncratically and even contrary to the expectations of their associates, they tend to perceive themselves as acting in a perfectly natural and culturally acceptable way. Rosaldo tells us, for example, that the Ilongots of the Philippines experience "no necessary gap between self presentation and inner self" (1984:146), and Ochs and Schiefflin (1984) note that the Kaluli of Papua-New Guinea make no distinction between an individual's acts and the motivations behind them. Likewise, Myers (1979) reports that the aboriginal Pintupi of Australia make no distinction between the expression of personal feelings and the performance of social roles. Their self-concept includes those close to them, and even the word for "oneself," *walytja*, also means "kin" and "one's own." The same merging of self and close others has been cited in other hunting societies as well. Balikci (1970) reports it for the Netsilik Eskimo, and Marshall (1961) describes an extreme emotional interdependence among the Kung Bushmen.

It is not that nonliterate people fail to perceive themselves as physically separate from others, or even that they do not reflect upon their own distinctness of character. Rather, in small traditional societies, it is rarely acceptable to justify one's behavior on grounds of personal motivation rather than on external agency or cultural precedent. Under the influence of such a morality, it is uncomfortable to perceive oneself as autonomous in the first place.

As a result of mental habits such as these, which occur in culture after culture, most nonliterate people have little trouble believing that they are acting rationally and maturely in terms that their culture recognizes, even when it seems to the outsider that their behavior is arbitrary, self-centered, and a fertile source of conflict. It is a matter of viewpoint. "The very terms they use in their accounts of how and why they act," continues Rosaldo on the Ilongots, "place emphasis. . . on the ways in which all adults are simultaneously autonomous and equal members of the group" (1984:147).

There are of course limits and exceptions to this rule. In situations where a member of a nonliterate small society finds himself among strangers, he is likely to feel extremely self-conscious about his actions. Also, nowadays many formerly isolated nonliterate peoples have been exposed to the beliefs and attitudes of people from industrial cultures, and have been encouraged to question the traditions of their ancestors. As I will discuss in the next chapter, such culture contact tends to promote self consciousness.

We must also be careful to put aside our Western ethnocentrism and recognize sharp distinctions between *nonliterate* and *literate nonindustrial* peoples. Self-concept and views of maturity in the traditional agrarian and pastoral Islamic, Hindu and Buddhist societies of the world, for example, are closer to those of the Christian West than to those of nonliterate society.

By "individuation" and "autonomy" in simple cultures, then, Radin and Malinowski could not have meant Western-style self-consciousness and insistence upon the right of free choice. Rather, they were writing about the pursuit of prestige. Privilege in nonliterate society is not equally distributed among adult members, but carefully allocated on the basis of position in the organization of the tribe. One wields power and influence largely on this basis of the statuses one occupies, and only secondarily on the basis of one's actual abilities. Anthropologists have since their earliest observations noticed changes in status corresponding to sequential stages of the life cycle (a point to which I shall return in chapter 12), but these changes have little to do with either age or ability. To illustrate this, Fortes (1984) uses the example of a twenty-year-old Tallensi man who could not punish his six-year-old relative for a grievous transgression, because the latter was his functional "father" according to the local rules of kinship! To pursue prestige and honor, then, does not mean to place oneself aside from one's fellows, but to draw closer to them, to enact more faithfully the ideals by which one and all live.

Nonliterate Maturity

Adulthood and maturity, then, are in practice the same. Do nonliterate people then deny any difference in *quality* of performance? Of course not. In culture after culture, the "good person" is recognized and valued. The difference between nonliterates and the rest of us is in the degree to which they place the blame or credit—the causal location, if you will—for performance *outside the individual*. Acts, and to some extent even emotions and thoughts, that are unacceptable in a social sense are thought to be caused by agents external to the person. This principle is best stated by Meyer Fortes, who studied the religions of West Africa in all their rich detail and found the idea of *fate* to be the lens that brought nonliterate cultures into focus:

> It is a law of nature that some people must fail in the whole or in parts of the task of becoming social persons. The predicament this gives rise to is interpreted, given moral value, and brought under control in the interests of society and of the individual, by means of the beliefs and rituals focused on the notion of predestiny, or Oedipal fate. (Fortes 1959:40)

Success, then, is seen as the working out of a good prenatal destiny, and failure as the opposite. Fortes found this system of belief over vast sections of West Africa, including the Tallensi and the great kingdoms of Benin and of Dahomey. Developmental failures—such major and lasting obstacles to social maturity as character disorders, infertility, poor hunting or fighting skills, illness, psychosis, and just plain bad social relationships—are caused by external agents like witchcraft, the influence of spirits or ghosts, or bad luck. It is an idea that is well expressed in the equally widespread habit of *ensuring* maturational success through the performance of rituals designed to control these external forces. (The prevalence of these beliefs in modern literate societies is another issue I shall say more about later on.)

The nature of individuality differs from society to society in the nonliterate world, just as it does in the industrial world. On the whole, however, nonliterates tend to regard every normal adult as "mature," although some adults are more successful than others. The tendency is therefore for every individual to pursue his or her own personal predilections and private dreams, knowing what will happen if the rules are broken too often or too flagrantly. To say that the social rules are respected is to misplace the emphasis. The social rules tend to be seen as the only possible way of understanding human action. If they cannot be fulfilled, this proves the interference of an outside agency. What is it that distinguishes nonliterate man from literate man, then, with respect to views of maturity? Two things: a relative emphasis on the fundamental equality of all normal adults, and the crediting to conscious external forces of differences in achieved social standing.

Maturity and Knowledge in the Conscious Anthropomorphic Universe

A close look at the Tallensi, or the Trobrianders, or the Ilongots, or the Kaluli, then, reveals a collection of morally equal individuals, each in his or her own way struggling to maximize the good things of life—honor, security, love, excitement—through the hatching of plots, the making of deals, and whatever is recognized by the culture as respectable hard work as well. All this takes place in small, face-to-face communities of people who know one another rather intimately, and who share a common knowledge about most of the important aspects of life—things like how to address an elder, how to make a canoe, perform such-and-such a ritual, find such-and-such a medicinal plant, or communicate with such-and-such a spirit. The holding of power tends to be strictly prescribed according to traditional ranking systems based on sex, age, and kinship connections; outside these prescribed structures, it is difficult for most people to get much ahead of anyone else. One must rely on a very small inventory of goods, materials, and ideas, and on one's own physical strength, eloquence, and powers of perception.

There are of course many strategies by which one goes about the competitive achievement of social standing in nonliterate society, but in order to really understand these struggles we have to look closely at the nonliterate concept of personal power, what it is and how one gets it.

As I mentioned in chapter 1, the conditions of nonliterate life lead naturally to the conclusion that the universe is conscious, and that its consciousness is of the same basic type as that of human beings. Since nonliterate people have relatively few ways other than memorization to accumulate knowledge, any individual can know practically anything that the society as a whole knows. There is no way of knowing what the society has forgotten. The nonliterate picture of the universe is therefore static in the long run, cyclical in the short run, and homogeneous throughout. In the absence of scientific explanations of why natural phenomena like stars, plants, and clouds behave the way they do, it is natural to assume that they have their own personal reasons, like people. This helps to explain, among other things, the commonly noted nonliterate idea that words, which make sensible the thoughts of their speakers, have the ability thereby to control events. Campbell (1964:112) discusses this as an early origin of the biblical story of creation beginning with the word of God. The idea of a pervasive but unseen consciousness is found also in the common fiction among nonliterate peoples that one person cannot ordinarily know the motivations of another any more (or any less) than he can know the motivations of anteaters or dust storms.

In such a world, there is an interpenetration of the normally sensed world of everyday action, and the normally unseen world of spirits and ancestors. Writing of the Australian aborigines, Bellah is struck by "the very high degree to whch the mythical world is related to the detailed features of the actual world. Not only is every clan and local group defined in terms of the ancestral progenitors and the mythical events of settlement, but virtually every mountain, rock, and tree is explained in terms of the actions of mythical beings" (1970:20).

Given the competitive nature of nonliterate society, it makes sense also for people to protect whatever private knowledge they have from being bandied about. Knowing what I myself want, and how I intend to get it, gives me a degree of power over my competitors if I keep them in the dark. If I can find out what someone else is up to, I am ahead of the game as long as I keep this knowledge to myself and my close allies. I am even further ahead if I can find out what other people *in general* are up to, and I really have something if I can discover the secrets of the nonhuman world as well, or if I can even convince others that I know those secrets. The nonliterate notion that we live in a conscious universe that protects its secrets jealously is preserved in many myths of literate cultures, including the biblical story of the Fall (Adam and Even stole knowledge from God and had to be punished), and of course the Greek myth of Prometheus, who stole fire from the gods and spent eternity paying for that, too. The knowledgeable person, then, is a seer or a shaman if people trust her; if they do not, she is a witch. Many people are a little of both.

Given this view of competition, it is hardly surprising that nonliterate cultures nearly always have a well-developed lore on the pursuit of knowledge. Techniques of persuasion and debate, memorized texts and rituals, and skills of perception and recognition are highly prized. Perceptual skills generally include the achievement of nonordinary states of consciousness, in which one can participate in the consciousness of the spirits, of animals, or of events that are far removed in space and time.

> Primitive religious action is characterized not, as we have said, by worship, nor, as we shall see, by sacrifice, but by identification, "participation," acting out. . . . The distance between man and mythical being, which was at best slight, disappears altogether in the moment of ritual. (Bellah 1970:28)

Among many native North American peoples, the establishment of such communication links with the nonhuman universe was a prerequisite for full tribal maturity; but in hundreds of other societies, ancient and modern, such techniques are routinely known, practiced, taught to the deserving, and carefully protected from the undeserving. Today this lore remains largely unexplored by psychologists, partly because, as I will discuss in later chapters, modern Western society is almost unique in its contempt for nonordinary states of consciousness as sources of knowledge. But as a source of information about the working of the human mind, the lore connected with the seeking and control of "visions" is vast and fascinating. It involves the use of emotional arousal through fear, pain, anger, and excitement; the alteration of brain chemistry through fasting, drugs, and diet; the control of neurophysiological processes through meditation, repetition, and sensory "driving"; the enhancement of recall through the use of behavioral, perceptual, and sensory cues; and elaborate combinations of these whose complexity challenges the scientific achievements of modern literate societies.

The Transition to Modern Views

In the next chapter, we shall take up in detail the transformation that befell maturity as a moral concept following the development of literacy and trade. It will be important to keep in mind that prevailing ideas are rarely replaced through this kind of transformation, and that this is no exception. Fortes's choice of a title for his study of primitive belief is instructive: *Oedipus and Job in West African Religion.* The words remind us that we can understand neither the classical Greeks nor the Old Testament Hebrews without reference to the primitive ideas upon which their belief systems were built.

3. Transcendence of Death: Maturity in the Ancient World

Writing and The Transformation of Culture

Writing was probably invented independently in a number of different civilizations. The unique ways of writing developed by the Chinese, the Maya of Central America, and the Phoenecians suggest this as much as the vast distances between them (Sampson 1985:46-47, 77). But the written word always seemed to appear in close association with other major changes in the way people lived, changes that were undoubtedly part cause and part effect of the new skill. There are many fine archaeological reconstructions and historical interpretations of the change, and a full exposition of it hardly belongs in this book. Because the evolution of maturity was intimately bound up with this change, however, I must say a few words about those features of it that seem to have had the greatest effect on man's vision of man.

Of key importance in the shift from primitive culture to civilization was man's ability to produce and preserve a large surplus of food and other essentials. Having a reliable surplus of food, a condition that developed slowly through the domestication of plants and animals and the improvement of storage techniques, led to increased population, made occupational specialization possible, and freed large numbers of people from subsistence work (cf. Harris 1959). It led to stable distinctions in wealth and class on a large scale as well. These developments in turn made it possible for masses of people to live together in political states, which had centralized authority and a complex division of labor. Surplus also stimulated trade and travel, encouraged sturdy buildings and even monumental works, and of course made warfare on a grand scale an irresistible possibility. Many of these things in turn encouraged the keeping of records. Traders needed to know how much they had of what, and who owed them how much. With writing, kings and noblemen could achieve wider and longer lasting reputations, a fact that stimulated struggles for power and at the same time elevated the prestige of writing. As trades grew more complex and effective, it was important to systematize their lore, and of course there was the development of trades like religion and politics that depended almost exclusively on brain work. The individual or society that could write could do all these things more effectively than those who could not.

Writing was a two-edged sword when it came to the preservation of cultures, however. While it increased possibilities for social control by standardizing information, it also preserved and spread new, dangerous, and even heretical ideas that might bring about dramatic change.

The Hero and the Mystic

Man's view of himself and the universe was gradually transformed by these new developments in a number of ways, two of which are especially interesting to us here. First, there was a great elaboration and refinement of the concept and practice of a behavior complex that involved the search for power (and ultimately for immortality) through the practice of extraordinary feats of strength, courage, and cunning, a complex that led Campbell (1964) to call the period from 1500 to 500 B.C. the Age of the Heroes. Second, there was the emergence of the idea that knowledge was something that transcended ordinary human experience—something absolute, unchanging, and mysterious. This idea, which I referred to in chapter 1 as the Conscious, Transcendent Universe, led to a parallel elaboration of the search for power (and immortality) through the cultivation of mental abilities.

Heroism was probably stimulated by several conditions of life in early literate societies. With the development of social classes, some individuals were freed from the mundane activities of making a living, and could devote themselves to heroic activity as a full-time job. In doing this, they might attract followers who were similarly at leisure, thereby multiplying their social impact. The large masses of people brought together in the new cities and states made this kind of activity especially attractive, since they provided an audience. New technologies like horsemanship and armor further increased heroic spectacles, as did the new preoccupation with large-scale warfare. The material rewards of heroism also became considerable. If you led a victorious army, you were likely to get more than a few yams from your grateful king.

But perhaps the greatest stimulus to heroism was writing. As the deeds of heroes got recorded (often after considerable exaggeration), their audiences extended outward in space and onward in time. Unlike the primitive hero, whose name and biographical details faded rapidly and whose deeds quickly merged in memory with the mythical exploits of other ancestors, the hero of literate society achieved a degree of immortality. Thereafter, he became an inspiration to younger generations. With time, heroic activities and their written accounts became important properties of the heroes' cultures, and whole societies could compete in producing such men (and occasionally women) and such deeds. As we shall discuss in the example of pre-Socratic Athens, heroism became the raison d'etre of a whole social class, and continued to be throughout the Middle Ages and the Renaissance. The "Vita Activa" as a form of maturity had been born, and the concept of development would never be the same.

The development of the Conscious, Transcendent Universe led to another form of heroism, a very different form called the "Vita Contemplativa." This change was stimulated by many of the same things that led to "Vita Activa" heroism, but it probably occurred a little later. Whereas heroic myths are found in preliterate societies and appear in the first records of newly literate ones, fully developed spirituality takes some time. Bellah (1970:22) refers to this process as the "phenomenon of religious rejection of the world characterized by an extremely negative evaluation of man and society and the exhaltation of another realm of reality as alone true and infintely valuable," and locates it in the "first millenium B.C., all across the world." Karl Jaspers speculates that it reached its full flowering somewhere between 800 and 200 B.C., when writing had already been known for two thousand years:

> Many extraordinary developments were crowded into this epoch. In China lived Confucius and Lao-Tse, and all the characteristic Chinese philosophical tendencies were born; such thinkers as Mo Ti, Chuang-Tze, Liadsi, and innumerable others were at work; in India it was the period of the Upanishads, of Buddha, and, just as in China, every philosophical possibility was then developed, including scepticism, materialism, sophistry, and nihilism; in Iran, Zoroaster taught the dramatic cosmology of the struggle between Good and Evil; in Palestine, it was the age of the Prophets, from Elijah to Isaiah, Jeremiah, and Deutero-Isaiah; in Greece, it was the age of Homer, of the philosophers Parmenides, Heraclitus, and Plato, of the dramatists, of Theucidides and Archimedes. (Jaspers 1948:598)

And what had touched off this flood of consciousness? Jaspers goes on:

The new element that appeared in this epoch was that man became aware of existence as a whole, of his self, and of his limitations. . . . he set himself the highest aims; he experienced the absolute in the depth of selfhood and in the clarity of transcendence. (ibid.)

But why? And why at this time? The questions of course are not new. In the early 1960s, for example, sociologist Alvin Gouldner and psychologist Robert Peterson took an interest in the apparent association between civilized technology and a highly developed "apollonian" religious ethics. They carried out a statistical analysis of the relationship in modern societies between measures of social and technological complexity on one hand, and the development of religiously sanctioned moral self-restraint on the other. In their view, religously based "apollonian" codes of ethics followed, in the early development of civilization, upon an epidemic loss of faith in the primitively conceived "natural order." It was a condition that followed naturally with social stratification and social heterogeneity, with their accompanying diversity of personal experience and social strife. The perception of oneself as essentially different from others became a common experience among the masses for the first time in the early agricultural states, Gouldner and Peterson argue, and this led to a turning-inward of consciousness. These conditions, in turn, led to the need for an *impartial* system of ethics, and from there to the invention of all-knowing gods (Gouldner and Peterson 1962).

I have already said I agree with the idea that nonliterate people are, compared with ourselves at least, disinclined to be self conscious. But I have some difficulty with the idea that transcendental religion and ethics developed largely as a result of civic heterogeneity and strife alone. Why would oppressed majorities not see easily through a theological system that conveyed so many privileges to the theologists themselves? Rather, I believe the source of the new self-consciousness lay mainly in the effects of writing and of the technological changes that accompanied writing, on the human consciousness. First, there was the problem of scale. Written records, trade goods, monumental buildings, massive conquests and population movements impressed upon the individual his insignificance in the scheme of things. A universe of such scope and scale could not possibly be the anthropomorphic universe construed by the mind of nonliterate culture. It would seem impossible that ordinary knowledge of the human kind could take it all in, much less predict it, plan it, or control more than a tiny corner of it. There had to be a transcendent consciousness, otherwise the whole system was impossible to explain; worse yet, it was liable to go wrong.

Second, writing and its associated changes introduced an equally important problem with respect to the nature of time. The nonliterate's time is cyclical, for the most part. Everything, including souls, is recycled endlessly, and there is little or no cumulative change in the world. Durable records of both the written and the stonework varieties, on the other hand, project an image of time as unquestionably linear, at least in the short-run span of a few centuries. If families, towns, kingdoms, ways of life disappear forever, how is man to find meaning in the evanescent world around him? To understand the seriousness of this issue for early literate man, it is important to remember that he lacked our modern sense of the *age* of the universe, and logically concluded that it was of very recent origin and might very well have an even shorter future. This question of man's role in such a universe, and the question of ultimate causality, together laid the cornerstones for the cataclysmic transition that ushered in a new way of thinking about human life and maturity.

> The symbol systems of the historic religions differ greatly among themselves but share the element of transcendentalism that sets them off from the archaic religions; in this sense they are all dualistic. (Bellah 1970:32)

Hebrews: The Revitalization of Myth

Between about 1300 and 500 B.C. a small group of seminomadic people in the area around what is now Israel invented a religion and a set of literary techniques with which to teach it. Both were totally new, from a primitive point of view, and they still offer the basic answers to all ultimate questions, including the goals of human development, for about half the world. In a thousand subtle ways of which we are seldom conscious, most of us think like ancient Hebrews. The explanation for the remarkable achievements of the early Hebrews lies in their adaptation to a particular kind of geographical and cultural environment.

In the formative period of Jewish culture and religion before the period of the prophets, that is, the fifteenth and fourteenth centuries B.C., the people whose origins are traced in the Old Testament lived in a region called Canaan. This area was hilly and semiarid, with a fairly sparse, seminomadic population. It was criscrossed by trade routes, lying as it did between the major population centers of Mesopotamia and Egypt. Gordon calls it "the crossroads of all the great cultures of the day" (1965: 92). Culturally, it was broken up into many small valleys holding ethnically related but jealously autonomous people who continuously fought each other over territory and trade, much like the situation in the Middle East today.

The Jews were one of these groups, speaking a dialect of the widespread Canaanite language. They, like their neighbors, were farmers and herders, but the aridity of the region required them to abandon land often, and to rely on trade with distant peoples for many of the necessities of life. Since they used asses for transportation (the camel was just coming into use, but the people of Canaan had no camels) they could not stray far from water, and did a good deal of travelling from town to town along well populated trade routes. In the towns, they formed an element of a culturally mixed occupation that was considered riffraff by more prosperous and settled peoples, but they absorbed a great many ideas from these cultures, especially from Caphtor in the west, Mesopotamia in the north, and Egypt in the south.

Early Jewish life, then, had three elements that were to play a crucial role in the shaping of a new idea of self and maturity. First, the Jews were exposed to writing and learned it early. It was important to them as merchants, and it helped them to maintain their traditions in a mobile, polyglot world. Second, they were exposed to a great many different ways of life, a situation that seems to stimulate the development of high cultures as no other situation does. Third, they were in constant conflict with other tribes over territory, even driven repeatedly from their homeland. The patriarchs, concludes Gordon, "were wandering merchants from the North Mesopotamian part of the Hittite Empire" (1965:132). Ordinary Jews were forbidden to own land at this time, although the patriarchs overcame this by virtue of their great wealth.

This set of circumstances gave them, and their neighbors, an abundance of problems, as the Old Testament clearly documents. With such a variety of beliefs and loyalties to choose from, such shifting boundaries and antagonisms, such movement and dispersal of their people, they found their identity as a tribe strained to the breaking point and their leadership in disarray. Two of the main problems of cultural survival, internal cohesion and boundary maintenance, demanded radical solutions in this environment.

Although many other peoples were in a similar situation, the Jewish response had some unique elements. They developed a religious identity of great appeal, a set of myths and rituals that embodied and transmitted this identity effectively, and a literature that made the whole system extremely portable. This solution did not spring forth in its modern form, of course, but developed gradually through a series of ups and downs, many of which are richly recorded in the Bible itself. Abraham made important contributions, particularly the custom of circumcision, which distinguished Jews physically from other Canaanite-speaking people. The story of the Flood and Noah's sons helped to establish the superiority of the Jews over their close cultural kin in Canaan. The Egyptian bondage resulted in serious social disintegration, so that they emerged, as W. F. Albright says, "not as a homogeneous body, illustrating a fixed social type of known character" but as a group of mixed origins, held together "by their remarkable history and their religious zeal" (1969:97). Mosaic Judaism was a fanatical and passionate religion—a movement, really, in the height of its fervor.

The conquest of Palestine and Judea that ushered in the period of the Kings (probably about 1200 B.C.) gave Judaism a great grip on history, as it allowed the building of temples and the identification of the people with the land. But the problem of cultural identity was far from over. Other tribes occupied the territory still, and their subjugation was accompanied by intermarriage and cultural borrowing; hence the repeated references in the Old Testament to the decay of Jewish worship and the purging of foreign elements. Even the House of David "was shot through on the distaff side," says Albright, "with pagan elements" (1969:101). The crisis of cultural cohesion exploded with the separation of Judea and Jerusalem under Rehoboam and the subsequent Babylonian exile of the Jews in 586 B.C.

Life as experienced by the Hebrews, then, challenged traditional ideas about man's relationship to his fellow men. In contrast to the hunter, or even the settled agriculturalist, the Jewish merchant spent most of his waking life in contact with people who believed and conducted their lives in ways alien to his own. He had to adapt to this, and he could not rely upon the nonliterate's faith in the identity of person and behavior. There was no place where he felt at home in the sense that other people do, no soil in which he felt his being fully established. Kin and community were all he had, and their solidarity and continuity were always under pressure from outside influences.

To understand the psychological effects of this, let us look at a sensitive analysis of a similar cultural situation from the modern world. Exploring the mental habits of people in urban Morocco, anthropologist Clifford Geertz was struck by the image of chaotic individualism he found there. On closer questioning, he found that in the marketplace, people related to each other not on the basis of personal characteristics at all, but on the basis of simple stereotypes assigned according to religion and ethnicity. These were the "boundaries" of selfhood, and the details were never questioned. Geertz called this the "mosaic" approach to selfhood: "What makes the mosaic work is the confidence that one can be as totally pragmatic, adaptive, opportunistic and generally ad hoc in one's relations with others as one wants without any risk of losing one's sense of who one is. Selfhood is never in danger because, outside the immediacies of procreation and prayer, only its boundaries are asserted" (1984:133-34).

Under these circumstances, the Jews developed a personal relationship with their own ethnic God, a relationship that told them at all times and in all places who they were. Worship was no longer propitiation, a mere adjunct to coping with the environment by other means. It was no longer merely an expression of one's group membership, or an ecstatic sense of release from suffering and care. It was still all these things; but first and foremost, it was simultaneously the expression of one's private personhood and a communion with the *one* transcendent consciousness in the universe. Through worship, the individual would survive time, which

God held the power to reverse. The Hebrew prophets had built a direct link, via ethnicity, between the individual and the transcendent universe.

Monotheism was not a new idea, nor by any means was the doctrine of cosmic tribal supremacy, nor the threat of Armageddon. In fact, there was probably only one major element of Jewish religion that was really unique, and that made all the difference. The new element was the idea of sin. It is impossible to understand modern Western ideas of character and maturity without understanding the idea of sin, and it is a concept quite unique to the cultural descendants of the early Hebrews.

Sin is really a complex idea. In order to feel sinful, one has to believe that there are absolute moral laws in the universe, which operate independently of human agency, and which affect everybody in a powerful and personal way. This is quite different from the primitive idea of fate. Fate is the preordination of circumstances according to unseen forces over which one has little control. It is largely whimsical and amoral, and there is no point in brooding about it. Sin, of course, is the notion that one suffers because one has broken a rule and deserves punishment. It is an idea that makes little sense to nonliterates, because the idea of *absolute law* is alien to them. If one transgresses against cultural rules in nonliterate society and gets caught, one suffers the consequences of immediate retribution. Perhaps one's entire family or village will be the object of revenge at the hands of one's outraged enemies; but no psychological guilt is implied in these relationships at all. The sense of sin is something new. It comes from a combination of three features of ancient civilization we have already mentioned—namely, the linear concept of time and permanent change; the awareness of a transcendent consciousness that guides the universe; and the social organization of the state, with its hierarchical class structure and its specialized occupations.

In the early literate world, with its chronic large scale warfare both within and between societies, it was easy to see that some groups and societies were prosperous, while others suffered slavery and even extinction. It was a barbaric world, with the powerful enforcing their will violently and often arbitrarily on the weak. One is reminded of the fateful words of Rehoboam that split the kingdoms of Judea and Jerusalem, "My father chastized you with whips, but I shall chastize you with scorpions" (II Chron. 10:11).

The ideas of obedience to arbitrary rule and punishment for rebelliousness were extremely important in this world, as they had not been in the nonliterate world. In this world of social stratification, the oppressed were continuously in danger of the psychological pain that attends alienation and cynicism; in order to escape such pain, as Anna Freud (1936) explains, they were often found to identify with their oppressors and assume the guilt for their own oppression. This tendency is shown in many studies, from Bettelheim's (1943) work on the Nazi concentration camps to Lerner's (Lerner and Lerner 1981) experiments with social justice.

The question is, how does this guilt get transferred to the cosmic realm? Again, we can rely only on our imagination in trying to reconstruct psychological processes that occurred very gradually several thousand years ago, but something like the following seems likely: It is a tragedy that people die and do not come back to life—a tragedy discovered in the literate world. If the cosmos is ruled by an all-wise and all-powerful transcendent consciousness, there is nothing arbitrary or accidental about such facts. Therefore death must be part of the plan. But why would something so tragic be inflicted upon man by the transcendent universe? It must be a punishment for something man did; otherwise one is stuck with the unbearable conclusion that the cosmos is capricious and cruel. Under the circumstances, the idea of sin—and specifically the Hebrew idea of *original* sin—is extremely powerful.

Here we have the basis of sin as a cosmological concept. It is an important part of our cosmology because it offers an explanation for an important existential question. But the idea of sin also plays another important function: It explains personal feelings of *guilt* that arise out of the alienation of the individual in complex societies. This is a subtle fact about sin that takes some explaining, but it is an important fact, because it accounts for the power of the concept as a catalyst for the formation of religious movements, as we shall see.

I mentioned that the Jews functioned in a culturally mixed milieu, where social relations were often regulated by stereotyped expectations based on race, religion, and ethnicity. This is a very different situation from what one finds in a primitive society, where the other actors on life's stage are all people whom one knows intimately as individuals. The mixed milieu of the Casbah produces a kind of privacy, in which the individual's feelings about himself and others are generally irrelevant to the social business at hand, and in any case are easy to conceal. The individual actors feel that their *selves* are not really involved in many of their social transactions. As Geertz pointed out, this means that each person is free to present himself however he wishes in any given situation, as long as he does not obviously violate the broad expectations others have of him *as a Jew*, or as a Hittite or a Philistine or whatever. But what if there were some social relationship in which all his self-presentations were simultaneously open to scrutiny—in which his secret inner identity were completely revealed? All the deception, all the inner contradiction, all the doubt and anxiety would no longer be simply a personal problem, but would also be a social problem. Moreover, if this relationship were not merely human, but existed on the plane of the cosmos, and the knower of one's individuality were an infallible consciousness, these hidden feelings and self-knowings would damn the individual to a sense of overwhelming unworthiness.

And this is exactly the relationship of the ancient Hebrew to his God.

Yet I do not believe it is the concept of sin alone that accounts for the success of the Jewish approach to the problem of the transcendental cosmos. Powerful as their theology was, I believe it was also partly the literary genius of the Jews that eventually raised Judaism to the stature of a world religion. In their texts, the ancient authors managed to achieve a synthesis of biography, history, and mythology. The people in the Old Testament are real people, not the superhuman heroes of earlier legends. One can identify with them. Many of the events are historically accurate, and the places and people themselves identifiable. This synthesis raised human life to the level of cosmic drama. It rendered cosmic forces concrete by focusing them on the everyday events of society. It immersed the reader or listener in a suprahuman time frame and made him a participant in the inner workings of the cosmos. While recognizing the new linear concept of time and the ephemerality of human life, it nevertheless gave man a place in eternity. To grasp the enormity of this feat, one need only contrast the Old Testament with the Homeric epics. Magnificent as Homer is, one finds the Bible more intimately human and at the same time more cosmically awesome.

The Hebrew achievement gave articulate expression to the literate era's conception of maturity. The knowledge needed for wisdom was now of a special type, a transcendental type embodied in sacred writing. There were degrees of maturity, corresponding to the degrees of one's under-standing of this new knowledge. The mature individual was typified by Job—not the "lucky" Job with his many cattle and his seven strapping sons, for such is a primitive maturity; not the virtuous Job, who conducted the rituals faithfully and was generous and kind; but the Job who knew God's power and understood his will, who bent his life, in other words, to the cosmic plan. In the Middle Ages, Job inspired such magnificent mystics as Gregory the Great and Saint Francis of Assisi.

Hebrew spirituality thus moved the Western concept of maturity closer to the Vita Contemplativa, but it took the New Testament to complete that movement. Most of the heroes of the Old Testament were sterling examples of the Vita Activa. Saul, David, and Solomon were of this type; violent, sometimes boastful, sometimes crafty and deceitful, but undoubtedly closer to the permanent, transcendental reality than the ordinary soul. Meanwhile, in the fifth century B.C., a parallel and equally consequential assault on the primitive mind was taking shape in Athens.

Greeks: Maturity and the Inner Guide

In the sixth century B.C., the Ionic philosophers of the Eleatic school were engaged in debate with the primitive mentality of their predecessors on the nature of the universe. Xenophanes found it necessary to argue the unlikelihood of anthropomorphic gods. "If oxen and horses, or lions, had hands," he said, "and could paint with their hands, and produce works of art as men do, horses would paint the forms of the gods like horses, and oxen like oxen." (Copleston, 1962a:64) The Eleatics were also concerned about the number and variety of causal agents in their world, and argued that everything was reducible to one unified, all-embracing principle. Parmenides, the founder of the school, and a teacher of Socrates, held that the sensible world is a mere manifestation of an absolute reality, and that that reality consists in ideas, or concepts, that can be discovered through systematic contemplation and logic.

This was the view of man's relation to the cosmos that set the Greeks off from the rest of the world, and that gave them their permanent place in the thought of Western civilization. If the Hebrews offered the literate Western world a link to the cosmos through literature, the Hellenic Greeks offered an equally important link through self awareness. Each solution to the problem of a transcendental universe has its own advantages. The Hebrew way is more vivid and passionate, and therefore appeals to more people, but it does require a good deal of humble self-abasement. The Greek way is simple and elegant. There are no massive texts to be memorized or arcane sayings to be interpreted; once its straightforward principles are grasped, anyone who can stand several hours a day of brutal self criticism can be a philosopher. Perhaps this is why the two systems never really merged (in spite of the medieval scholastics, whose chief mission was to merge them) but remain distinct teachings today.

Like the other Greek city states of the sixth century B.C., Athens was a society with a vigorous public life that centered on the closely interrelated pursuits of war, politics, and religion. Industry and commerce were important for survival, but their importance in spiritual life was minimal. They developed, as Vernant says, "in every case more or less on the periphery of the city-state, being somehow extraneous to the civic community" (1980:6). This "civic community" was made up of free and equal adult male landholders, who devoted most of their time to the worship of the civic gods and performance of civic rituals, to public political debate, and to fighting wars. Their wealth went correspondingly into public buildings and festivities, weapons and armor, rather than luxuries. They lived (if you'll pardon the expression) a Spartan life. Merchants and manufacturers were mostly noncitizens, and the daily work of farming, housekeeping, childrearing, spinning, weaving, cooking, and fetching-and-carrying was done by women and slaves, who were considered constitutionally inferior to freemen. Philosophy, needless to say, had to do with freemen.

The Greek city-state of the time had a structural problem just as the Hebrew tribe did, but it was a different kind of problem. Since the Greeks owned land they had no trouble finding their identity as a people in their local geography and material culture. Although they lived cheek-by-jowl with foreigners in their cities, their language, gods and rituals, customs and mores were known and revered over a wide area, so *that* was not so much of a problem. The problem was that they saw themselves besieged on all sides by other hostile city-states. Vernant (1980) calls their view of life "agonistic," and notes that ritual battles were even characteristic of their festivals. This made them quite dependent on the dedication and solidarity of their fighting men, and they needed an ideology and a way of life that would assure these qualities.

This is a need that conflicts with certain natural human tendencies. In addition to their civic pride, most men have family ties which often conflict with civic duties, and most have a sentimental attachment to life and limb that occasionally interferes with their blood-lust. The Greek solution to this problem was a way of life that offered every freeman an equal chance at heroism through the pursuit of politics and war (the Vita Activa), and at the same time severely limited the influence of the family on its sons.

The young man's chance at heroism was assured by the system of education, which taught boys how to fight and how to debate. The purpose of warfare was not to destroy the enemy, but to exact concessions and to prove moral superiority by winning battles. It was, essentially, Homeric heroism transferred from the individual Achilles-type figure to the state itself. The importance of debate, an equivalent of verbal warfare, led to the development of Greek principles of logic. Whereas in less democratic societies knowledge was couched in esoteric terms and carefully guarded by elites, In Parmenides's Athens it was public and logical.

The system required that horizontal ties among equal freemen take priority over the vertical ties of generations in families. This is a problem that often plagues simple societies, and the Greeks evolved a solution to it that is very often found in societies with similar structural problems: age grading.

Age grading is the cultural practice of assigning specific social roles and statuses to specific periods of life. For example, in many African tribes, males are considered "children" until they reach puberty, at which time they become "warriors," a change that involves ritual transformation of the group of same-age boys. They will remain warriors until they marry, or until their fathers retire and they become "householders," and so on. This system serves to dampen interfamilial conflict, because it unites age peers and places them in conflict with other age groups. This is what the Greeks did. Plato's idea in *The Republic,* of taking boys away from their parents and raising them as wards of the state, was not as radical as it might sound. The Athenian state did in fact seclude boys from their families during a period of initiation, and it inducted every male into the army at a certain age. We can see other ways of limiting the power of families as well, in the institution of the oath of office (the Hippocratic Oath being a perfect example) and in the superimposition of the state gods over the family gods of the hearth.

Classical Greek culture, then, sought to unite man with the transcendental universe and to remove the sting of linear time by making every man a hero, although women and slaves would have to shift for themselves. The pursuit of heroic immortality was, of course, only one of many avenues of spiritual development. There were religious cults offering among other things transcendental experience through orgiastic rites and trance induction. We are familiar with the cults of Bacchus, of Cybele, and of Orpheus, for example. But because Greek spirituality stressed civic duty as *action*, not belief, religious heterodoxy was rarely an issue.

The Socratic Revolution

Although the Eleatic philosophers revolutionized philosophy, along the lines we have been discussing, in the sixth century B.C., it is not the Eleatic school to whom Western civilization owes its greatest debt. An even greater intellectual revolution is represented by the works of Plato and Aristotle in the fifth century B.C., and it is the influence of those works that concerns me here. The Eleatics hit upon a method—logic—for the achievement of contemplative heroism, but they did not really question the ethical foundations of Greek civilization. The Socratics of the following century did something so unprimitive it has rarely been achieved in philosophy since. They made the basic assumptions of their own culture the subject of discussion and invention.

It is difficult to convey the importance of the Socratic revolution. Without it, philosophy and social science as we know them would be impossible, because we would not be able to see the structures of our own belief for what they are—mental habits, susceptible to logical analysis and deliberate revision. The history of Western civilization would probably be quite different without this ability, as it was a major force in the transition from the Middle Ages to modern times. This discovery bears emphasis here, because it reinforces the central argument of this book—it is an outlook we must keep in the center of our educational process if we are to thrive as a society.

What was the Socratic revolution, then, and how did it happen? It began with the fall of Athens in 404 B.C., which marked the end of the Peloponnesian War. That event not only broke the power of Athens permanently, but touched off a moral crisis in the culture.

From the very first, Greek civilization had been inseparably connected with the life of the city-state; and the connection was closest of all in Athens. Therefore the effects of the catastrophe were, inevitably, far more than merely political. It shook all moral laws; it struck at the roots of religion. If the disaster were to be repaired, the process must start with religion and ethics. (Jaeger 1943:3-4)

The Homeric version of heroism, the fanatic religion of war across one's borders and political competition within them, had proven disastrous. The names of the great leaders—Pericles, Cleon, Alcibiades—now stood not for immortality, but for death itself. The Athenian people could no longer find their way to transcendental truth through the assumptions of their culture.

Plato was about twenty-three when Athens fell. He had already made the acquaintance of Socrates, an incomparable genius of magnetic personality, whose radical method offered the basis for the moral reconstruction of Greek culture that Plato undertook. For Socrates's method—dialogue, in which the teacher plays the role of student—was precisely the systematic questioning and clarification of deeply held assumptions. Because all cultural belief systems contain irrational elements and areas of self-contradiction, the effect of the Socratic dialogue is to introduce doubt wherever there once was culturally conditioned certainty. Moreover, the method accomplishes this without directly contradicting existing beliefs, thereby permitting ideas to enter public discussion that would be much too shocking if they were directly stated. It is an excellent tool for reform in a society devoted to intellectual talk. Using the Socratic method, then, Plato sought to make education and debate tools for self-examination, rather than for self-aggrandizement. He sought to move the repair of ethics to the center of moral teaching, and to loosen the powerful association in the Greek culture between piety—the worship of tradition—and *arete*, or excellence.

In order to do this, he had to offer people hope of a belief system worthy of their devotion: something more beautiful and more permanent than the old ways. In the light of this necessity, we can more clearly understand the Platonic doctrine of Ideal Forms, in which he taught that the principles of virtue, although accessible to discovery through introspection, belong to a realm of permanent reality different from the ever-changing world of the senses. The approach to this different reality is in essence Plato's theory of maturation.

Plato wrote about the development of character in several of his works—notably *The Republic, The Phaedrus,* and *The Symposium.* I shall deal mostly with the last, since it states his developmental theory most systematically.

The Symposium is a dialogue about love. In it, Plato puts his own ideas about maturity into the mouth of Socrates, who in turn credits *his* insights on the topic to a woman. The courtesan Diotema tells him that love is first "the child of poverty and plenty," because he who seeks it, having none, is poor; but he who is too poor lacks the desire to seek it. In other words, there is a stage of development that is prelove, namely, the stage of mere survival. The first stage of love proper is the erotic, where the love object is another person. This, as Arendt (1958) has shown, seems to refer both to the ontological stage of adolescence and to the social level of women and slaves. By their service to the passions and bodily needs of others, women and slaves lived lives that were completely bound to the organic cycle of birth and death. Their labor freed the citizens of the state for the more important work of fighting and arguing, and of course they served the well-being of the family, which was itself an object of religious worship. Carnal love is thus a positive virtue, and celibacy seems to have been illegal in Plato's Athens. Even friendship had a strong erotic quality, which the modern mind finds somewhat shocking.

So the love of one beautiful body spreads to the love of others, and finally to physical beauty itself, the embodiment of the temporal and moral. Then there arises, says Diotema, a desire for a higher kind of love, and the hero's attention turns to honor and power. Here is the preoccupation of the adult freeman of the time, the pursuit of what Arendt calls "beautiful words and deeds," the principle embodied in the myths and epics, and a necessary duty in the religious worship of the city—the Vita Activa. It is obviously superior to carnal love because, as we have seen, its products are immortal, but also because it requires training, wit, and courage, and because it is based on leisure derived from the labor of others.

This was probably the highest stage of maturity sought by most freemen. The Sophists, after all, taught philosophy as a technique for the acquisition of honor through verbal combat, and only incidentally as a vehicle for knowledge. But for Socrates, there was a fourth stage of development, the Vita Contemplativa, the love of wisdom. This stage was also obviously the privilege of mature freemen (and possibly their female playmates, like Diotema) because it required leisure *and* a state of moral purity reached by unending self-discipline and study. This level was not for everybody. Socrates had to insist continually that the purpose of philosophy was *not* the pursuit of heroic honor, but rather the opposite, the acquisition of humility through self-understanding. Moreover, the goal of Socratic philosophy was union with transcendental knowledge itself, and was therefore by definition never fully attainable, just as union with God was the unattainable goal of Hebrew maturity.

The four stages of Plato's theory of maturity present two parallel hierarchies; a temporal, developmental progression and a moral framework or ladder (Arendt 1958). Developmentally, childhood is the state of prealtruism. The child conforms in order to win approval most of the time, first from its real parents, then from its "inner" parent, or conscience. Sexual maturation and erotic love occur next, before one has acquired the educational and anatomic stature for serious heroic competition. As the individual personality develops, it requires intense personal dyads for its fulfillment. The dyad is the only social relationship in which one can be simultaneously selfish and altruistic (Simmel 1908). Finally, the stage of philosophic contemplation logically takes place in late life, when the mind is most experienced and the body is past its prime.

Turning to the moral ladder, we see that the self-centered life is the least desirable because it is the least durable. Its referent is the monad, and its values dissolve with the individual's death. Spontaneous and unreflective, it is taken up with the mundane, and is furthest from the transcendental. The next stage, personal love, survives the partners in the form of that which their love has produced (typically, children), and prepares the way for higher forms of selflessness. At the stage of honor and power, the locus of value is the whole society, and the time-frame is the whole history of that society. The Vita Activa produces words and deeds worth recording and recounting. It approaches the transcendental by altering the suprapersonal flow of history.

At the stage of philosophy, one seeks not just immortality, but union with eternity through the discovery and contemplation of timeless truth. The Vita Contemplativa is higher than the Vita Activa. This principle is seen also in the Allegory of the Cave, where Plato presents us with the problem of selfhood in literate society: In order to be fully developed, we must know of the existence of sunlight; once we do, we can never be satisfied with the firelit shadows on the cave wall. It is clear from Plato's treatment of maturation that he thought of the emotion of love as an innate human capacity—as that capacity which allows us to see the light of absolute truth.

The mature individual for Plato was, like Socrates, an introspective person, one who weighed carefully the effects of perceptions and ideas on his own inner experience. In this sense, Plato preserved the pursuit of passion, even ecstasy, that was so important for the pursuit of knowledge in primitive culture. The mature person, although outwardly self-controlled, was likely to have a sensitive and turbulent conscience, and to resist the implications of mere logic until he had weighed the deep internal effects of an argument.

Plato's greatest pupil, Aristotle, seems to have accepted the idea of the Platonic stages of development, but his ideal of maturity differed from his teacher's in at least one very important way. For Aristotle, the light of the universal truth was to be discerned not in that subtle attraction of the feelings that Plato proposed, but in the intellectual discernment of order in the perceptible world. The Aristotelian ideal was one of poise and harmony. For the perfect functioning of the intellect one needed to avoid emotional extremes, indeed, extremes of any kind. Inherently unstable, the emotions were to be tamed by rigorous self-discipline, to accept the dictates of reason.

If it still seems correct to say that there are two distinct forms of knowledge, an emotional form and an intellectual form, and that these two forms are often in disharmony, the fault of our confusion may lie in the unbroken preservation of these great Greek ideas in the history of our moral thought. When the Renaissance master Raphael sought to portray the spirit of his era in his fresco *School of Athens* in the papal apartments, this was the theme he chose. On the left side of the painting stands Plato, his right index finger pointing upward toward divine inspiration. To Plato's left stand the philosophers who appealed to the emotions and intuition. On the right, holding the palm of an extended hand downward in a moderating gesture, stands Aristotle; and to his right, the logicians, the geometers, the grammarians.

Moral Maturity and Everyday Life

At the end of this book we shall turn to the question of how these moral ideas have affected life and thought in later times. It is difficult to say how they affected the lives of ordinary people in ancient civilization, but their effects were probably subtle and indirect. For one thing, primitive ideas of fate were not much affected by the new thinking. The Old Testament, for example, has many examples of such ideas. It even appears that the ancient Hebrews believed in the power of the ancestors to affect the fortunes of the living, much as many modern sub-Saharan African peoples do. In the Book of Job, for example, we find Bildad the Shuhite doubting that Job's troubles have nothing to do with his prenatal destiny:

> "For inquire, I pray thee [says Bildad to Job] of the former age, and
> prepare thyself to the search of their fathers. For we are but of
> yesterday, and know nothing, because our days upon earth are a
> shadow. Shall not they teach thee, and tell thee, and utter words out
> of their heart?" (Job 8:8-10)

Bildad might be referring to a belief in the magical powers of the written word, or he might be suggesting a seance with the spirits of the dead; in either case, the ideas of an anthropomorphic universe and prenatal fate seem clearly implied.

Similaraly, a personified fate held great power over the imaginations of the Greeks and Romans at the height of their civilizations. The story of Oedipus, the Homeric sagas, the greatest Roman poetry betray a positive preoccupation with the idea. In the opening stanza of the *Aeneid* Virgil describes Aeneas as *fatō prōfugus*, "driven by fate." Roman prayers were regularly directed to Fortuna, *imperatrix mundi*, empress of the world.

The failure of individuals to reach normal maturity, then, was regarded in the classical world much as it had been in the primitive world—a result of outside interference or bad fate. As Maurice Charlton says of classical Greece, "Madness (in the sense of overt psychosis) was regarded as primarily due to possession by various malignant demons and gods. For example, when Hercules went insane, he was thought to be inhabited by Lyssa, the goddess of madness. When Orestes went mad after he had avenged the murder of his father by killing his mother Clytemnestra and her lover, his madness was acribed to the Furies. Interestingly enough, the possessing demons were usually regarded as female" (1967:12).

But this is not to say that the new ideas had no effect on life in the streets. All cultures contain contradictory ideas, just as individuals entertain contradictory goals and beliefs, but ideas that survive and flourish do so because they affect the way people think. The Jewish notion of integrity based on ethnicity led to great struggles to keep their religion and their culture pure in the face of many obstacles; whereas the Greeks simply absorbed pagan elements, diversifying and diluting their culture until it was absorbed in turn by the spread of Christianity. Greek admiration for scholarship and interest in the physical world, on the other hand, led to the spread of the Greek language, philosophy, art, and science throughout the Mediterranean and the civilized world. The Greek colony in India, Gandala, introduced their ideas to the East, with far reaching results. One can even find eighth century Buddhist statues in Japan that bear an uncanny resemblance to the gods of the Acropolis. The ethical foundations of Roman law and statesmanship, too, grew out of Greek ideas of the heroic dignity of free men. The effects of both the Hebrew and the Greek ideas on the Middle Ages were equally profound, as we shall now see.

4. *The Middle Ages: Decline of the Tribe*

The Middle Ages, Morris Bishop reminds us (1970), were really the continuation of the classical Western civilization (with its primitive peasant base) and the beginnings of the modern world, not a distinct period of history with its own unique traditions. There is not even general agreement on when the Middle Ages began or ended, a common date for the beginning being the year the barbarian Odoacer acceded to the emperorship of Rome, 476 A.D. The date is not really important here, since I am interested in the major turns of scholarly thought on maturity. The Middle Ages in Europe conformed to an overwhelmingly Christian teaching on human virtue, but it was neither a uniform nor a static teaching. The period from the fall of Rome to the Renaissance really encompasses two somewhat distinct cultures—an ecclesiastical one and a secular one—each of which passed through two main stages. The shift occurred in both cultures at about the same time, for slightly different if related reasons. The watershed was the twelfth century.

In the ecclesiastical tradition, the first stage was one of institution-building. The leading moral teachers had to struggle with an inherent conflict between a highly personal ethical ideal on the one hand, and a need for collective strength and continuity of the faith on the other hand. The patrist fathers from Paul to Augustine preached a spiritual quest in which ecstasy was promised as a reward for extreme asceticism—a tradeoff that was not likely to attract the man in the street to begin with, and was likely to turn away even many with high ideals in the long run. Yet without a steady supply of serious students, this ideal would not survive and spread. Monasticism evolved as the solution to this dilemma.

Monasticism apparently worked rather well. By the twelfth century, the church had become strong and orderly enough to tolerate some experimentation with new ideals. The monasteries had become centers not only of humble work and prayer, but of learned debate and inquiry as well. The result was a second stage of medieval religious ethics—a stage that centered on the problem of reconciling Christian and classical philosophy. This stage began in the time of Bernard of Citieux and Peter Abelard, and it culminated in the work of Aquinas, Bonaventure and Duns Scotus, about a century later.

In the secular tradition, the first stage was driven by the gradual expansion of population and exhaustion of unused land from the eighth century until the twelfth. The second stage coincided with the gradual replacement of the feudal knights, in most places, with the system of courts and kings.

The Christian Cultural Background

During the early phase of the Middle Ages, man's view of the cosmos did not change dramatically, but there were three features of early medieval religious thought that had major effects on our modern ideas of maturity. It is these that will occupy us here. First, there was the stark intolerance of the monastic movement for new ideas from any source, and the creation of institutions to enforce that intolerance and act as a brake on change. Second, there was the unification of religious belief across tribal boundaries, which resulted in the weakening of tribal loyalties. Third, there was the division of life into the somewhat contradictory spheres of the sacred and the profane, the former stressing the Vita Contemplativa view of maturity, and latter the Vita Activa.

Large changes in behavior that are indirectly related to survival are, as we saw in the case of the transition to literate culture, brought about only through the convergence of many pressures. Although technological innovations like the introduction of the horse collar and the water wheel gradually changed the way of life of the common people during the Middle Ages—especially after the thirteenth century—there had probably not been much change in their beliefs since the dawn of civilization. However, among the propertied, the literate and the powerful, one detects a shift early in the Christian era toward pessimism and away from identification with ethnic group or nationality. A spiritual emphasis on death and afterlife, and the identification of the individual with the supernatural, resulted in a kind of vacuum at the tribal level of life that was manifested in various ways. One manifestation was the ascendent power of the church over other institutions; another was the growth of monastic withdrawal from society as a way of life; still another was the excesses of corruption and brutality of the nobility. Latin was superimposed upon ethnic dialects in writing, diplomacy, trade and ritual; urban cultures evolved that transcended local customs in many of their institutions and ways of life; and elites of widely different ethnic backgrounds intermarried and formed alliances, often against rivals within their own cultural communities. (Interestingly, this decline in ethnic solidarity put the Jews of Europe in a very special position. Having preserved their cultural identity, they reaped the major handicap of standing out as ethnic "outsiders," as well as the major benefit of being able to use ethnic networks in trade and finance, just as they had done in their homeland, but now almost without competition from similar ethnic groups.)

The historical processes behind this decline of tribal or ethnic identification were various. One was the serious disorganization of the Jews and other peoples of the Levant around the time of Christ and his related success as a messiah. Christ presented his era with a model for thought and behavior that further weakened ethnicity as a source of personal identity. With the help of gifted interpreters like Paul, people were convinced that if they believed in Christ and followed his example, they would achieve a personal link with the transcendent universe, independently of their loyalty to their tribal traditions. Legions of prophets had tried the same thing before, and legions have tried it since, but few have succeeded as he and his fellows did.

Aside from the matter of the timing, mentioned earlier, Christ had several unique assets. One was the literary beauty of the Jewish writings. Another was his appeal to the antirational and antilegalistic spontaneity characteristic of popular pagan religion, as well as the adoption by his followers of the widespread pagan rituals of communion, sacrifice, and rebirth (Campbell 1964). Then of course there is the ethical beauty of Christ's teachings themselves, and the great power of his personality. The charisma of Christ was also a result of his personal qualities:

> A quick insight into the crux of any moral situation, dislike of any form of pretentiousness and a talent for deflating it, respect for the sincerity of simple people, the constant use of homely imagery to convey moral lessons, a fondness for humorous exaggeration, ability to escape from dialectical dilemmas and turn the tables on opponents by means of swift and effective repartee—these are the qualities most clearly portrayed in the gospels. (Parkes 1959:389)

In addition to the idea of poverty, which may have been borrowed from a contemporary ascetic Jewish cult called the Essenes, there were two features of Christ's teaching that, combined with the persuasive power of his person, helped to spread the new religion beyond the bounds of the

Jewish community, and gave it vitality as a supratribal unifying force. These were the twin ideas, largely alien to the pre-Christian West, of forgiveness, and of ritual simplicity.

The ideal of poverty counteracts tribal identification by weakening the group's control over individual behavior. Respect and social status are important means for enforcing group standards in a community. Most communities give respect and status for various achievements, including unusual abilities, exceptional procreativity, and the display and distribution of wealth; the desire for this approval keeps people busy at competitive projects approved by their culture. The ideal of poverty suggests that such projects are of no real value. If poverty itself is made a badge of group membership, as it apparently was among the highly ritualistic Essenes, one kind of social control is simply substituted for another. But combined with an attack on ritualism and a disregard for ethnic and religious antagonisms, the idea of poverty as preached by Christ promoted panhumanism.

The ideal of forgiveness serves the same ends by different means. Earlier thinkers (notably Socrates) had noted that revenge is morally inferior to the toleration of injustice, because it consists in adding wrong to wrong. But, as Hannah Arendt (1958) and Henry Parkes (1959) have shown, Christ took this idea a step further by adding that the very idea of resentment is wrong. If taken seriously, this removes a major motive for the maintenance of tribal boundaries. In tribal societies, aggression among cotribesmen is always regarded as a more serious offense than aggression against outsiders, a fact that leads to frequent hostilities and standing antagonisms across ethnic boundaries everywhere at all times. (See also the discussion of aggression in chapter 12.) The injunction to ignore such traditions, not only in deed but in spirit, separates the individual psychologically from his cultural institutions.

The concept of forgiveness had an even greater appeal when it was applied at the cosmic level. We have seen how the concept of *sin* was a price paid by the Jews for the patronage of an all-powerful, all-knowing God. Many cultures of the Mediterranean at the time of Christ seem to have been suffering from the conditions that produced personal alienation among the ancient Hebrews—heterogeneous, densely populated areas; rapid population movements; the anonymity of the individual in his daily life—and it is possible that the Hebrew idea of a personal relationship with God was a widely attractive one as an antidote to mass alienation. Aside from the fact that you could not just become a Jew, there was the problem of sin. The Jewish God was jealous and vengeful, not the sort who would attract many followers, alienation or no alienation. Christ's forgiveness changed that. By offering himself as the intermediary between God and man, he made the Jewish brand of personal communication with the transcendental universe possible, and at the same time offered a solution to the problem of sin entailed by that communication.

Finally, there is Christ's teaching against the extreme ritualism of the Jewish sects of his time. Ritual affirms and maintains narrow tribal boundaries by demonstrating group differences in belief, by drawing unfavorable attention to the uninitiated outsider, and by bolstering ingroup sentiment among the initiated. Christ's antiritualism seems to have been the basis for Paul's insistence, at first unpopular, that uncircumcised gentiles could join the Christian sect.

The decline of ethnic loyalty and the spread of Christianity went hand in hand, and it is often impossible to say which took priority. The earliest converts seem to have been urban craftsmen and tradespersons, and slaves (Parkes 1959:414)—those for whom tribal loyalties probably meant least to start with. Eventually, however, the decline and collapse of the Roman Empire and with it a great deal of the optimism that went with political order and technological progress probably soured many people on their own cultural values. Roman subjects found their cultures unable to stem the barbarian tides; barbarians found their cultures unable to sustain Roman levels of achievement in technology, statecraft, or the arts. The result was a succession of vigorous and learned antitribalists—the patristic apologists of the second to fourth centuries—from Justine and Athenagoras to Greogry of Nyssa and Ambrose of Milan.

The Vita Contemplativa: Saint Benedict's Rule .

Philosophically, the ideal of the warrior class, the Vita Activa, was never much of a match for the Vita Contemplativa in the Middle Ages. Before the twelfth century the Church defined maturity as the approach to God through self-denial and prayer. It was a monopoly that the priesthood guarded jealously, both through control of the monastic orders and through active discouragement of lay attempts at spiritualism. Wrote one medieval churchman, Peter Damian, to a prefect of Rome named Cinthius, "Take care that your zeal for the private prayer which perhaps you try to make does not lead you to neglect the duty of keeping good order among the people who have been entrusted to you" (Leclerq et al. 1982:98).

The contemplative ideal of maturity in this period was based on a mystical union with God through the medium of Christ. This union was made possible through the attainment of *grace*—what we would now call an altered state of consciousness—in which lifelong habits of thought, feeling, and behavior dropped away, and consciousness opened for the entry of the spirit of God. The writings of Saint John, Saint Paul, Saint Augustine, and the Pseudo-Dionysius were especially revered, wherein this altered state was described as an actual union with the mind of Christ.

This key idea, sometimes called *theosis*, is described in Paul's letter to the Phillipians:

> If there be any consolation in Christ, if any comfort of love, if any
> fellowship of the Spirit, if any bowels and mercies, fulfil ye my joy,
> that ye be like-minded, having the same love, being of one accord, of
> one mind.

and

> Let this mind be in you, which was also in Christ Jesus: Who, being in
> the form of God, thought it not robbery to be equal with God.

This principle of identification with Christ was greatly expanded and given
authority by a writer in the late fifth or early sixth centuries now known as
Pseudo-Dionysius. There is no known record of who the actual author of
these works was, but it is important that they were falsely attributed to
Dionysius the Areopagite, a disciple of Paul's, and therefore a voice of
enormous authority. Although the main effect of Pseudo-Dionysius was on
cosmology (he propounded the neo-Platonic concept of Ideal Forms), his
importance here is that he taught a technique of meditation which was
believed to effect spiritual union with God. The technique, which is
echoed in Greogry and in Saint Benedict's Rules, was one in which the
mind was emptied of all imagery, so that it became totally dark and still
(Leclerq et al. 1982).

A regimen for the attainment of this divine union was developed
throughout the period, but the most important handbooks were those of
Saint Gregory and Ambrose Autpert. Gregory laid down the ascetic ideal
and Autpert systematized and popularized the regulations for everyday life
in the monasteries, the practical and sensible "Saint Benedict's Rule."

Let us begin with Saint Gregory, whom Leclerq calls "the spiritual
father of the Middle Ages in the West" (Leclerq, et al. 1982:30). Gregory
was born in 540 A.D. and became Pope in 590. His extensive writings on the
spiritual life were the chief source from which the early medieval scholars
drew. Gregory praised both "action" in the sense of charitable work and
"contemplation" in the sense of meditation and prayer as the pillars of the
spiritual life, but there was no doubt that the latter was higher, and that
only a select few were elected by God to rise above the herd in their
approach to him through it. There was a paradox here, because Gregory
also saw union with God as the only legitimate goal of human life. All
pleasures of the flesh and all egotisms were to be shunned in pursuit of
spiritual maturity; the three most useful virtues were humility, patience,
and repentance, the last referring to the devotee's willingness to accept,
like Job, whatever suffering God offered him and to inflict still others upon
himself in order to tame his spirit. Christ was to be depended upon as
man's intermediary and model in this quest.

The asceticism of Gregory's prescription was not completely new.

Earlier Greek and Roman philosophers (notably Stoics such as Epictetus) had dwelt upon self-denial as the road to spiritual perfection. But the early Christian version was more extreme than the classic one, and it reinterpreted the goal: Whereas the Stoics sought mastery over the self in order to beautify and dignify life, the Christians sought an altered state of consciousness in which the old, secular self dissolved in readiness for God's command. The early medieval version of maturity is beautifully summarized in the epigram of Richard of Saint Victor, written in the twelfth century. It is, he said, "the clear gaze of a free spirit, suspended in wonder, on the marvels of wisdom" (*libera mentis perspicacia in sapientiae spectacula cum admiratione suspensa*) (Leclerq et al. 1982:335). Here the word "free" means "freed from the limits of conventional consciousness."

Needless to say, the goals that Gregory set for medieval man were almost impossible to pursue singlemindedly even in monastic life, let alone in the world abroad. Gregory and his predecessors were asking for ceaseless, exhausting, and occasionally even painful labor, and they could not even guarantee success. If the monastic movement were to succeed, it would have to be made more appealing. Starting in the seventh century, a standard set of sensible rules for the regulation of life in the monasteries gained popularity, and was soon widely copied. Saint Benedict's Rule, as it is now called, is attributed to an unknown abbot of Monte Cassino, but is best known through the edition of the Italian monk Ambrose Autpert (d. 784). Extreme austerity and self-inflicted torture were replaced with simplicty of life, with an emphasis on work, ordinary prayer, and the liturgy. The Rule regulated the relations among monks, and their discipline by abbots. Times for work, prayer, and worship were set down, as were the proper mental attitudes, postures, and procedures for each. Even deviations from the rules were dealt with. For example, if a monk were to suddenly receive the gift of spontaneous prayer (the so-called *donum orationis*), he was to report to the abbot, who would decide, after examining him, whether he should be excused from work.

Sober as this all sounds, early medieval monastic life would probably have seemed a bit chaotic to us. Following the suggestion of Pseudo-Dionysius, prayer was conceived as a search for complete inner silence, or "sabbath calm," in Autpert's words. The proper experience must have been profound, as tears were its surest outward sign; and it was apparently difficult to control, either in timing or intensity. But Saint Benedict's Rule contributed to a sense of peace and order in the monasteries, and a sense of spiritual well-being also. By means of the rule, the altered state through which one approached God was standardized and controlled. Hermitism was strongly discouraged, and in the communal life that resulted, spiritual development could be closely watched.

Institutions based on the Rule flourished throughout the Middle Ages, and with them the vision of maturity the early church fathers had described. The monasteries provided a living example to the epoch of the possibility of a fully spiritual life; it was this wellspring of spirituality, among other things, that led to the full flowering of Christian institutions and culture in the late Middle Ages.

As we have seen in the values of the nobility, the monastic ideal was not the only acceptable version of maturity, even in the early Middle Ages. It was not even the only *contemplative* form, as many of the saints' lives reveal. Rather, it legacy to later times is this: Monastic life and its systematic ideals provided an institutional link between the Conscious, Transcendant Universe and the individual consciousness. As such, it nurtured the contemplative version of heroism that had developed in the Hebrew and classical worlds. It promoted a set of attitudes compatible with the classical scholarship that began to stir in the twelfth century and culminated in the Renaissance.

Among modern commentators on medieval asceticism, Michel Foucault stands out as a thinker with stimulating new ideas. In his work on the history of sexuality (1978), Foucault portrays this period as one in which many of our modern habits of self-examination and self-control developed. He is particularly interested in the practice of *confession*, which was a regular part of monastic life before, and of lay Catholic practice after, the twelfth century. Confession, he tells us, became a principal method for eliciting and validating truth, not just in religious contexts, but throughout the life of Western man. As such, it helped to bring our private thoughts and feelings to the center of our concept of who we are, as social beings. It made us more self-aware, and thereby more self-controlling. Foucault's insight is a good one. Together with the concept of sin, the concept of moral self-awareness fostered by confession promotes the Western idea of the mature person as an autonomous, internally coherent spirit.

The Early Secular Tradition

Early medieval politics centered on the continuous bloody struggle over land, and the hegemony of the landed warrior in his fortified castle. Until about 800 A.D., the struggle was accompanied by vigorous population movements. Hellenic people moved into Asia Minor and the Balkan peninsula; the Moors moved into Spain; Celts invaded western Europe from the north; and waves of Slavs continuously pressed from the east. These movements came to an end after 800, however, and the settled populations of Europe began to grow (Elias 1982:30-33).

Eventually, the pressure of population on the land resulted in the collapse of the feudal warrior tradition, but the collapse was not complete for another three hundred years. Although many of the knights were pious in their way, they were for the most part primitive, uneducated people, whose lives bore little resemblance to the religious ideal. Their power—even their livelihood—depended upon a constant willingness to fight each other, and to levy tribute and keep the peace on their lands through the use of brutal force. As a result, the formation of coalitions among warrior nobles by oaths of fealty was their only means of security. It was neither tribal loyalty, then, nor the gentle ideals of the monastic life that kept what little peace there was among the nobility before the twelfth century.

The society of the early knights produced very little in the way of philosophy, and it is difficult to reconstruct their belief system. Judging by their way of life, their idea of maturity must have been similar to that of the pre-Socratic Greeks of Homer's time; like Odysseus, the ideal knight must have been brave, proud, sensitive to insult, crafty, intensely loyal to his friends and kin, strong, and quick to anger. This is, in fact, the picture we get from the Norse sagas and the Arthurian legends.

The Turning Point: Enter Civility and Love

Beginning in about 1100, a definite change began to take place in both the spiritual and the political life of Western man. Spiritually, Europe had become thoroughly Christian, not only in belief and ethics, but also in loyalty to the universal church. Politically, the filling of the land forced the collapse of the old feudal system and the rise to power of the great princes. The latter was a complex process, perhaps best described by Norbert Elias in his two-volume work on the history of manners (Elias 1978:1982).

According to Elias, the filling of the land meant that little could be gained by the small-scale warfare that had characterized political relations up to the twelfth century. The boundaries of the knights' domains tended to stabilize, with the result that the larger holdings, which included commercial enterprises and regulated trade, began to grow richer at the expense of the smaller ones. Increased population produced a labor surplus, which in turn stimulated crafts and the use of money. European society became more closely knit as a result of greatly improved transportation and commerce. Many of the smaller landholders, who depended on the barter economies of their estates, were victims of the inflation that inevitably followed the introduction of money, and they lapsed into relative poverty.

The peace and stability resulting from the religious unification of Europe further encouraged travel and trade, and pilgramage grew in popularity until it became a regular industry. It was an atmosphere in which the early medieval pessimism began to give way to a new enthusiasm and confidence. The period of heroic Christian works began—the crusades, and the building of the great cathedrals. Along with the new confidence, a new gentleness emerged in Western personality as well. The cult of romantic love flourished in the courts of the newly wealthy princes, and the cult of the Virgin Mary took firm root in popular religion, as witnessed by the dedication to Our Lady of the great early cathedrals—Chartres, Paris, Amien, Laon, Rouen, Rheims. The rise of a leisure class at the great royal courts stimulated the growth of courtly manners, and the ideal of the "cultivated person" as a new type of Vita Activa maturity. Kenneth Clark calls this period "one of the three or four great leaps forward in history" (1969:35).

Naturally, the new confidence was soon reflected in man's conception of man. Secure in their faith and free to travel, Christian scholars began to discover new intellectual material with which to beautify their faith. They began to turn to the pagan classics of Greece and Rome, and especially to Plato. It was a tendency that was carefully watched, and frequently denounced, by conservative church leaders. But the time for classical scholarship had come, and there was no turning back.

One of the first great medieval thinkers whose ideas of maturity clearly rested on Platonic ideals was Bernard of Clairveaux. Bernard was a contemporary of the great Peter Abelard. He entered the Cistertian monastery of Citeaux as a youth in 1112 and was later made abbot by virtue of his exemplary life and his impressive and prolific pen. Although he regarded himself a traditionalist and an adversary of the progressive Abelard, Bernard's approach to spiritual maturity was an important departure from that of earlier scholars. He subtly shifted the emphasis from the Gregorian negatives of self-abnegation and self-denial, toward the more positive ideal of love. Bernard taught that self-love is natural for man, and is the first stage of love for God. As the soul matures, the individual first opens his heart toward his fellow man, in charity, then toward God for the sake of his own salvation, and finally toward God in pure selflessness. He also seems to have agreed with Abelard's interpretation of Christ's mission as a sign of God's love, rather than as a cosmic sacrifice for man's cosmic sin.

Bernard and Abelard had an influence on medieval thought that strikes us today as modern. It was modern in the sense that it was relatively accepting of ordinary human nature and even sought to bridge the gap between man and God by bringing the latter a notch toward compassion. In Bernard's choice of *love* as the engine that drives spiritual development, and in his sequence of developmental stages, he echoes not the works of Gregory or any medieval Christian text so much as *The Symposium* of Plato.

That Bernard's Platonism was no mere oddity, but the early sign of an intellectual movement, we see in the thought of Saint Francis of Assisi, and in that of the greatest literary figure of the middle ages, Dante Alighieri. Saint Francis (b. 1181) was a frail-looking man with an air of delicate spirituality about him, but he was more of a doer than a thinker, and his success at founding a monastic order based on strict rules of poverty kept him too busy to write much. His ideas were developed by his disciples, the most talented of whom was Saint Bonaventure. Francis had held that the three great enemies of spiritual development are pride, sexuality, and greed. These correspond to Plato's three stages of unenlightened development, the love of honor, eros, and materialism. Saint Bonaventure further elaborated Francis's ideas by borrowing Plato's notion (which we shall discuss in chapters 7 and 12) of the three parts of the soul—vegetative, appetitive, and intellectual—as providing the "threefold path" by which God is sought.

Dante was thoroughly educated in both the Christian and the classical scholarship of the time, and proceeded to write an allegorical story of the process of human spiritual maturation, *The Divine Comedy*, based on earlier medieval models of spiritual quest. He was so impressed with the Platonic ideas that he began and ended his masterpiece with them. In the opening stanzas of *The Inferno*, we read,

> Scarce the ascent
>
> Began, when, lo! a panther, nimble, light
>
> And cover'd with a speckled skin, appear'd;
>
> Nor, when it saw me, vanish'd; rather strove
>
> To check my onward going; that oft-times,
>
> With purpose to retrace my steps, I turn'd.
>
> The hour was morning's prime, and on his way
>
> Aloft the sun ascended with those stars,
>
> That with him rose when Love Divine first moved
>
> Those its fair works: so that with joyous hope
>
> All things conspired to fill me, the gay skin
>
> Of that swift animal, the matin dawn,
>
> And the sweet season. Soon that joy was chased.
>
> And by a new dread succeeded, when in view
>
> A lion came, 'gainst me as it appear'd,
>
> With his head held aloft and hunger-mad,
>
> That e'en the air was fear-stuck. A she-wolf
>
> Was at his heels, who in her leanness seem'd
>
> Full of wants . . .

On his developmental journey, Dante finds his way blocked by the Platonic-Franciscan trio, the leopard of Lust, the lion of Pride, and wolf of

Avarice. Aided by the classical poet and symbol of the intellect, Virgil, however, he eventually finds his way through Hell to Paradise. And having reached its apogee he ends his poem,

> As one
>
> Who versed in geometric lore, would fain
>
> Measure the circle; and, though pondering long
>
> And deeply, that beginning, which he needs,
>
> Finds not: e'en so was I, intent to scan
>
> The novel wonder, and trace out the form,
>
> How to the circle fitted, and therein
>
> How placed: But the flight was not for my wing;
>
> Had not a flash darted athwart my mind,
>
> And, in the spleen, unfolded what it sought.
>
> Here vigour fail'd the towering fantasy:
>
> But yet the will roll'd onward, like a wheel
>
> In even motion, by the Love impell'd,
>
> That moves the sun in Heaven and all the stars.

Again the origin is clear. Dante tries to comprehend his vision intellectually and almost fails, until he is rescued by divine love, and experiences the union of his intellect, his emotions, and his will—the three parts of the Platonic soul. Meanwhile the "circle" and the "wheel" symbolize his achievement of integrity as well as his union with the universe. It is also typical of the new spirituality of the time that Dante reserves the highest level of Paradise (level 10, above the level of Christ and of the Divine Essence) for the Virgin Mary, and the guide who explains to him this exalted level is of course the platonist Saint Bernard of Clairveaux.

Bernard, Abelard, Bonaventure and Dante sought to soften and humanize Christian ideas of maturity, and they found Platonic wisdom attractive. But they did not seek to justify classical scholarship on the nature of man, perhaps because they found the transcendentalism of Plato so compatible with what was already accepted as the metaphysics and ethics of their time. The medieval students of Aristotle had a very different problem. Aristotle was less mystical, more confident of the power of the human intellect to penetrate the crucial secrets of the universe. And it was an Aristotelian, Thomas Aquinas, who first succeeded in the struggle to normalize classical scholarship.

The Dominican Aquinas (1224-1274) lived and worked in an atmosphere of controversy about the problem of classical scholarship. His teacher, Albert the Great, was a student of the Greeks, and wrote a popular introduction to theology (which is what a *Summa Theologica* is) that drew heavily on them. In Paris the Averroists, led by Siger de Brabant, were contending that philosophy and faith could not be reconciled, which put them in hot conflict with the Augustinians, eventually led by Aquinas. Pope Gregory X disliked the uproar, and blamed the classics; but Aristotle was the winner, and the next pope (Innocent V), though short-lived had been a student of Aquinas.

Aquinas was, like Bernard, an optimist on the subject of human nature. He thought of man,

> as tending naturally and inevitably towards his perfection, towards the actualization of his potentialities as man, towards his final end or good. (Copleston 1955:224)

This optimism stemmed from his view of man's tendency to seek happiness, and to seek it with the help of an intellect by means of which he can discern order in his surroundings, and thereby understand his own basic task in life and the means to accomplish it. The task, of course, was union with God. Although Aquinas saw the passions as natural, like Aristotle he mistrusted them, and he urged their strict obedience to reason. He and his Greek teacher parted company in a few respects, however. Thomas held that full maturity could never be attained by reason alone. To understand the will of God, one needed three qualities of character beyond the power of the intellect to sustain: faith, hope, and charity.

Aquinas was by no means the only important philosopher of his time. In the Renaissance universities there were chairs of Scotism and Nominalism as well as Thomism. But Aquinas's fellowship with the Renaissance is striking in many ways. He had struggled to legitimize classical erudition as a normal process in the pursuit of maturity. He had proposed that man's path towards virtue is lit by an inquiring intellect, keen to detect God's plan in the regularities of nature. He did not disagree with Richard of Saint Victor's vision of "a free spirit, suspended in wonder," but where the early medieval emphasis was on the wonder, Aquinas's was on the free spirit. In chapter 8, we shall look more closely at Aquinas's description of the process by which maturity unfolds.

The Ideal of the Courtier

Among the medieval elite there were many spiritual repercussions of the new humanism. One was a passionate and individualistic quest for a sublime life, beyond the tawdry confines of the local estate, through asceticism, heroic action, and just plain fantasy. As the Dutch philosopher Huizinga put it,

> In aristocratic periods . . . to be representative of true culture means to produce by conduct, by customs, by manners, by costume, by deportment, the illusion of a heroic being, full of dignity and honour, of wisdom and, at all events, of courtesy. This seems possible by the... imitation of an ideal past. The dream of past perfection ennobles life and its forms, fills them with beauty and fashions them anew as forms of art. Life is regulated like a noble game. (1954:39)

This picture contrasts with the one Foucault painted of the Middle Ages, from which he excluded the notion of life as art (1984:370). He may have been thinking mainly of the pre-1100 period, but in any case he does not discriminate between the two forms of maturity that developed in the classical world and lasted until modern times. The Vita Activa form leads easily to grandiosity, and needs to be recognized as the medieval partner of the Vita Contemplativa, about which Foucault has written eloquently.

In the medieval courts, the goals of maturity were at first essentially those of the Hebrews as radicalized by Christ, and those of the Greeks. From the Hebrews came monotheism and sin; from Christ came the individualistic quest for redemption; from the Greeks came the ideal of valor and the concept of "life as art."

The increasing dependence of the lesser aristocracy on the powerful princes, the growing wealth of the latter, and the decline of warfare as a way of life resulted in a growing circle of idle people at the courts, whose sole occupation was to curry favor with the princes. This was the crucible in which the modern notion of "refinement" took shape. Courtiers were eager to distance themselves from the coarse, brutal rusticity of their origins. Books on manners began to circulate, and they are often revealing. From thirteenth-century works on table manners, for example, we have the following:

> Those who like mustard and salt should avoid the filthy habit of putting their fingers into them.
>
> A man who clears his throat when he eats and one who blows his nose in the tablecloth are ill bred, I assure you.
>
> May refined people be preserved from those who gnaw their bones and put them back in the dish.
>
> (Elias 1978:86)

This new emphasis on manners appears much more in line with our modern ideas about maturity, but it did not assure a uniformly genteel society. Contradictory views were held on such important principles as the dignity of labor, the status of the poor, the moral value of violence, and the qualities of maturity. The church regarded labor as a valuable form of punishment, to be endured for the purpose of spiritual instruction; while the laboring classes were seen by the nobility as scarcely human. In a passage that could have been written by Plato, Chastellain, historiographer of the Dukes of Burgundy, attributes "no great qualities to merchants and laboring men as they are of a servile degree," giving them the admonition to practice "humility, diligence, obedience to the king, and docility to the lords." The virtues of the lords he records as "veracity, courage, integrity, and liberality" (Huizinga 1954:5). The church was required by its economic dependence on the nobility to look the other way on the oppression of the working classes.

A similar ethical confusion surrounded attitudes toward wealth and social status. The nobility regarded wealth as a means to heroic stature, while the monastic orders saw it as a temptation to be resisted at all costs, and the clergy pursued it zealously in the name of God. The seeds of change in this culture were many, and among them were its schizophrenic devotion to heroic megalomania and self-abnegation at the same time, which finally led to an intellectual revolt among the learned. The values of the Middle Ages are still with us in the twentieth century, but not exactly as they were in the fifth century.

Of chivalry and aristocratic heroism, we have already mentioned its individualism, its artificial reliance on past civilizations for standards and contempt for contemporary reality, its brutality and its emphasis on form. The knightly pursuit of the Vita Activa was couched in the spiritual language of the church and tacitly supported by the church hierarchy. The twelfth-century English philosopher John of Salisbury lists the functions of the knightly class: "To protect the church, fight against treachery, reverence the priesthood, fend off injustice from the poor, shed blood for your brethren, and make peace in your province" (Bishop 1970:73).

At first the church held herself aloof from the direct condoning of warfare, but the crusades changed that between the eleventh and the thirteenth centuries. During this period, the clergy took an increasingly active role in war, as we can see from the development of the religious ceremonies accompanying knighthood. Prior to the thirteenth century, as in ancient Greece, any freeman who could afford the paraphernalia and the leisure to train for war could set up trade in the knight business, but this was out of step with the new growth of court society. It gradually became necessary for a *real* knight to be "dubbed," in a religious ceremony that typically included the blessing of his weapons, a confession and communion, and sometimes a prayer vigil attended by priests. Leclerq says that this ceremony "had some points in common with the consecration of virgins [antithesis of sexuality and heroism again] and the coronation of kings"

(1982:278). At any rate, it resulted, among other things, in the restriction of knighthood pretty much to hereditary succession and princely favor.

Before the twelfth century, warfare had been the chief means of forcing life up toward heroism. Now the cultivation of manners began to suggest other paths. Court life brought dependent, aristocratic men into contact with socially superior women, with the result that romantic love began to appear as an ideal. Prior to the twelfth century, it had not been uncommon for a knight to discipline his wife by punching her on the nose (Elias 1982:78), but the conditions of court life gradually changed this. At the same time, the Greek equation of the feminine with the inferior life of the body seems to have continued. In addition to the example just given of the similarity of dubbing and the consecration of virgins, one can cite the old English epic *Beowulf*, which underscores the tragedy of the hero's death by giving the role of his dirge singer to a toothless old woman who "lives on because her life is made up of daily survival" (Fowler et al. 1982:29). The notion was of course reinforced by biblical values of male superiority.

Neither was the Vita Activa vision of maturity entirely confined to the courts. A kind of profane scholarship reminiscent of sophistry also provided opportunity for heroic competition. In twelfth-century London, Bishop tells us, scholars of several cathedral schools met in churches to "dispute logically and demonstratively in syllogisms" (1970:269). For some at least, the object was to show off. These schools taught the "seven arts," which included the *trivium*—grammar, rhetoric and logic—and the less important *quadrivium*—arithmetic, geometry, astronomy (that is, astrology), and music. In the thirteenth century, several continental universities began "clerical tournaments," in which scholars took turns challenging the world to theoretical debate.

Popular Culture

The crusades, the spread of trade and pilgrimage, and the building of the cathedrals showed a change not only in the power of the church and the conception of spirituality, but also in the degree of lay involvement in spiritual life. Improvements in farming, trade and industry in the twelfth century began to create a kind of middle class, who had more leisure for study and contemplation. Sculpture, architecture, and other forms of art helped to popularize spiritual ideals as the Christian culture flourished. At the same time, the growing wealth of the churchmen and monks, and the narrow orthodoxy of conventional preaching, led to popular desire for church reform, and heretical movements like the Cathari, the Waldenses, and the Joachimites also attested to a growing involvement of the laity at this time.

In the thirteenth century the combination of the new devotion to the intellect and the growing involvement of the laity in spiritual life registered with many churchmen as a danger sign. New efforts were made to purify popular belief, including the reforms of the Fourth Lateran Council, which in 1215 standardized confession for all faithful of both sexes. The new developments stimulated a countermovement called the "Devotio Moderna" in the late fourteenth century, in which the central message was the dangers of intellectuality and the importance of spiritual *action*—the humble, self-denying life.

This movement appeared just when printing was coming into use and people of leisure were beginning to read, and its effect was great. The most widely printed and widely read book of the time, other than the Bible, was a Devotio Moderna work called *The Imitation of Christ*, probably written by Thomas a Kempis in about 1400. Its lesson was the antithesis of the new humanism that had emerged in the works of Saint Albert, Saint Thomas, and Duns Scotus. It portrayed man as thoroughly and hopelessly sinful, and preached withdrawal from the world, meekness, mistrust of learning and the intellect, suffering, self-abnegation and self-loathing, humility, chastity, and constant vigilance against evil temptation.

What the Western world now saw was the institutionalization of the late medieval problem epitomized by Aquinas—the schism between the piety of the intellect and the piety of the emotions. On each side of the schism was a concept of maturity; on the one side the pure soul, the tearful monk of Saint Benedict's Rule, striving to clear his mind of vain ideas in order to receive as a gift the pure light of God; on the other side was the tireless student, burning the midnight oil over the esoteric products of human genius. It is a division that still remains between fundamentalist and humanist views of man, between self-denial and self-affirmation, between conservatism and creativity. Paradoxically, the conservative view was probably the greater stimulus to the ethical revolution of the Reformation. The Reformation was at first largely an attempt to rescue the purity of early Christianity from what appeared to the conservatives at least as a lack of humility and self-denial among the monastics and clerics of the sixteenth-century Catholic church.

On the Eve of the Renaissance

Many of Western man's ideas about maturity survived the Middle Ages more or less intact. The Vita Activa was as vigorous as it had been in ancient Greece, and the Vita Contemplative still held court in its ivory tower. The Conscious, Transcendent Universe with its profound dualism and its strain toward ascetic purity was still taken for granted. As in the ancient world, too, the primitive belief in fate continued; in fact, it was to be given new meaning and influence by the Protestant revolt, which translated it into the doctrine of predestination.

As in the classical and primitive worlds, too, the failure of maturation was attributed largely to outside influence, as the medieval word "lunatic," meaning someone under the influence of the moon, indicates. There seemed to be no moral approbrium attached to madness, and lunatics were either allowed to roam about freely, or were treated with the same solicitation that was reserved for the sick, unless their madness was thought to result from spirit possession. In the latter case, either exorcism or burning was the treatment of choice.

The two fundamental human purposes that had introduced the Middle Ages—the active goal of warlike heroism and the contemplative one of knowing God's will—had remained the same throughout the period. And why shouldn't they? Cosmic time was still linear and short, social inequality was still an accepted fact of life, and the cosmos was still the product of an infinite and arbitrary consciousness. But something had happened to the idea of maturity that would shatter irreparably the fabric of medieval life and thought. The Vita Contemplativa had grown less ascetic; the Vita Activa had grown less violent; and both had grown more intellectual. New tolerance had allowed the entry of ancient ideas and new habits of mind. And with the growing interest of the laity in spiritual self-perfection, the line separating the active and contemplative lives had begun to blur.

5. The Loss of Hierarchy: Passion and Restraint

The Rebirth of Vanity

T he end of the Middle Ages, like its beginning, was a process, not an event. The fall of Constantinople to the Turks in 1453 is a popular place to put the final punctuation mark, but by then the turning that we call the Renaissance—the turning of Europe toward the high learning of pagan antiquity—was already well under way. It is easier to characterize the way man's view of man changed in the Renaissance than to explain it, since there were so many influences. The church had grown extravagant in corruption, commerce was opening Europe to foreign influences, and the Black Death and the Hundred Years' War of the fourteenth century had reduced the population and raised the living standard. The modern professional army was beginning to replace amateur knighthood, printing was creating a large literate class outside the monasteries, and Marco Polo had been to China. Court life, exhausted by its own overblown ritualism, had devised a form of nature worship that, while laughably artificial, nevertheless encouraged an occasional look at the planet of man's residence. At any rate, human self-consciousness was on the move again.

A glance at the literature of the fourteenth century, especially the writings of Bocaccio and Chaucer, shows the stirrings of the new consciousness; these writers were concerned with the details of everyday life and the personalities of ordinary people, not just with the relationship of man to the transcendental. In exposing the basic contradictions of medieval society, they helped to open it to rational criticism as well. But perhaps the best way to appreciate the Renaissance change in consciousness is to look at the pageant of Italian painting, from Giotto's mastery of perspective in 1304, to the thoroughly modern work of Michelangelo and his contemporaries of the sixteenth century. What one sees is not just the progress of technique and the expansion of styles and subjects, but the transformation of the human face and figure way beyond anything achieved by classical Western cultures. The people in the first Renaissance paintings are archetypes, emotionless, expressing in grace of feature, pose, and drapery alone the artists' visions of an abstract ideal. Gradually, beginning with a secondary figure here and there (for example, the angel in Filippo Lippi's *Holy Family*) they come to life. By the time of Michelangelo, emotion and human character have stealthily invaded the faces until consciousness dominates, and the figures are now real men and women, elevated to holiness through the artist's insight into passion, rather than through his ability to avoid it altogether. It is the story of civilization's shift of focus, from the purely transcendental back to the personal and temporal. In the Dutch and Flemish masters, one sees the same new emphasis, together with the dramatic shift in subject matter, from the strictly religious and heroic to the strictly prosaic and familiar.

There is no doubt that the Renaissance painters and intellectuals were interested in nature, and in man as a natural creature, in a way that scholars had not been since classical times. It took a bit longer, for some reason, for the sensitive portrayal of human emotion and character to emerge in literature than it had in art, but by the time of Shakespeare's *Hamlet* (1600), a modern style of insight had been reached, as the great playwright himself showed again in *Othello, King Lear,* and *Macbeth.* It would be tempting to use Shakespeare as a model for his age on the subject of maturity, but he was primarily an artist and an entertainer, not a philosopher, and he often bent ideas to fit his dramatic needs. Throughout his tragedies and histories, however, he seems to say that a man's life is determined by his character, not by impersonal fate or outside agency. The individual is a unique purposeful agent, and as Casca says in *Julius Caesar,* "...every bondman in his own hand bears / The power to cancel his captivity" (act 1, scene 3, lines 101-2).

It was precisely this note that Martin Luther sounded in his letter *Concerning Christian Liberty* to Pope Leo X in 1520, a document that established the principles of the Reformation. With careful scriptural documentation, Luther pointed out that the Christian soul is absolutely free of any moral necessity other than obedience to God's will, and that God needs no intermediary other than Christ to get his message across. It was a message frequently preached by the Apostle Paul: "Christ is the end of the law for righteousness to every one that believeth" (Rom. 10:4). Singlemindedly bent as he was on righting the evils of the Catholic church, Luther was probably not fully aware of the transition in human self-consciousness into which his ideas fed. He certainly could not have predicted either the breakup of the church or the spectacular rise of secular individualism to which his ideas added momentum.

The intellectual atmosphere into which Luther's ideas diffused was a divided one. On one hand was a growing alarm over human depravity and the decay of institutions; on the other hand was a burgeoning optimism toward natural human qualities unfettered by institutions. The individualism of the Renaissance has been compared to that of the Greeks, but it was much more radical than that. The Greeks were tribalists, but the Middle Ages had deeply eroded tribalism, leaving individualism adrift of its cultural moorings to an extent that would have made the Greeks seasick.

If there is a single principal upon which the Renaissance change in consciousness can be said to turn, it is the redefinition of hierarchy, making it less an accepted condition of social life. In the classical and medieval worlds, the idea of a Transcendent Universe was closely linked with the idea of a special consciousness or art that could alone decipher it. Although the Greeks tried to integrate philosophy and life for the small class of free landholders, they were apparently not successful even in this limited attack on hierarchy. In the Middle Ages, full maturity was the privilege either of kings (the Vita Activa) or of monks who withdrew from society to climb the ladder of knowledge. In the Renaissance, a complex web of changes breached this ancient principal of hierarchy; the rediscovery of ancient learning, and its spread through books and travel, opened questions about the privileges of religious and political elites. The corruption of the Catholic church further undermined the spiritual authority of the priesthood. Changes in warfare and transportation led to a more fluid dynamic of wealth and power, which encouraged men to challenge temporal authority.

As a result of these and other changes, the pursuit of full moral maturity came out of the monastery and the court, and began to live in the cottage, the shop, and the street. Renaissance humanism was a call to all men to begin living in their daily lives the highest values of their culture. The Reformation was a similar call to the Christian faithful—to make every detail of their lives a form of worship, and as Casca suggested, to "cancel their captivity" with their own hands.

The rise of trade and banking in the fourteenth century, particularly in Italy, is well known. The combined expansion of travel, literacy, and wealth ushered in the era of the merchant princes. Together with the erosion of the Catholic church's centralized authority in the fifteenth century, this helped to free men's imaginations and abilities, to create once more the ideal conditions for the Homeric style of heroism, whereby the individual could aspire to rise through personal ability to fame and power. And that is exactly what scores of clever people did.

The manners and morals of the temporal princes came fully into the center of society's interest. The Greeklike passion for politics and war, long fettered by asceticism, bloomed with new vigor. A proud and violent type of personality grew popular, a type who bore no resemblance at all to the Gregorian or to the Thomist ideal, and who lacked even the superficial piety of medieval royalty. Alberti, whom Kenneth Clark calls the "quintessential early Renaissance man," recounts in his life story how the strongest horses used to stumble under him, and how he could throw farther, jump higher, and work harder than any other man. Cellini, too, left an autobiography of a character most of us nowadays would call pathologically vain and impulsive: a roaring furnace of a person who often fell ill from the heat of his emotions, who was given to beating his servants, murdering his enemies, and avenging with criminal destructiveness the slightest insult. In 1529, a handbook even appeared for this style of self-aggrandizement— Machiavelli's *The Prince*. Heroic maturity was indeed the rage—or one of the rages—so much so that the popes themselves helped set the example.

The Golden Mean

Never had there been a greater need for a moderate, sensible vision of maturity, a philosophy and pedagogy that would produce self-conscious personalities, immune to the lust for crude power and ignorant adulation. Typical of the tendency of cultures to embody mutually contradictory ideals, the Renaissance not only produced such an ideal of moderation, but eagerly sought it and heaped accolades on its most gifted champions.

The most talented of all the Renaissance proponents of self-consciousness and self-control was Desiderius Erasmus. A classical scholar, essayist, satirist, and close friend of Sir Thomas More, Colet, Martin Luther, Albrecht Durer and Hans Holbein, Erasmus was the most venerated man of his time. Henry VIII of England, Francis I of France, and Charles V of Spain pressed him to accept court positions; three popes (and what popes they were!) wrote him letters full of veneration; five universities vied to get him on their faculties. An opportunity to meet with Erasmus was, in the early sixteenth century, enough to confer celebrity among the learned (Zweig 1934:100).

Erasmus was born in Rotterdam in about 1466. In 1487 he entered the monastic school at Steyn, attracted not so much by the pious life as by the library there, which was one of the finest in Europe. Later he was ordained a priest in the Roman Catholic church, studied at the University of Paris and travelled widely throughout Europe (partly to stay clear of the Black Plague). He retranslated the Greek Bible into Latin, wrote a cross-indexed guide to classical scholarship, and generally made himself so useful to the scholarly world that his books were soon in great demand. His popularity, however, was only partly due to his erudition and his admirable style. Erasmus refused to attach himself to any powerful person or institution in an age when power was practically everything. In other words, he lived the value of self-reliance that he preached in his works. Since moral truths must be proven by example rather than argument, Erasmus's works merely made him famous; it was his life that made him inspirational, a quality he shared with his less-lucky friend, Thomas More.

Aside from his exemplary self-reliance, Erasmus made two contributions to the history of maturity. First, he continued the work of the late Middle Ages in reconciling Christian piety and classical scholarship. Second, he was a humanist in the modern sense of the word: he studied human nature closely as Bocaccio and Chaucer had done, and integrated his philosophy with his findings on human behavior.

The first contribution of Erasmus is seen clearly in his *Manual of the Christian Knight*, published in 1503. A somber and pious work, in tone something like *The Imitation of Christ*, the *Manual* preaches that the world is a dangerous place for human souls, and sets forth instructions for spiritual self-defense. Contrary to the Devotio Moderna view, however, Erasmus moves away from self-abnegation toward self-respect through scholarship. The Christian knight, he says, has two weapons against evil: prayer and learning. The personality that results from these methods is self-respecting, self-sufficient, self-controlled, modest, wise, and free of avarice and pride—qualities that were also extolled in other contemporary works such as More's *Utopia*, and that shine forth with increasing power in seventheenth- and eighteenth-century views of maturity.

Erasmus's humanism is best reflected in his satiric work, *The Praise of Folly*. It is hard to believe this sparkling comedy was written by the author of the somber *Manual*. In fact, Erasmus claims to have written *Folly* in seven days while recovering from an illness, and it may represent a side of his character that was rarely seen. In form, *Folly* is a lecture, or rather a sermon, delivered by Dame Folly, in praise of herself. Aping the self-congratulatory autobiography so popular at the time, Dame Folly first explains, quite convincingly, her importance for those who seek a worthy life. Lust, vanity, and the capacity to fail, she reminds us, make life sweet and human company endurable. In attacking hyperintellectual and puritanical attitudes, Erasmus shows his affinity with the Platonic respect for emotion, and his scepticism of the Stoic self-denial and Aristotelian rationalism popular at the time:

> Everyone admits that all the emotions belong to Folly. Indeed a fool
> and a wise man are distinguished by the fact that emotions control
> the former, and reason the latter. Now the Stoics would purge the
> wise man of all strong emotions, as if they were diseases; yet these
> emotions serve not only as a guide and teacher to those who are
> hastening toward the portal of wisdom, but also as a stimulus to all
> virtuous actions.... Seneca strips the wise of absolutely every

emotion; yet in doing so he leaves something that is not a man at all. (Erasmus [1509] 1946:67)

In the second part of the *Folly*, the viewpoint of the author inexplicably shifts. Here Dame Folly boasts of her enormous following, and we find to our surprise that she is really evil after all: The hypocritical burghers, the lazy and ignorant monks, the idly frivolous gentry, the pompous and vain scholars, the rapacious merchants—all the characters whom the author really loathes—are sycophants of Folly! It is difficult to interpret Erasmus's motive here, but the shift could not be accidental. I believe Erasmus was aware of the schizoid consciousness of an age that idolized both unbridled self-indulgence and saintly restraint, and that the structure of *Folly* is meant to demonstrate the human capacity for self-contradiction. One can read it as a deliberate demonstration of the plasticity of language and the relativity of values.

The Reformation

Such a reading of the *Folly* would be consistent with Erasmus's attitude toward the Reformation. Although he hated the corruption of the church and campaigned eloquently for the concept of autonomous conscience as against blind obedience, he condemned the actions of Martin Luther and his followers. Erasmus could see the violence inherent in the breakup of the church, and felt that no mere ideology was worth it. Quoting Cicero, he said, "An unjust peace is preferable to the most just of wars" (Zweig 1934).

The early humanists like Erasmus and More upheld the virtue of self-control and simplicity, and explicitly condemned excesses of either the ascetic or the libertine variety. The Protestant reformers, on the other hand, tended to prefer extremes. The humanist reaction to the Renaissance excess was essentially conservative. The Protestant reaction was visionary, driven by a somewhat hysterical conviction of the consequences of those excesses. The age of the earth would not be discovered until the late eighteenth century, and until that time, most people thought the cosmic game might be over any minute. Those who feared the changes that were taking place interpreted them as the End itself and were often driven close to panic, as shown by the scores of witchcraft trials throughout Europe in the fourteenth and fifteenth centuries, and by the mass religious conversions of the sixteenth and seventeenth centuries. Lest optimism should subvert their souls, wealthy Elizabethan ladies wore as necklace pendants *mementi mori*, or "reminders of death," in the form of tiny coffins containing jewelled skeletons.

In the Judeo-Christian tradition, the concept of sin stands always on hand as a lightning rod for the feelings of despair that afflict large sectors of society during periods of upheaval. The Protestant reformers of the time were extreme in their insistence on self-mortification and the essential evil of humankind. In order to comprehend the enormous difference between these two competing moral views of man—the Renaissance and the Reformation views—compare these two passages on the raising of children, by leading exponents of each view:

> My judgement is that men go the wrong way to learn their children to pray, [wrote John Bunyan, author of *Pilgrim's Progress* and one of the most successful puritan reformers of the mid-1600's.] It seems to me a better way for people to tell their children betimes what cursed creatures they are. (Durant and Durant 1963:209)

> If the mind be curb'd and humbled too much in children, [wrote the Enlightenment's chief spokesman John Locke in 1692,] if their spirits be abas'd and broken much, they lose all their vigor and industry...dejected minds, timorous and tame...very seldom attain to any thing.... He that has found a way how to keep a child's spirit easy, active, and free, and yet at the same time to restrain him from many things he has a mind to do...has, in my opinion, got the true secret of education. (Locke 1692:35)

There were, then, three basic views of maturity in the Western world of the sixteenth century, each of them highly individualistic in its own way. The Reformation hero was ascetic, tuned in to the transcendental consciousness, proudly aloof from human frivolity and humbly obedient to God, awaiting death and Armageddon, savagely loyal to a truth revealed by scripture (properly interpreted) and prayer, rebellious if his beliefs were questioned, contemptuous of all worldly titles and wealth, and bent on labor and simplicity as measures of God's grace.

The view of the Renaissance hero was life-as-art. It was elitist, intellectual, optimistic and worldly. At its best it produced the magnificent portrayals of the human spirit one sees in the Louvre, the Uffizi, the Vatican. At its worst it was Louis XIV, exceedingly vain and violent, a kind of Achilles with cannon.

The Renaissance scholar understood the dangers in these extremes, and advanced a maturity of moderation, tolerance for human frailty, and solid self-reliance guided by an educated intellect. Such a vision combined Vita Activa and Vita Contemplativa aspects in a vision of maturity that transcended the horizontal bonds of tribal loyalty and the vertical bonds of civic and religious authority. Castiglione's 1528 treatise, *The Book of the Courtier* listed not only swordsmanship, conversational wit, and courage as requisites of maturity, but also modesty, control of the passions, and a striving for knowledge and spiritual growth. All in all, it was a confusing time in which to grow up.

Renaissance Confusion: The Case of John Milton

Things would have been simpler if the divergent ideals of the time had been parceled out to distinct sectors of society—if Homeric heroism had been confined to the nobility and the popes, and hysterical asceticism to the Protestants. But such was not the case. Perhaps the best illustration of the schizoid belief system of the late Renaissance is the personality of one of its greatest artists, John Milton. Born the son of an educated London clerk who was nonetheless a God-fearing Protestant, Milton was destined to have what we would now call "identity problems." "In the Milton home," record the Durants, "the Renaissance love of the beautiful mingled with the Reformation passion for the good" (1963:212). The mixture was to be violently stirred by the political winds of the Protestant Revolt in England. The result was a masterpiece, Milton's epic poem *Paradise Lost*, a work that forever enshrined the ethical confusion of the time.

Hot-headed and incredibly megalomaniacal, Milton strikes us as a caricature of the Renaissance hero. Having shown early brilliance of mind, he was sent to Cambridge, where he engaged in a fistfight with one of his tutors and ultimately left in disgrace, refusing to take the required Oath of Loyalty to the Anglican creed and liturgy. He mastered Greek, Hebrew, Latin, and French so thoroughly that the Long Parliament recruited him to be its secretary, and he executed the office with an unrestrained literary brutality that must have made even the feistiest Roundhead cringe. Of the Bishop of Exeter, Milton wrote that his feet and socks "stink to heaven," and when rebuked for such language he likened himself to Christ, whom, he said, "speaking of unsavory traditions, scruples not to name the dunghill and the jakes [privy]" (ibid.:220). At the time of these self-indulgent outbursts, our hero was running a puritanical private school for boys in London, and theorizing pedagogically, "There is not that thing in the world of more grave and urgent importance throughout the whole life of man than discipline[!]" (ibid.:221).

Milton would have been a mere buffoon, except that he was unquestionably a brilliant poet, a fact of which he himself was only too aware. He believed that poets like himself were "the voice of God, and prophets divinely inspired to teach mankind" (ibid.:223), and he said of his masterpiece that its purpose was "to paint out and describe...the whole book of sanctity and virtue" and to accomplish no less than "as the choicest wits of Athens, Rome, and Modern Italy, and those Hebrews of old, did for their country" (ibid.:221).

The work did indeed bring out the character of its time, but it was an effect quite unlike what Milton had intended. In *Paradise Lost*, the now-blind poet sought to paint the Puritan image of God in tones that the spirit of the Renaissance could revere. With the musical ear for English poetry that rivals Shakespeare's, Milton set the whole thing to cadences and turns of phrase that still leave the reader breathless. His aim, he said, was to "justify the ways of God to man," and in order to accomplish it, he brought to bear his full-blown Renaissance insight into human character and sensitivity to human emotion.

The result is a moral disaster. Confronted with such a clear and compelling image of the Puritan God, modern man can only cringe with embarrassment. God is portrayed as a haughty aristocrat who first deprives mankind of knowledge for no more reason than to impress him, then leads Adam to break the taboo in order to teach him a lesson by punishing him and his descendents for eternity! The world can no longer absorb the image of the Renaissance hero projected to the cosmic plane. We have learned enough of the humanistic tradition to feel that knowledge is man's birthright. Pride is a natural companion of ability. Power is an adjunct of intelligence and nobility of character. Says Milton's sympathetic interpreter Christopher Ricks, "Ever since Milton retold the story of the Fall, that story has gradually become less and less essential to the Christian faith" (Ricks 1968:xxiii). The Durants put it more bluntly: "Who can help but sympathize with Satan's revolt against such an incredible sadist [as Milton's God]?" (1963:238).

What we see here is an attempt to bring together two distinct forms of consciousness in a single form of expression. The failure of *Paradise Lost* illustrates simultaneously the internal moral contradictions of the age, and the human ability to live with contradictions as long as they are kept in separate packages. Milton's identity confusion is still with us in the twentieth century, and it still challenges those of us who would be fully self-conscious, as we shall see.

The Age of Reason

That Milton was able to give voice to his era was not much to his advantage. If identity confusion was not enough, when Charles II was restored to the English throne in 1660, Milton almost lost his head for his pugnacious Protestantism. But troubled times often provoke profound thought, and even while Milton was pouring vitriol on England's royalists, one of them, Thomas Hobbes, was quietly inventing modern psychology in the safety of France. A difference of character greater than that which separated the two men would be hard to imagine. Hobbes was a quiet, deliberate man who strove for cool, surgical logic in all his thought—and achieved it. He was an Oxford graduate whose broad knowledge and calm intellect had brought him in close contact with some of the greatest thinkers of his day—Francis Bacon, Ben Johnson, Galileo, Rene' Descartes—and whose loyalty to the British aristocracy had him tutoring them in exile. His writing was spare, economical, and admirably clear; his ideas led him straight away from the Bible. The only important possession he shared with Milton, it seems, was the wrath of the Catholic church, and that was for a totally different reason.

Hobbes was a deist. For him there was no transcendent consciousness. Rather, the universe was a machine, and virtue consisted of the laws by which the machine operated. We could know virtue, up to a point, because our minds were also machines, whose function allowed us to deduce order from the perceived effects of orderly processes. But there was no such thing as free will. "In deliberation," he said, "the last appetite or aversion immediately adhering to the action or omission thereof is what we call the will" ([1651] 1910:343-344). In such a universe, any natural phenomenon that tends to keep things (and people) in order, is desirable; Hobbes was not the least bit surprised that the Roundheads had made a mess of English society. He was always welcome at the court of Charles II, in spite of his bald head and drab garments, which made him look like a Puritan. The king used to say to his friends when he caught sight of the aged Hobbes, "Here comes the old bear to be baited" (Durant and Durant 1963:561).

Hobbes's radical deism made little impact on man's concept of man (although Marx and Freud ended up with similar ideas about the will), but his model of the mind as a machine was a radical leap that transformed psychology altogether. He probably got the idea partly from his conversations with Galileo, whom he met in 1636, and partly from reading the popular works of the late medieval philosophers Duns Scotus and William of Ockham, whom we shall discuss in chapter 9. Galileo's contribution was the convincing demonstration that the behavior of natural phenomena conformed to machinelike laws. Scotus's and Ockham's contribution was the idea, borrowed from Aristotle, that all knowledge is ultimately based on sense experience, and that rational abstraction from experience constitutes all we can know of truth in general. Hobbes's formulation of these ideas as the basis for a science of psychology was clearer and more radical than others', however; here we must note the moral effects of his legacy. If the universe is a machine and the mind is merely one machinelike part of it, it would follow that the *best* mind is that which performs its mechanical functions best; the same could be said for the best society. In fact, this came to be a leading concept in modern views of maturity.

There have been many ideas since Hobbes on the role of conscience in ethics; there have been reactions against the mechanistic view of man, and certain pre-Hobbesian models of maturity have continued to thrive. But look at some of the moral offspring of Hobbesianism. The next two centuries or so were dominated by a picture of man in whom passion and reason are locked in mortal combat, the latter being clearly the superior moral force. The Age of Reason was a period studded with brilliant philosophers like Locke, Hume, Kant, Spinoza, Bentham, and Mill (and poets like Alexander Pope) who thought this way. Hobbes's model transcended the more elitist ideas of the Greeks and the Middle Ages by reviving Averroes's "psychic unity of man," the belief that all human minds function essentially alike—a cornerstone of modern participatory government. Utilitarianism, the ethical system that swept the remnants of feudal rule away, is essentially based on the Hobbesian machine.

Finally, look at our modern views of maturity. The mature person of the twentieth century may be "in touch with her feelings," but the phrase only underscores the importance of rationality. What would you think of somebody who was "in touch with her reason?" This is quite a contrast to the dominant medieval, Renaissance, and Reformation views of the ascetic supplicant who sought divine instruction *and* of the man of action who returned all slights to his honor with explosive violence.

Naturally the new Man of Reason did not evolve in a social vacuum. In the seventeenth century, subtle but important changes were taking place in the class structure and the family life of northwestern Europe. An examination of textbooks on manners shows that the medieval and Renaissance strain toward life-as-art was beginning to be replaced by the idea of "distinguished mediocrity" (Aries 1962:388), where the field of endeavor was not the noble court, but society at large, and the contestants were the youth of the growing middle class. As middle-class life grew more respectable, family privacy increased, and parents took more care to influence their children's morals (Stone 1977). John Locke's 1692 essay on education, quoted earlier, still strikes the modern reader as basically sound. He teaches the cultivation of mutual respect between parents and children, the careful choice of sober and well-educated tutors, a system of control based on reward rather than punishment, and a reasonably loose rein to allow "natural" development to unfold. The image of human nature as basically rational and good fit with the new models of class and family in which bonds of affection were important, and in which the rationally educated individual could rise in a rationally ordered society. Here we see the beginnings of the "performance-oriented society" that accompanied the Industrial Revolution.

Developmental Failure

The Enlightenment emphasis on rationality and performance drastically changed ideas about developmental failure. No longer did a conscious universe manipulate the fate of the individual as it had in earlier ages. If moral excellence consisted in the effective functioning of the human machine, flaws in that functioning became signs of moral failure. The idea was reinforced by the epidemic spread of syphillis throughout Europe, with its debilitating psychological effects, but the association was merely coincidental. For the first time in history, madness and mental incapacity were looked upon as loathsome and shameful diseases, and the insane were treated accordingly. The first *Zuchthaus* was opened in Hamburg in 1620; the Hôpital Général opened by decree of Louis XIV in Paris in 1656. Here the insane were gathered in chains, among the poor, the crippled, orphans, the retarded, and the sick, without the benefit of medical care. Four years after its opening, the Hôpital Général housed six thousand people.

But the Hobbesian machine did not sweep away earlier models of human nature altogether. Our modern views incorporate Hobbes, but they also include contrasting principles of thought—romantic principles—that developed in reaction to the mechanical rationality of the Enlightenment.

6. Modern Times:
Maturity as Mental Health

T he collapse of premodern hierarchical views of the cosmos, of human nature, and of the social system that accompanied the Renaissance not only led to new definitions of maturity based on individualism and self-reliance; it also led to institutions that were based on, and in turn fostered, those new definitions. The new churches fostered a sense of civic responsibility in the parishioner; the new businesses fostered complex long-term planning, requiring self-betterment and competitiveness. The passion for learning nurtured schools, which in turn exposed children to the principles of competitive self-betterment at younger and younger ages. New ideas of the dignity of the individual led to architectural and residence patterns permitting greater privacy, which fostered new definitions of intimacy and self-expression.

But the simultaneous growth of individualism, equality, and rationalism produced powerful strains in the emerging modern society. Rationalism, with its search for universal laws, promoted equality but frequently conflicted with religious and artistic self-expression. The competitiveness born of individualism produced terrible new inequalities in society, and the ideal of self-reliance allowed those inequalities to fester into open conflict. The demand for self-improvement levied by egalitarian ideals became for many a crushing burden that robbed life of the dignity those ideals were meant to guarantee.

The Romantic Rebellion

As the Enlightenment gave way to the industrial revolution and the development of mass society and participatory government, ideals of maturity reflected these strains. Against the rationalist threat to spiritual spontaneity, and the egalitarian-competitive threat to the spontaneity of the body there developed a romantic maturity. To the Enlightenment notion that all men, although autonomous, are basically alike, the romantic movement counterposed the absolute uniqueness of the individual soul. To the rationalist philosophy that proposed the deduction of truth and justice by logical operations from strict adherence to sense experience (Hobbes, Locke, Hume) or to sober introspection (Descartes), romanticism offered the evidence of the transcendental, carried forward from classical and medieval thought.

The romantic view of man has three closely related components: an ethical one, an epistemological one, and an aesthetic one. Ethically, it is derived from Protestant pietism, which preached the unique relationship of the individual soul to God—the "priesthood of all believers"—and from the nature-worship of Rousseau. It is an insistence upon the integrity and dignity of the individual body and spirit, against the rationalist tendency to dissect, which can result in the complete denigration of the spiritual element. We have seen the tendency toward such ideas in Erasmus's *Praise of Folly*, but Erasmus was a devoutly religious man, and for him true sentiment had been Christian sentiment. The new romanticism required fresh ethical foundations.

The Hobbesian revolution went so far toward the destruction of religion, among English intellectuals at least, that in 1730 Montesquieu wrote, "There is no religion in England. If anyone mentions religion people begin to laugh" (Clark 1969:269). This situation left a vacuum in the emotional life of the educated elite, and the English poets and painters began to turn to nature for emotional inspiration. Rousseau was the first man of genius to be deeply affected by the English naturalism, and he developed a convincing philosophy from it. Where the British empiricists had essentially banished the soul by making human experience "nothing but" a stream of sense impressions, Rousseau put things the other way around. He elevated those sense impressions to the status of divine inspiration.

Epistemologically, romanticism is a belief in the validity of emotional and intuitive experience, and an attempt to show the limitations of the intellect as an instrument of knowing. From the many statements of human nature that might be called counterintellectual, then, the romantic are those that grew out of the Enlightenment tendency to rely on personal experience as opposed to religious or philosophical doctrine. The romantics were those Enlightenment thinkers who discovered through inquiry and introspection that the most profound moments of life are the ones that most defy intellectual analysis—the vividness and power of spontaneous emotion; the apprehension of beauty, truth, justice, love; the relationship of man to nature; confrontation with death; hatred; vengeance; the reliability of intuition; the unity of diverse things and separate lives. It is the attitude expressed by Wordsworth in the lines "Our meddling intellect / Misshapes the beauteous forms of such things, / We murder to dissect," and in Blake's "To see a world in a grain of sand, / And a heaven in a wild flower . . ."

Aesthetically, romanticism is a glorification of the natural, the subtle, and the ineffable, as against the artificial, the clear, and the logical. The mature person is sensitive to his natural and human environment in a way that allows him to appreciate not only natural grandeur itself, but refined human embellishment of it in art, poetry, and music, and the beauty of honest human nature as well. From this aesthetic romanticism come many of our contemporary attitudes toward our natural environment, toward human society, and toward sexuality and the family.

Romanticism and Science

Romanticism and rational philosophy might have parted company permanently, the way philosophy and revealed religion did, had it not been for the work of Immanuel Kant. Thanks to Kant, the basic truths of human nature revealed by the romantics have retained their relevance for philosophy, and are an integral part of our modern intellectual view of man.

The romantic rebellion left philosophy in something of a shambles. Hobbes and the empiricists had destroyed the Transcendental Universe, forcing us to rely upon the intellect alone for knowledge of absolutes. Without reviving God, the romantics pointed out the futility of the intellect as a guide to ultimate knowledge or maturity. It hardly seemed, by the late eighteenth century, that a science of ethics was possible, and the alternative—moral anarchy—did not look good given the human capacity to err. Under the circumstances, the temptation was great (and still is) either to reject the Enlightenment and return to dogma, raw power, and superstition as moral guides, or to reject the romantic insights and insist that science have the last word.

It was this situation that prompted Kant to begin his "critical philosophy," starting with the *Critique of Pure Reason* in 1781. As the first clear statement of both the relativity of all human knowledge, and the human capacity to transcend one's own relativity by studious self-awareness, Kant's work marks the beginning of all truly modern ethical philosophy. Kant rescued reason as a basis of maturity without trying to revive its claim to absolute knowledge. He did this by showing that, while we cannot know ultimate justice or reality, reason can give us the knowledge we need to maximize the accuracy of our judgements about the long-range effects of our actions, and can show us the *relative* universality of ethical norms.

Thanks to Kant's advances in psychology, romanticism could be assimilated in philosophy and the sciences. From the standpoint of psychology the most important romantics were the German philosophers C. G. Carus (1789-1869), G. H. von Schubert (1780-1860), and A. Schopenhauer (1788-1860), and the Swiss I. P. V. Troxler (1780-1866), and their literary colleagues of the so-called Bildungsroman school.

The common concern of these writers was a unique, inborn, intuitive faculty in every human being that contained the seeds of the individual's full moral maturity. It was an idea that had been anticipated by Meister Eckhart and Saint Albert in the thirteenth and fourteenth centuries. As we shall see in later chapters, it was also a product of the emerging consciousness of human antiquity and kinship with the animal world, and was undoubtedly influenced by G. W. Leibniz (1646-1716), who taught that the ultimate source of things was not a uniform *matter*, but rather a heterogeneous *activity*, and that minds were the fundamental expressions of this diversity, which nevertheless contained the idea of the universal Truth innately within them from birth.

In a somewhat similar vein, Carus held that human character was the result of the epigenetic development of "primordial phenomena," and he sought to develop a "genetic method" for tracing behavior to its primordial roots (Ellenberger 1970:203). His ideas closely resembled Plato's discussions of the union of the soul with the transcendental Absolute, but he proposed a new mechanism, which was to have enormous weight in our modern thinking—the notion of the Unconscious.

Troxler's and von Schubert's psychologies were closely parallel. They held that full maturity was prefigured in every developing person, as the expression of his or her "true self." For both writers, the teleological unfolding took place through a series of stages that resembled Plato's discussion of love in *The Symposium*. For Schopenhauer, the unfolding of character was essentially dictated by the unconscious development of a sexual instinct; full maturity awaited the individual's consciousness of his impulse life. The Bildungsroman school (of which Hermann Hesse is a modern example) centered on the portrayal of heroic lives as a series of epigenetic developments, in accordance with the romantic logic.

Kant's discovery, however, had a much wider effect than the stimulation of holistic psychology. For over a century, it served as the moral basis for education in Western civilization. It is a distressing fact that modern students of the social sciences usually earn their doctorates in America without the slightest idea of what Kant did. His work has been largely ignored in American science—including psychology—since the turn of the twentieth century. As I will discuss in chapter 10, scientific precision is now rarely seen as a tool for shaping moral excellence. At best it has become a form of art or entertainment; at worst a tool for the achievement of celebrity, comfort, and power. Perhaps this outcome is an indirect result of the decline of heroism in modern concepts of maturity.

The Romanticism of the Body: Freud

As we have seen, the seventeenth and eighteenth centuries witnessed the development of the middle-class family as a private, autonomous unit, held together by strong bonds of loyalty and affection, and dedicated to the pursuit of its own social success. The romantic movement encouraged this tendency, by glorifying the emotional quality of interpersonal relationships. If people were indeed unique, and the rapture of personal intimacy was a valid form of transcendental experience (as medieval chivalry had held), so much the better for a form of social organization based on such intimacy. The mature person was one who loved another selflessly; his relationship with another was itself the expression of transcendental truth and proof of the unfolding of personal character. Now the stage really was set for the era of Industrial Man.

By the beginning of the nineteenth century, most of the essential elements of modern maturity had been laid down. The ideal was the hard-working, self-reliant, self-controlled, logical, egalitarian, loyal, emotionally warm individual. Yet one more important moral challenge arose out of the economic and social conditions of the late eighteenth and early nineteenth centuries. This was the shift from *heroism* to *success* as the goal of maturation, and the concomitant greatly increased pressure for *strict control of sexual and aggressive drives* as a feature of the mature personality.

For our purposes, the important changes that accompanied the industrial revolution in England and America in the century following 1760 were: (1) the rapid development of industrial cities and commerce, with corresponding increases in economic opportunity for the well educated; (2) changes in the nature of family life in the middle class, with greatly increased privacy, and systematic investment in the upward mobility of the family through the children's marriage and education; and (3) a gradual improvement in public health, resulting in lower infant mortality and longer marriages.

The most significant fact about the industrial revolution for the individual was that *it was the first time in history that an average child could reasonably expect to surpass his parents in wealth and social standing through his own efforts.* Of course not everyone would succeed. Of course there had been upward mobility in earlier eras. But it was the improvement of the odds that made the difference. The improved odds offered no guarantees, but they offered a reasonable challenge. Education, reputation, social contacts, intelligence, thrift, and industry could be wielded confidently for social advancement. The increasing wealth and privacy of middle-class families meant that they, especially, could put their time and resources into the acquisition of these commodities by their children. The quality of the children's upbringing, schools, marriages, and friends could be controlled, and the outcome could make or break the family's fortunes.

The difficulty was that this required a redefinition of the role of sexuality and aggression in social life. Upward mobility required two new skills: the careful husbanding of family resources, and a carefully controlled aggressive self-interest in work. Let us look at the emotional demands of these skills.

With lowered infant mortality rates, the management of family resources in turn required the limitation of family size. Since social advancement also meant class hypergamy (marrying upward) or at least the avoidance of class hypogamy (marrying downward), the marriage of a man often had to be delayed until he was secure in a career; there could be no sowing of wild oats by either sex. Thus the decline in infant mortality and the increase in living standard in England resulted in a gradual rise in fertility rates until 1862, when the rate was 35 per 100,000. Within a single generation (from 1878 on), fertility rates had begun to drop, first among the upper classes, and then gradually among the lower echelons of society. In 1890, for example, professionals had the smallest family size, with an average of 2.80 children; salaried employees averaged 3.53 children; laborers, 5.11. Within two generations, average family size fell by roughly two-thirds (Quadagno 1982:31-32).

There were two interesting results. One was the new role of sexuality in private life. A necessity appeared for the severe suppression of sexual impulses, not only outside of marriage (an idea for which there was ample religious precedent), but within marriage as well, an idea incompatible with prevailing eighteenth century wisdom, which held that "orgasm, even female orgasm, was necessary . . . to maintain physical and emotional well-being" (Smith-Rosenberg 1978:215). The other result, in some ways contradictory, occurred in public life. The control of sexuality became a matter of continuous and shrill public concern. From the mid-eighteenth century on it was regulated, evaluated, dissected, and disinfected, until it became a mass neurotic obsession (Foucault 1978; 1984a: 292-334). The stage was set for the rise of the famous Victorian morality, preached by a century of educators who taught that strict sexual self-control, not only of behavior but of fantasy, was a necessary prerequisite for moral maturity. The champions of this new repressiveness were mainly male educators, and their targets were largely young, middle-class men entering on paths to new urban careers. "The images and symbols of the male moral reformers," says Smith-Rosenberg, " . . . provided an ideal sexual regimen for a newly urbanized middle class that had suddenly to reverse the procreational practices of the past two centuries" (1978:243). A pervasive idea grew up in the middle class that the natural erotic tendencies of the young could be stunted if children were simply shielded from any kind of sexual stimulation, including information about sexual behavior, emotions, and anatomy. In the high school literature before about 1920, "excruciating obliqueness...marked discussions of sexuality" (Kett 1977:237).

Foucault has shown, in his three-volume work on the subject, that there was a great deal of academic and medical interest in sexuality throughout the Victorian era. From this he has concluded that we must "abandon the hypothesis that modern industrial societies ushered in an age of increased sexual repression" (1984:327). Given the population trends and their economic implications, the undeniable tone of moral alarm that marked most writing on sexuality, and the vigorous and continual attempts to censor overt sexual pleasure from Victorian education, art, literature, and theater, I am surprised that Foucault draws this conclusion. Would it not make more sense to conclude that the outpouring of a learned discussion on the subject was stimulated by the general state of anxiety it provoked in the Victorian mind—an anxiety derived from the association of sex with economic failure, among other things?

In the Victorian anxiety over sexuality we see history at its most cruelly ironical. For at the very time that sexuality had become the specialty of ill-informed social engineers, upward mobility was also undermining the role of parental authority in marriage. Young people were freer to choose marital partners, freer to decide on a marital lifestyle, more dependent on a marital partner for emotional support, and less emotionally equipped to make a marital choice. The middle class Victorian nuclear family was self-sufficient as no other nuclear family had been in recent history; having more privacy, it had greater influence on the emotional lives of all its members than had earlier families. The result, as we now know, was not sexual innocence, but sexual neuroticism among the middle class. In an atmosphere of sexual repression, it was an ideal breeding ground for guilt. It was another period of upheaval, this time characterized by severe conflicts between social goals and personal impulses, and as before, the Judeo-Christian concept of sin stood ready as a link between personal suffering and social acceptance. The nineteenth century saw another wave of religious conversion, and the development of many new sects.

Aggression became an equally severe problem, with the development of upward mobility as a way of life. In eras when social standing was fixed or severely limited at birth for most people, competition for wealth and status took ritual forms that removed it from everyday life. As we saw in the Middle Ages, labor, far from being a matter of pride, was considered an unpleasant necessity or a form of self-torture. Guilds regulated prices, wages, and advancement; markets were regulated by law, and competitive bargaining took place only in ritual settings—fairs, for example—set apart from normal activity. "Success" was a word that referred to tournaments and wars, diplomatic negotiations and trade voyages, and the activities of the "devil's dominion," the bazaar. In the eighteenth and nineteenth centuries, open competition diffused throughout everyday life until a great part of social interchange was governed by it. Labor, as the means by which social standing was achieved, became the principal source of men's identities. Competitive work made it necessary for people to shift often and accurately from aggressive to cooperative attitudes, and vice versa. This problem of the relationship of aggression to maturity is an especially complex one, and I have reserved chapter 12 especially for it.

It was these twin problems, stemming from the redefinition of sex and aggression, that led to the innovative ideas of the human body's great romantic philosopher, Sigmund Freud. While saving Freud's developmental theories for a later chapter, let us look at his effect on the moral idea of maturity.

"To love and to work" are Freud's famous criteria of maturity. What he meant, of course, was that the maturing middle-class person of his era, the turn of the twentieth century, faced many challenges, of which two were most difficult: to be able to love *in a particular way* and to work *in a particular way*, dictated by the class culture. The individual needed to be in full control of his passions. Both sex and aggression had to seek narrowly defined, socially appropriate targets. But paradoxically, in order to accomplish this vigorous self-limitation without paralyzing guilt, the individual had to recognize his own destructive and antisocial impulses and accept them as normal. The idea of maturity returned once more to the Platonic ideal of self-understanding.

At first glance, the self-understanding proposed by Freud seems very different from the goal of Plato's philosophy. Plato taught that the human soul contains knowledge of transcendental truth and beauty, and that insight will lead to (or rather *toward*, since the Ideal is never reached) union with the eternal values of the universe. Freud's goal appears much more prosaic: simply to live in harmony with one's self and society. But on closer inspection, the distinction between the two views begins to fade. For Freud, insight brought one closer to the understanding of one's own basic nature—a nature that geological and biological science had shown to be unimaginably ancient, and that seemed likely to last practically forever. It was an understanding that promised a transcendent view of human history and gave the individual the means to control those internal forces that lay at the foundation of human injustice and failure. In short, Freud's solution to the Victorian problem of love and work was no less than the answer to the existential question of maturity itself: What is the meaning of life? The understanding and control of one's own animal nature—the self-design of one's own humanity. It is a process that harkens back to the importance of self-love proposed by Bernard of Clairveaux, to the basic soundness of the human reason proposed by Aristotle and Aquinas, and to the idea of a fully developed self-waiting-to-be-born, found in the German Romantics.

The materials for this modern view of maturity had been drawn equally from the romantic rebellion that began with the thirteenth-century German mystics, and from the rational-empiricist tradition that began with Hobbes. The former viewed man as the unfolding of a particular transcendental destiny; the latter viewed him as the product of impersonal natural forces. The intellectual catalyst of this magical synthesis was, of course, *On the Origin of the Species by Means of Natural Selection,* published by Darwin in 1859; the theory of natural selection was an idea so profound in its implications for human nature that no moral vision of maturity could ever do without it from then on. Natural selection permitted the solution of the Victorian dilemma by morally neutralizing sex, aggression, *and* social repression. The lesson Freud drew from Darwin was that the essence of evil lay *neither* in passion nor social constraint, but in men's ignorance of the relationship between these two forces. In more ways than one, *Genesis* was stood on its head.

Mass Society and the "Psychopathology of the Average"

In the twentieth century, Western society entered a new phase of development, sometimes referred to as "post industrial" (Bell 1973). Many of the problems of sexuality and aggression that plagued Victorian man were simply solved for him by the new technological and social developments following the First World War. For one thing, birth control became simpler and more effective, reducing the problem of sexuality. For another thing, as capital came to be concentrated more and more in the hands of enormous multinational corporations, upward economic mobility became both more general (through mass employment and higher wages) and less spectacular (through the restriction of opportunities for the entrepreneur). Riesman's (1950) "other directed man," the group-conscious team member of the corporation, began to replace the "inner directed man" of the industrial revolution. The tasks of sexual and aggressive self control became less prominent.

Meanwhile, several other important economic and social developments affected prevailing definitions of maturity in the twentieth century: material abundance, standardization, mechanization, and specialization. Material abundance and the standardization of goods through mass production raised the level of material affluence for all but a small minority in Western society. More important, this technical revolution raised *expectations* for material abundance, and altered definitions of justice to include a safe and comfortable lifestyle for everyone. Social legislation led the way to pensions, medical insurance, welfare, the medical treatment of the insane, and the rehabilitation of the "culturally deprived." This meant that full social development was supposed to be available to everyone who had the character and energy to pursue it. Poverty and ignorance were no longer legitimate excuses for the failure to mature.

At the same time, mechanization greatly reduced the amount of labor needed to produce material abundance, with the result that: (1) more time and effort went into the production and sharing of information; and (2) a wider *variety* of goods became available for the purpose of cultivating individual style (Bell 1973). In the mid-1800s the average worker spent an estimated thirty-five hundred hours per year at his job. By the mid-1900s automation raised labor productivity to the point that the average worker was spending about two thousand hours per year at work—a drop of some forty-five percent (Harris 1971:218). This meant paid vacations, sick leave, and shorter hours. These developments, in turn, meant universal education for at least eight and often twelve years per person—enough for a flying start at intellectual maturity—and after that, time to study, think, plan, and cultivate the finer things of life. It meant the further development of ideals of family life and heterosexual intimacy. Together with material abundance, it meant the cultivation of personal taste, and the expression of that taste through lifestyle.

Specialization—the proliferation of knowledge by means of expertise in all fields—meant rapid technological change. The effects of this on ideas of maturity have been diverse and subtle. One of the most important effects was the marriage of social success and technical education. We have seen that the idea of social success largely replaced heroism as a measure of maturity in the industrial revolution. I believe that technical education in our culture results in a thorough moral relativism—a self-critical awareness of one's own limitations, and a corresponding respect for the abilities and views of others—that has come to be closely associated with maturity itself. This trend has led to greater tolerance of differences, but also to profound moral apathy.

Given the modern sense of maturity not as heroism but as decent mediocrity, Western society has reached a stage of political and technological development such that the basic necessities of a fully mature life are—or should be—available to everyone. We have the means at our disposal as a civilization to eradicate hunger, poverty, disease, and ignorance. Our laws recognize equal opportunity for self-development throughout all levels of society; governments spend a great deal in an effort to administer those laws fairly. And yet, a casual glance at modern Western society reveals that the promise of a morally mature society is, if anything, as distant as ever. Few would dispute the idea that the major social and personal problems of our time stem not from a lack of resources, but from the inability of most people to achieve the insight and self-control called for in the modern concept of maturity. Why do many fail to make use of free education? Why do marriages fail? What is the origin of the crime, delinquency, alcoholism, domestic violence, labor unproductivity, and madness that plague modern societies, to say nothing of the failure of the political and judicial systems to administer justice, preserve the environment, or avoid the unimaginable expense and folly of arms production and war?

Our egalitarian ideals no longer allow us to chalk this up to natural differences in endowment. In an interesting way, mass society has reproduced two of the important conditions bearing on the conception of maturity in primitive society: social equality (or the ideal of it), and faith in human consciousness as the means to ultimate understanding. These similarities have driven us back to the problem faced by primitive society in accounting for developmental failure. Equality means that the ideal of maturity is not heroism but social success. Faith in human understanding means that failures are not to be explained by the machinations of a transcendental consciousness, but by natural processes that should be tractable to discovery and control. What concept will do in a society that has ceased to believe in an anthropomorphic universe and cyclical time?

Disease.

I am not sure who started the idea that averageness was itself a sort of illness. Erich Fromm (1955:16) finds the concept in Spinoza's *Ethics* (1677); Freud used the phrase "collective neuroses" in *Civilization and Its Discontents* (1930), while Fromm himself prefers the softer term "socially patterned defect" (1955:15). Perhaps Abraham Maslow, one of the fathers of that peculiarly modern form of consciousness we call self-actualization, said it best: "What we call 'normal' in psychology is really a psychopathology of the average, so undramatic we don't even recognize it ordinarily" (1968b:16). Maturity is the normal state of development for an adult in our society. Failure to achieve it is a form of illness. The point has been driven home by the application of modern mental-health standards to the masses in modern society, with predictable results, as exemplified by Marvin Opler's scientific conclusions about New Yorkers: eighty percent of the residents of that city suffer from one kind or another of "emotional disability" (1967:265). Could this be because the poor devils live in an unusually pathological environment? Apparently not: the Leightons studied a rural county in Nova Scotia, with the same results: Only 18.7% of the population were free of psychiatric symptoms (Leighton et al. 1963:121).

And what is this sanity that is so difficult to achieve? There are essentially two traditions in modern psychology that seem to stem from the Enlightenment and the romantic lines of thought, respectively. The Enlightenment position is egalitarian and, on the whole, empiricist. It holds that most adults are reasonably mature, or would be if their material and social needs were adequately provided for. It draws its standards from the observation and measurement of personality among the socially well-adjusted. Examples of this view are found in the works of Gordon Allport, Benjamin Bloom, and Jack Block. Allport, a leading personality psychologist, describes the mature person in terms of the skills one needs in order to have friends and stay out of social trouble: (1) an interest in other things and people; (2) warmth and friendliness; (3) self-acceptance; (4) a fair grasp of reality; (5) awareness of limitations and a sense of humor; and (6) a philosophy of life (Allport 1961:275-307). This is a *functional* definition, based essentially on the idea of the mind and society as machines, as proposed by Hobbes. The inclusion of a "philosophy of life" refers not to an inner spiritual quest, but merely to the fact that modern societies are heterogeneous in beliefs and values, and the individual without a set of standards by which to navigate will be susceptible to confusion and depression. It eschews notions of the transcendental, either as a teleological goal toward which maturation tends, or as an inner *daemon* demanding satisfaction. Likewise, Bloom (1964:227) gives as "prized characteristics in a society" those which "enable the individual to adapt to a rapidly changing society as well as those which enable the individual to secure some measures of happiness in his life." Block based his ratings of subjects' adjustment on the "resourcefulness, versatility, and resilience of individuals in creating and responding to their life encounters" (1971:84).

The romantic view has strong roots in the psychoanalytic concept of maturity as freedom from repression. It is exemplified best, perhaps, by Carl Gustav Jung, Carl Rogers, and Erich Fromm. For these giants of modern developmental psychology, the unique, irrepressible, and quite incommunicable Self is the core of maturity and the path of its attainment. It is Meister Eckhart, C. G. Carus, Troxler and von Schubert. It is elitist and intellectual, drawing upon for its standards not the successful and well-adjusted insurance salesman or housewife, but the spiritual leader, the visionary, the artist (while avoiding the equation of character and occupation). Of the basic needs of man, Erich Fromm wrote:

> Those needs which he shares with the animal—hunger, thirst, need for sleep and sexual satisfaction—are important, being rooted in the inner chemistry of the body, and they can become all powerful when they remain unsatisfied.... But even their complete satisfaction is not a sufficient condition for sanity and mental health. These depend on the satisfaction of those needs and passions which are specifically human...the need for relatedness, transcendence, rootedness, the need for a sense of identity and the need for a frame of orientation and devotion. (1955:67)

More recently, the romantic tradition has stimulated a view of :urity White (1976:508) calls "the liberated person." Many modern writers, notably Charles Reich in his 1970 bestseller, *The Greening of America*, and Robert Lindner in *Prescription for Rebellion* (1952) have carried forward the idea of an irreducible self, whose suppression through social conformity constitutes a kind of disease. This movement drew impetus in America from the Vietnam War, during which many highly conscientious, altruistic, and socially successful individuals found themselves in open rebellion against the conforming majority.

It would be a mistake, however, to think that the kind of maturity advocated by present-day romantics is the same as the kind Rousseau and his peers had in mind. If we look at the romantic art and literature of the eighteenth and early nineteenth centuries, we can see that the sensibility that produced that art is no longer widely accepted among the educated classes. The heroic paintings of David, Tiepolo and Gericault, the poetry of Byron and Wordsworth and Blake, so admired a century and a half ago, now strike us as naive, even at times banal. We are more at home with Goya, and with Goethe. What has happened?

The change in us is the firm establishment of *the blasé attitude*, and it is the result of a vastly more stimulating environment than the early romantics knew. Most of us live in great cities, where our senses are constantly bombarded with stimulation, much of it foreign to our understanding or our taste, or to both. Even those of us who rarely venture into the city are in close contact with urban life through the press, television and radio, the telephone, and the rapid comings and goings of our urban consociates. As a result, we have learned to defend ourselves against too much stimulation, too much sensivity to others' needs. We are wary, aloof, and self-protective in a way that our ancestors were not. The effect has been described best by Georg Simmel:

> There is perhaps no psychic phenomenon which has been so
> unconditionally reserved to the metropolis as has the blasé attitude.
> The blasé attitude results first from the rapidly changing and closely
> compressed contrasting stimulation of the nerves. From this, the
> enhancement of the metropolitan intellectuality, also, seems
> originally to stem. Therefore, stupid people who are not intellectually
> alive in the first place usually are not exactly blasé. A life in boundless
> pursuit of pleasure makes one blasé because it agitates the nerves to
> their strongest reactivity for such a long time that they finally cease to
> react at all.(1902:413-414)

Simmel goes on to talk about the compounding effect of mass culture and money economy, which rob things of their individuality and value for urban man; and to describe the attitude of reserve, whereby the blase attitude expresses itself in relations among urban people. But in the passage given here, which was written at the turn of the twentieth century, we already see several interesting ideas. In addition to giving us an accurate account of the causes of modern reserve, Simmel (1) shows the link between the romantic values (sensitivity to, and interest in, environment) and the blasé attitude; and (2) shows how the blasé attitude comes to be equated with intelligence and sophistication, and so becomes a valued aspect of maturity.

The value of sensitivity is still with us, then, but it has been redefined. Sensitivity to the ordinary, the hackneyed, the obvious, the easy or cheap, is childish. The modern romantic cultivates sensitivity to that which is rare. By contrast, the Enlightenment view of maturity tends to classify a robust interest in anything and everything within reason as a sign of health.

In summary, the views of maturity seen in the Enlightenment and romantic traditions, are strikingly different. Yet they present quite accurately, I think, the ethical implications of two contending emphases in psychological science that emerged from their corresponding early modern roots—the philosophic emphasis representing the romantic tradition, and the scientistic emphasis representing the Enlightenment. I will say more about this polarity in chapter 10. However, the mid-twentieth century did see several attempts to reconcile these two principles of causality within the strictures of the Nonconscious, Lawful Universe, but with varying emphasis on one causal factor or another; I shall reopen the problem of synthesis in chapter 12.

Christianity

Ninety-five percent of Americans claim to believe in God (Bellah 1970:41), and any account of modern norms of maturity must at least try to deal with religious ideals. This is difficult, because the main effect of the Enlightenment on religion has been to radically individualize belief. The death of the Conscious, Transcendent Universe, and with it spiritual hierarchy and metaphysics, culminated in Kant; but that was only the beginning of the shift to modern personalized religion. Since the nineteenth century, the central source of culture and belief in the industrial countries has been public education, not the church, and public education has been closely wedded to empiricist science. Modern man must fight against his education in order to develop an understanding of the limitations of the empiricist point of view. As such, he is inclined to be sceptical of any metaphysical doctrine, and to prefer to construct his own personal solutions to questions about ultimate values. There are those, to be sure, for whom this liberal education makes little sense, and for whom pre-Enlightenment Christianity still has value. Their beliefs are examples of the persistence of old solutions to the basic questions, as are the examples of astrology and astral soul-travel. When I speak of modern religion, I speak of religion that addresses the present historical situation.

In this historical situation, organized religion has little choice but to be tolerant of doctrinal scepticism, and to accept the role of its ministry as one of providing raw materials for the construction of the myriad private faiths present in any given church on Sunday. Modern churches try to provide an atmosphere in which each individual feels free to confront his own limitations without excessive shame or guilt, and in which he can receive comfort for his existential longing. It is a role similar in many ways to that of the psychotherapist; in many ways it reinforces the concept of maturity as mental health. The spiritually healthy person in modern religion is one who is free of chronic crippling psychological pain, and who is able to love, work, and handle the other responsibilities of citizenship and family life.

Gains and Losses of History

Our brisk tour of moral maturity has arrived at its exit point as the twentieth century draws to a close. If we reflect on what Western humanity has gained and lost in the four or five millenia behind us, we find much on both sides of the balance. Our big loss has been the moral certainty offered by the Conscious, Transcendent Universe. As I will discuss in chapter 13, this leaves us with great difficulty in defining maturity without reference to cultural norms, and consequently in accounting for moral excellence in our midst. The extent of human efforts to avoid this fate through the ages should serve as some measure of its seriousness.

On the positive side, we have grown incomparably more intimate with the universe of our ordinary sense experience. This achievement of natural science has united each of us with the rest of mankind in three ways: first, because it provides a highly useful and highly communicable way of looking at the universe, it extends and democratizes knowledge and the power based on knowledge; it transcends and weakens the barriers of language, tradition, and personal experience. Second, it teaches the common origin and biological unity of our species and the falsehood of philosophies based upon other conceptions. Third, it offers us the brotherhood of accidental companions on a strange voyage, the chance to see ourselves as tragical/comical coimprobabilities all facing the same uncertainties with the same lack of preparation and ability.

Finally, history has shown us the necessity of historical self-consciousness. Since Kant, maturity requires honesty and clarity about the limitations of our own understanding and the understandings bequeathed to us, not only to minimize self-delusion, but to maximize the effectiveness of our value choices. An empiricist psychology is no longer a mature psychology, morally or otherwise.

PART II

The Evolution of
Developmental Theory

7. Before
Developmental Theory

From Maturity as an Ideal to Maturation as a Process

In chapter 1, I mentioned that moral ideas about maturity are only loosely related in history to theories about how people actually mature. Now we have examined the main periods and trends in Western ideals of maturity, and we are ready to look specifically at developmental theory.

The main steps in the evolution of the ideal were these: In non-literate societies, maturity tended to be equated with adulthood, and failure to achieve it was generally attributed to influences outside the individual. With the shift to writing and the concept of a transcendent consciousness, cultures like those of the classical Greeks and the Hebrews tended to view moral maturity as a stepwise approach to an ultimate knowledge that was infused into awareness from some superhuman source. Human consciousness was thought to resemble that of the universe in kind, but to be much more limited in extent and clarity. With the Enlightenment came an erosion of faith in the ability of man to intuit universal absolutes, and maturity came to be equated by the empiricists with self-control, intelligence, and learning; the romantics retained the ancient belief in a spiritual guide. In modern times, as faith in absolute knowledge has continued to erode, we tend to equate, as our preliterate ancestors did, maturity with the achievement of "normal" adulthood. However, the ideals of each era have been retained as the new ones have been added, so that we now have a complex and sometimes confusing set of ideas about moral maturity.

Each of these ideas set limits on the range of developmental theories that made sense. Within these limits, however, was a good deal of room for variation. In the following chapters we shall see that the Hebrews preferred the study of ancient texts as a source of inspiration and guidance; the Greeks preferred introspection (and discipleship based on it); the early Christians sought an altered state of consciousness pleasing to God; the late medieval scholastics returned to the study of texts; and the Enlightenment ushered in the era of systematic scepticism and empirical enquiry that still guides most scientific psychology and pedagogy.

Even within these broad traditions there are important disagreements. Right in the midst of Hebrew scholarship, we find the book of Ecclesiastes, with its primitive admonition that human efforts at wisdom in general are useless, and that most useless of all is scholarship! Among the Greeks, Plato trusted the emotions as a source of inspiration; Aristotle and the Stoics shunned them like the plague; both opinions are represented in modern developmental psychology. To fully understand the evolution of thought about the maturation process, then, we must start again at the beginning.

"Development"

The idea that living things and other natural phenomena "develop" is as familiar to us as the idea that each of us is the same person on Friday that we were on Wednesday. It is so natural an idea that we have to spend some effort to be conscious of what it means. We habitually think of development as a natural law that we need only take into account in order to make sense of the world. We are used to the notion that one should understand the specific developmental processes of specific things and creatures, but the question What is development? may strike us as a little metaphysical, like the question What is gravity?

Actually, both questions might help us to understand ourselves. Development and gravity are examples of the core ideas of our culture, ideas with which we automatically and unconsciously make sense out of our experience. Like most such ideas, they are drawn not from sense data alone, but from deep traditions of perception and thinking; they differ among people with different cultures. They are also answers to emotionally charged questions about the meaning of life, the nature of justice, and the origins of knowledge. The questions What is development? and Why do we believe in it? are by no means idle or esoteric; they are important fragments of the larger question Who are we?

To "develop," then, means "to go through a process of natural growth, differentiation, or evolution by successive changes" (Webster

1984), or to go through "orderly, organized change toward a hypothetical ideal" (Kagan et al. 1978:5). But we are merely substituting words for words. What do the words mean? First, "development" refers to something "natural," which in our culture is another way of saying something orderly, predictable, and unavoidable under ordinary circumstances—something inclined to happen the same way over and over. Second, although it involves unspecified changes, the changes are linear, not circular or oscillating (they end up somewhere other than where they started), and they involve an increase rather than a decrease in the qualities we think of as typical or ideal for the person, being, or phenomenon in question. "Decay" is not a form of "development," or vice versa. In the absence of any notion of an ideal end-state, we are forced to speak of any process simply as "change," never as "development." It is for this reason that we have had to look carefully at ideals of maturity before we could think clearly about maturation—a form of development.

Our look at the history of moral maturity has indicated why twentieth-century Western man is attracted to the idea of personality development, and why other cultures might not be. We think of time as linear, not cyclical, and our image of nature is more machinelike than personlike in its assumption of process, machines being both more accurate and less whimsical than people. Other cultures have not always shared these assumptions. The task of the next several chapters is to understand a bit more fully what we *do* mean when we say people "develop," and why, in a historical sense, we think people develop the way we think they do. I have already mentioned that our concept of development is only loosely related to our ideals of maturity. Moreover, both the concepts of process and the concepts of end state are only loosely related to what strike us today as empirical facts. This is exactly what we should expect, once we realize that all knowledge is a mixture of custom, desire, and observation. To know something about the ingredients of our knowledge is to know something about ourselves.

Predestination: The Nonliterate and Ancient Worlds

In chapter 2, I argued that in nonliterate societies maturity is seen as the inevitable result of growing up, and that the problem in such societies is how to explain the failures of maturation that occasionally occur. I showed that failure is attributed to conscious forces external to the individual. Given such a view, the modern idea of personality development makes little sense. In the nonliterate view, consciousness does not "develop," it simply "is." The idea of consciousness developing would strike people in such cultures in the same way the idea of things and people materializing out of thin air would strike us. The failure of people to achieve a mature state of consciousness must be, and is, the result of deliberate interference from outside—the influence of some other consciousness that distorts the natural tendencies of the victim.

In such a universe, nothing happens according to chance or accident; everything is willed. The future is contained in the *intentions* of the present. We might argue that this is not so different from modern ideas of natural epigenesis, of genetic "codes" and organic "plans," but there is an important difference. The intentions of the nonliterate universe are of the same sort as the intentions of human beings. They are self-conscious, passionate, and whimsical. They can be engaged in dialogue by anyone who speaks their language; and, of course, they can be influenced by persuasion, threats, and coercion.

In such a universe, every human life is in constant danger of interference from some outraged consciousness or other. Every individual must be constantly vigilant against such interference; he must surround himself with means of warding it off or removing its effects. This kind of protection is one of the chief functions of magic and ritual—the other functions being the collective protection of the group, and the pursuit of gain.

Magic and ritual make perfect sense, given this worldview. If every event is intentional, and all causality is conscious in a human way, then the same maneuvers that persuade or dissuade people will affect events similarly. Good fate is attracted and secured by polite and beautiful speech and gesture, fine art, perfume, delectable food and drink, and promises of service. Bad fate is dissuaded by curses, threats, and the infliction of pain, discomfort, and disgust.

Given the nonliterate worldview, there is little notion of intrinsic change in individual personality; therefore little attention is given to fostering or shaping such change. A great deal has been written about rites of passage, often from a modern literate viewpoint that such rites are meant to bring about or direct internal developments in the celebrants. Although good arguments can be made that rites of passage do in fact have such effects, and although at least some individuals in nonliterate societies undoubtedly know this, I doubt that this is the main conscious purpose of performing such rites. Rather, I agree with Fortes (1959) that the rites are meant to *influence fate*, which might otherwise interfere with spontaneous maturation.

There is plenty of ethnographic evidence that most nonliterate people think of maturation as a spontaneous event, rather than a developmental process. Alfonso Ortiz, for example, has written a particularly detailed and sensitive account to the worldview of the Tewa Indians, pueblo dwellers of the American Southwest. Ortiz tells us that the Tewa use the term *seh t'a,* meaning "hardened," or "dry," to distinguish older children from those up to the age of six or seven who have not yet attained the age of reason. Thus, to be not yet *seb t'a* is to be innocent or unknowing. I might sketch the general reasoning process involved here as follows: to be innocent is to be not yet Tewa; to be not yet Tewa is to be not yet human. (1969:16)

Once the child "hardens," moreover, it becomes at once fully Tewa. In the same vein, an aged Chagga on the slopes of Kilimanjaro told Sally Falk Moore, "You can tell what character a child will have at the age of seven to twelve. Then they do not change any more" (1978:49). Paul Radin also concluded from his wide survey of nonliterate beliefs that primitive people generally view character as fully formed in early childhood, and see no intrinsic internal development thereafter. As I mentioned in chapter 2, there is only an incidental correspondence between age and authority or responsibility in the nonliterate world. Often older and more experienced individuals are denied responsibilities granted to younger ones. Fortes records that aging Fulani are required to "return to the jural and economic dependence of childhood" regardless of their skill and knowledge, once they have relinquished their family headship (1984:107). We can best get the flavor of this view by letting primitive man speak for himself. Here is an Ojibwa grandfather speaking to his grandson about life:

"My son, as you travel along this road (the road of life), do not doubt it. If you do you will be unhappy and you will injure yourself. But if you do everything I tell you well, it will benefit you greatly.

"My son, the first thing you come to as you travel along this road will be a ravine, extending to the very ends of the world, on both sides. It will look as though it could not possibly be crossed. When you get there you will think to yourself, 'Grandfather said that I was, nevertheless, to pass across.' Plunge right through and you will get to the other side.

"Now this ravine means that sometimes in life you will lose a child and thoughts of death will come to you. But if you pay attention to my teachings you will be able to go right on and find the road of the lodge on the other side. If you do not try to go beyond, if you get frightened and dwell upon your loss too much, this will be your grave.

"After you have crossed the ravine you will see the footsteps of the medicine men who have gone before you marked very plainly in the road. Step into them and you will feel good. . . .

"As you pass along the road, evil birds will continually din into your ears and will cast their excrement upon you. It will stick to your body. Now do not brush it off and do not pay any attention to it. If you paid attention to it you might forget yourself and brush it off. That would not be right. Life is not to be obtained in this manner.

"The evil birds have the following meaning. The fact that you have joined the medicine lodge signifies that you would like to lead a good life. Now as soon as you have joined the lodge, the work of evil tattlers will begin. They will say that you have done things contrary to the teachings of the lodge. Perhaps a bit of the bird's excrement will fall on you. Don't brush it off without a thought. Some people might even claim that you had said that the lodge was no good. However, even then you must not forget yourself and blurt out, 'Who said that?' and get angry. Keep quiet and hold your peace.

"As you go along, you will come to a great fire encircling the earth and practically impossible to cross. It will be so near that it will scorch you. Remember then that your grandfather had said that you would be able to pass it. Plunge through it. Soon you will find yourself on the other side and nothing will have happened to you.

"Now this great fire means death. Your wife will die. Go through this as well as you can and do not get discouraged. This fire will be the worst thing that you have to go through. You will have been living happily and then, without warning, your wife will die. There you will remain with your children. Bear in mind, however, what your grandfather said and plunge straight through. On the other side you will find the footprints of the medicine men.

"After a while you will come to tremendous perpendicular bluffs which hardly seem surmountable. Think again what your grandfather said and you will then soon find yourself on the other side of these bluffs and quite safe.

"These bluffs mean death. As you travel along the road of life you will find yourself alone. All your relatives, all your loved ones, are dead. You will begin to think to yourself, 'Why, after all, am I living?' You will want to die. Now this, my grandson, is the place where most encouragement is given for it is here most needed. This is the most difficult of all the places you will come to. Keep in the footsteps of the medicine men and you will be safe. The teachings of the lodge are the only road; they alone will allow you to pass this point safely." (Radin 1927:86-89)

Charming as the old man's words are, several things about them strike us as distinct from our own way of thinking. First, there is no notion of development in his vision of the "road of life." The young man who sets out and the old man who survives life's trials are exactly the same person. No matter how many times death is encountered (and I left one out for brevity) it is experienced the same way, and the same formula is used for meeting it. All the important events are external; none of them unfolds from within the individual.

Second, the course of life is known ahead of time. The old man must have had a vision or conducted a clairvoyant voyage to be able to speak with such certainty about events (for example, the sudden and unexpected death of the young man's wife). Nothing happens by chance. Fate is the master of all.

Third, there is the importance of tradition—the steps of the medicine men and the way of the lodge. As all lives are in general repetitions of the same cycle, so the ways that have worked in the past are the only certain ways. Fate can be managed, to some extent, and the wise men are those who have learned the techniques of its management.

Fourth, the grandfather relies on magic to protect his grandson. He arranges a good fate in advance, not by praying for it, but by *predicting* it. His prediction has the same ontological status as fate itself—the conscious intention to secure a certain outcome. Hence, the grandson need only remember (that is, make conscious again) the prediction in order to assure its realization. We would be inclined to say that this is nothing but good psychology, because the confidence it conveys will help the young man to bring about the desired result through his own action. But I do not believe this is what the old man meant. He meant to *cause* a certain outcome by *intending* it, and by securing the cooperation of the chief participant in his intention. This is the essence of ritual and magic.

Finally, we moderns will sympathize with the grief of the young man as he experiences the deaths of his loved ones, but we might wonder why it is considered so difficult for him to survive those deaths. The answer lies in the nature of death in an anthropomorphic universe. For us, bereavement means the loss of a love object, usually as a result of accidental or impersonal natural causes. It is difficult to deal with emotionally, and often enough results in illness or death of the survivor. In the primitive world it means these things also, but it means something more. Death is never due to accident or impersonal nature. Nature and causality are conscious and purposeful. Death therefore results from the direction of conscious anger at the survivors by an external agent, and it means the relative weakness of the survivor's power as compared with the power of the agent. Unless the death is diagnosed as witchcraft or outright murder and is avenged (which happens often in many primitive societies, too), the bereaved is in the psychological bind of the survivor of an unpunished murder. He must accept that he is helpless in the face of premeditated evil. If you or I were in that state, we would probably need some help to avoid serious damage to our egos.

This last point, incidentally, helps to illustrate the usefulness of the idea of predestination in primitive life. Although destiny is conscious and intentional, sometimes it cannot be undone. Perhaps its cause cannot be found; perhaps it is the result of extraordinarily strong forces. The old man's prediction of the evil events in the grandson's life helps to establish their inevitability, and to relieve the youth of blame. Perhaps it is the functional beauty of this worldview that accounts for its appearance throughout the nonliterate world, and its survival in our own culture, down to the founding of modern psychology.

Causality in Classical Civilization

In chapter 3 we traced the changes in worldview that accompanied the appearance of writing and civic politics. We noted that man's sense of time shifted considerably from cyclical to linear models, and that consciousness, although still an a priori quality immanent in the universe, was now thought to be gradable into various levels, from stupidity to transcendental wisdom. This view led naturally to the idea of *teleology*, that is, the idea that transcendental wisdom (The Good, The Beautiful, The True) stood as goals, toward which human consciousness strove. Although somewhat more "modern" in its recognition of change, this idea was not yet "developmental," because it did not propose that change unfolds naturally according to innate laws of the organism. Rather, it proposed that transcendental consciousness reveals itself somehow to the ready mind, and acts as a map in the search for maturity.

I believe this worldview was widespread throughout the early literate world. The recognition of its effects allows us to understand some interesting things about the relationships among ancient schools of thought, and about their influence on later ideas. For example, the idea of teleology suggests that the transcendental consciousness must be revealed to man through some specific medium, whose study would be the natural path to wisdom. Specific ideological traditions can be identified with specific ideas about what this medium was. For the Jews, the medium was the written word. Through the study of their history and mythology, one learned the mind of God, and qualified as a teacher of men. For Pythagoras the medium was mathematics, for Aristotle it was physics (meaning the study of natural phenomena), and for Plato it was introspection. For the so-called mystic religions such as the cults of Dionysus, Orpheus, Cybele, Moloch, Baal, Mithra, and the rest, the medium was the altered state of consciousness appropriate to the deity. This "ecstatic" group of beliefs is especially important for understanding modern psychology, because of the fate that befell the systematic pursuit of religious ecstacy during the Middle Ages and afterwards.

I mentioned in chapter 2 that most nonliterate societies cultivated achievement of nonordinary states of consciousness for the purpose of wresting knowledge from the jealous consciousness of the universe. These same techniques were carried over into the early classical period for the achievement of union with the transcendental superhuman cosmos. Early Christianity was one of these ecstatic religions; there was no formal priesthood, and the ability to know God and to preach was conveyed through the direct, ecstatic experience of salvation. Parkes (1959) says that this direct empowerment of the individual believer was the chief reason for the popularity of early Christianity, but I am sceptical. There were many popular transcendental cults all around the Mediterranean at the time, and it is hard to see how the experiential element could have given the teachings of Christ their victory. Campbell records, for example, that the ecstatic cult of Mithra "was the most formidable rival of Christianity both in

Asia and in Europe, reaching as far north as to the south of Scotland" (1964:255). In a sense, direct identification with a deity as a source of spiritual maturity actually grew in stature during this period. Knowledge of transcendental wisdom created a kind of ontological chasm between the saved and the damned, a chasm that had not existed in primitive society with its cyclical concept of time.

The establishment of a church hierarchy and a professional priest-hood during the Middle Ages resulted in the control of spontaneous mystical experience, and in the development of both a practice and a theory of spiritual gradualism. This fact undoubtedly helped to prepare the ground for the reemergence of pre-Christian rational philosophy in the twelfth century. I shall return to this point in the next chapter.

When one thinks of the contribution of the classical world to psychology, one immediately thinks of the Greeks, and of rationalism. Aristotle in particular was a rationalist, and he spent a good deal of effort trying to work out a logical relationship of the psyche to the sensible world—a relationship, in other words, that would avoid the necessity of mystical vision. He believed that the soul is the "basic metaphysic perfection of the organic body and its faculties" (Galdston 1967:30), in contrast to Plato's idea that the soul is immortal, and derives its character from the transcendental consciousness. Here I find myself agreeing with Emerson, that Aristotle "Platonizes"—that the difference between the two philosophers on this issue was largely one of language, not of basic conception. Galdston quotes David Knowles (1962:212) to the effect that Aristotle failed "to harmonize the seemingly incompatible views of the soul . . . as simply a metaphysical 'form' and as a mind-substance existing in its own right." I think the problem, and the distinction between philoso-phies, largely disappears once it is clear that both thinkers started with the premise that "things" are inseparable from "consciousness," and that "ideal form" is another way of talking about the *intentions* of "things." To say that the soul is the ideal form of the body and its faculties, then, is simply to say that those substances have their own intentions and that they partake of the intentions of the transcendent universe—which does not seem to me so different from Plato's ideal *telos* toward which people are drawn. Nor, I believe, is the humoral theory of Hippocrates and Galen an exception to the attribution of consciousness to the universe. These great physicians had no idea of the chemical or microbiological dynamics of the "humors." Rather, they simply tried to identify the precise location of the conscious universal elements that participated in health and disease. This fits well with the Aristotelian notion that consciousness itself is material, and with the Ionic philosophers' theory of correspondences, which we shall meet in chapter 8.

We saw in part 1 the great influence of Plato on medieval and modern ideas of moral maturity. Plato was unusual for his age, first because he was interested in the process of the mind's development, and second because he actually observed developmental stages, as I mentioned in the discussion of *The Symposium*. Was Plato then a developmentalist? Not in the modern sense. Plato held that the human soul was an entity, with an existence and qualities of its own somewhat independent of the body. In keeping with the three levels of love, he divided the soul into three parts; the *vegetative* part (located below the waist), corresponding to the animal instincts and appetites; the *will* (located in the breast); and the *reason* (located in the head). Plato was inconsistent on the immortality of the soul, and on whether its parts were detachable one from the other. He seems to have been certain that the *reason*, at least, was immortal, and that it was unique to each individual. At any rate, the elements of maturity, apparently, do not come into being through the process of maturation, but already exist a priori, and respond to objects with attraction or repulsion, teleologically. Why do some free men stop short of spiritual maturity, then? Plato attributes the failures to "stupid upbringing." In *The Republic* he suggests that this can be eliminated by standardized education. He was well aware of the effects of parental influence on the shaping of character, and even thought of the idea of studying character development through biography (Charlton 1967:14).

To Plato's great credit, then, he did notice that people go through orderly stages in their ascent toward spiritual maturity. One begins by loving a single beautiful body, then learns to love other bodies like it; then graduates to the love of an honorable deed, then others of its type; then loves a beautiful idea, and finally loves Beauty itself. The progression from self-centered to altruistic to contemplative maturity is a familiar one in modern psychology. We can recognize, for example, the concept of the progressive "sublimation" (and how Platonic the word itself sounds!) of psychic energy in the developmental theories of Freud. But, like the primitives, Plato and his Greek contemporaries saw both success and failure as regulated by conscious, external agencies, not by the unfolding of a developmental plan. This part of the Greek contribution is alien to modern psychological thought because the Greek view accepted the idea of revealed truth.

The Greek concept of the continuity of transcendental spirituality and civic action was rooted in the political organization of the Hellenic states, which ideally gave every free male citizen a chance to achieve immortality within the framework of his civic institutions. Those institutions prompted a quest for a philosophy in which politics, war, and spiritual maturity formed a unified system governed by a single set of cosmic rules, which could in turn be discerned by the well-educated citizen.

In the early Middle Ages, the institutions and the ideas of maturity changed, to form a different symmetry. Christianity was based on the Hebrew concept of the transcendental as a God who spoke directly to a spiritual elect, rather than as an ideal immanent in human consciousness. This conception made the pursuit of the transcendental a highly specialized way of life, which in turn promoted a separation of political and spiritual action. In the new system, the split between the monastic and the temporal ways of life was expressed ideologically in the split between the Vita Activa and the Vita Contemplativa as maturational ideals. According to Saint Gregory, the temporal prince had a chance at spiritual maturity, but Gregory rejected the Greek equation, and portrayed civic life as a hindrance to the highest aim, not a forward step.

The interdependence of ideology and way of life can be seen even more clearly from the fate of Greek psychology when it was reintroduced in the late Middle Ages. The practical virtues of the well-regulated temporal life—what Aquinas called the Natural Virtues of reasoning, skill, wisdom, temperance, and justice—remained somewhat irrelevant to the pursuit of maturity by the impractical path of contemplation and prayer. In the hands of Ockham, philosophy—the study of these natural virtues—and the-ology—the study of received Truth—split completely; and finally, in the Enlightenment, transcendental concepts of maturity ceased to have any serious place in scientific psychology.

At the same time, the Greek suggestion of a continuum binding human justice and absolute values was expressed in the image of the pious nobleman or king, who prayed for guidance in his civic duties; today the same idea can be seen in what Bellah has called American "civil religion," the vague notion that our elected officials guide us wisely to the extent that they, and we, are God-fearing people.

8. Developmental Metaphysics: The Middle Ages

The Essential Unity of Things

Plato's interest in human lifespan development was unusual for premodern times. Before scientific inquiry had begun to reveal the evolution of things, Western man held a rather static view of the universe, and rarely seemed interested in complex natural processes. The Ionic philosophers of the sixth century B.C. had had a habit of classifying everything according to a vast system of correspondences, in which all natural phenomena were seen as the expression of a small number of principles. There were the Four Humors of the body, the Four Seasons, the Seven Planets, the Four Elements, and so on. Each item of a given type (season, planet, humor, element), was thought to correspond, by virtue of some principle of unity, to an element of another type. There was a planet for each season, a season for each humor, and so on. In the absence of scientific theory, it gave a kind of tidiness to the universe. Plato's four developmental stages, and his three parts of the soul, may have drawn to some extent from this earlier tradition.

At any rate, the Middle Ages was strongly influenced by this view. The thinkers of the time accepted such images as the Great Chain of Being, in which every creature was given a place in a single moral progression, from God and the angels down to the worm and the flea. Astrology, alchemy, and the ubiquitous number magic of the time (three wishes, seven black cats, nine lives) were based on the Ionic notion of the universe as a tight-knit enterprise. Of course this system extended to the stages of human life—originally the idea of a Byzantine philosopher named Fulgentius in the sixth century A.D. (Aries 1962:21), who drew on an ancient and therefore unimpeachable source, the *Aeneid*. As far as the scholarship of the Middle Ages was concerned, that settled it. Fulgentius's idea of seven ages of human life was accepted and repeated ad infinitum, right down to the seventeenth century, where it appears in Shakespeare's *As You Like It* and in Henry Cuffe's *The Difference of the Ages of a Man's Life*.

This business of immutable correspondences and fixed stages of life was really a variation on the primitive idea of predestination. Just as the thinker of nonliterate society was led by his conviction of a conscious, anthropomorphic universe to see the hand of fate or the machinations of the ancestors or spirits in the unfolding of lives, the medieval mind visualized linkages between synchronous events involving stars, thunderstorms, battles, and bee stings.

The Spirit Quest

One might suspect from this that the Middle Ages was a period devoid of theorizing about developmental processes, but such is not quite the case. Monasticism, after all, centered on spiritual quest, a kind of activity we would now think of as developmental; the monastic teachers recognized that it involved some sort of process within the human spirit. But unlike the Greeks and us moderns, they preferred to rely upon introspection and the testimony of authorities, rather than upon systematic observation, to understand this process. There was no shortage of models that could have been studied in the search for knowledge about the topic. The times were teeming with saints great and small, and the modern mind naturally assumes that the actual process of their spiritual enlightenment would have been a subject of intense interest to the pious. But a comparison of the developmental ideas of the time on one hand, and the biographies of the saints on the other, shows a certain absence of influence. A case in point is the matter of spontaneous conversion.

Many of the greatest saints achieved the heights of inspiration not by gradual progress along the prescribed paths of monastic discipline, but by spontaneous leaps into the arms of God, often while in the midst of the most uninspiring activity. Saint Francis of Assisi heard the call of God while on a drunken toot with a group of his friends. The friends found him standing in the road, "his face so changed that they scarcely recognized him" (Englebert 1965:22). When they asked him what was wrong, he slyly replied that he had been thinking about marriage. Among other brilliant spontaneous enlightenments one could list those of Saint Paul, Saint Augustine, Saint Anthony, and Saint Ignatius—the last having been a swashbuckling knight in the height of his valor, his enlightenment the result of a musket ball through the legs!

Given the impracticality of the advice that people should drink and fight as much as possible in the hope of following Saint Francis or Saint Ignatius, one would still think that the fact of spontaneous conversion would have been treated systematically in the spiritual thought of the time. There are probably several reasons why it was not. Parkes (1959) reminds us that the ecstatic basis of Christian belief began to come under suspicion in the middle of the second century. At that time there was no formal priesthood in the church, and missionaries preached, like Paul, from the basis of their own inspiration. The number of fake luminaries who sought an easy living in this way finally reached such proportions that preaching itself came under question in the absence of a certification procedure. Once a church had been organized that could oversee the needed certification, it was greatly in the interest of the monastic orders that spiritual development should be explained as the gradual result of a consistent and sober way of life, not of an intense and idiosyncratic personal experience. If everyone were Saint Francis, there would be tens of thousands of inspired monastic orders, and little need for even one.

Second, it was important for the orders, and the church itself, to have some control over the *contents* of spiritual experience. As we have seen, clerics discouraged laymen from too much spirituality, probably because this helped the church to keep a monopoly on theological truth. The devil, people were reminded, had a way of disguising himself as his adversary in order to inspire false conversions.

Official suspicion of spontaneous spiritual experience became the source of a good deal of inquisition and witch burning at various times during this era. The virtual exclusion of such experience from scholarly writing on spiritual development, and the focus of that writing on self-discipline and meditation, is interesting for two reasons. First, as I mentioned in the last chapter, this spiritual gradualism created a natural link between the medieval scholastic mind and the disciplined thought of the Greeks, a link that must have helped to focus and solidify the classicism that reemerged in the Renaissance. Second, spiritual gradualism contributed somewhat paradoxically to the triumph of science and industry in the seventeenth to nineteenth centuries, and especially to what we think of as scientific psychology. Serious treatments of transcendental states of consciousness, including William James's *Varieties of Religious Experience* (1898), most of the depth psychology of Carl Jung, and such modern works as Maslow's *Religious Values and Peak Experiences* (1970) are regarded largely as curiosities in modern courses on developmental psychology. This is in spite of the fact that ninety percent of a sample of 488 world cultures have one or more institutionalized forms of altered consciousness in their normal repertoire of behaviors (Bourguignon 1973:11), and that modern surveys in the United States consistently reveal that a third of the population is affected by them in spite of cultural admonitions not to be (Thomas and Cooper, 1978).

What is disturbing about the lack of academic interest in these facts is that it discourages us from inquiry into a well-known source of moral development. Observers as diverse as Pitirim Sorokin (1954), Margaret Clark and Barbara Anderson (1967), Abraham Maslow (1951), and Adam Curle (1972) have noticed that many, perhaps most, unusually altruistic and morally self-conscious people have achieved insight through nonordinary mental states.

Meditationist Theories

As we saw in chapter 4, there were two main periods in medieval thinking about maturity, the first—we can call it the meditationist phase—was based on the pursuit of an altered state of consciousness. The second, or scholastic phase, was based on a combination of reason and meditation. Each phase had its own theories about spiritual maturation.

The basic idea of the meditationist phase was the primitive idea that God is attracted by certain behaviors and states of mind, and will choose the moment to reveal himself to the seeker who attains these correctly. Saint Paul, Saint Augustine, the Pseudo-Dionysius, and Saint Gregory the Great were among the most important teachers on this attainment, and they were carefully interpreted and commented upon throughout the Middle Ages. After the twelfth century, the interpreters, who included such luminaries as Aquinas and Scotus, became more intellectual. But earlier teachers avoided such scholarly games as logical proofs and references to pagan authorities, and were simple and practical. Saint Gregory's works were typical, and had the greatest impact on early medieval developmental theory.

Gregory often described activities, feeling-states, and mental images that would lead the student toward the state of grace. Quiet humility was the affective state most pleasing to God; he stressed the attitudes of passive contemplation, charity toward others, indifference toward one's own body, and resignation to achieve this state. On the matter of mental imagery, Gregory warned against efforts to image the figure of God, who he said was incorporeal and unimaginable, except as an impression of pure light. On the positive side, he emphasized the figure of Christ, whose role was to intercede on one's behalf with God. Christ was described as shining but solid, like brass or silver; the devotee was encouraged especially to meditate on the Passion of Christ, "since in his passage from the flesh to the glory of the spirit, he accomplished what men aim at in contemplation: to go from the visible to the invisible, from what is without to what is

within, from faith to understanding, from the humanity to the divinity"
(Leclerq et al. 1982:16).

A continuity with nonliterate ideas of the life course is quite clear in
Gregory's work. For one thing, he is preoccupied with the problem of
warding off evil influences, in order to give good fate a chance, just as the
Ojibwa grandfather in the last chapter sought to protect his grandson
against the influences of death and envy. For another thing, he relies on a
kind of magic to fix a desirable future. As the old Ojibwa sought to impress
upon his pupil's consciousness a preordained success brought about by
the old man's intention, so Gregory sought to fix the devotee's attention on
the person of Christ, whose promise of salvation might fix the future for the
devotee.

What is *not* primitive about Gregory's thought, is of course the
transcendental nature of his God, and his belief in a hierarchy of spiritual
capacity. Although he distinguishes dozens of different kinds of listeners in
his instructions on sermon-writing, his overall anthropology lists three
levels: laymen, whom he calls "the children of the church"; clergy, whom
he refers to variously as "shepherds," "teachers," or "rulers"; and monks
and nuns, the spiritual elect. He believed that anyone, even a layman,
could eventually attain the withdrawn and contemplative life that would
lead to spiritual perfection; but he recognized that the activities of normal
daily life greatly distract one from this narrow path. Charitable work among
men helps to prepare the spirit for meditation and prayer, but in itself will
not lead to the highest state of consciousness in which one attains grace.

Scholastic Theories

There is a paradoxical quality to the lives of the meditationist
teachers. Although they were themselves erudite, they saw little value in
scholarship as a means to salvation, instead putting their trust in prayer,
work, and the ascetic life alone. We have seen how this began to change in
the twelfth century. At first it was just a matter of willingness to borrow
ideas from the pagan classics. The great professor of Paris, Peter Abelard,
and the prolific Cistertian Abbot Saint Bernard were innovators, not so
much because they discussed the redeeming value of love—Dionysius had
done that—but because they shifted emphasis away from ascetic self-
denial, and used the concept of love as Plato had used it, as a natural
human emotion that is enjoyed first for its own sake, and only later leads
the aspirant on the first steps toward Grace. This kind of tender humanism
reached fuller expressions in the following century, with the work of Saint
Francis, Bonaventure, and Dante. It is clear, for example, in Bonaventure's
formula for meditation, a series of "steps from purification to illumination":

Thus do thou distinguish the steps that lead to the way of union:

let vigilance make thee attentive, for the Bridegroom passeth swiftly;

let confidence make thee strong, for he cometh without fail;

let desire enkindle thee, for he is sweet;

let fervor raise thee up, for he is sublime;

let delight in him give thee repose, for he is beautiful;

let joy inebriate thee, for he is the fullness of love;

let attachment unite thee to him, for his love is full of power.

And mayest thou ever, O devout soul, say to the Lord with all thy heart:

I seek thee, I hope for thee, I desire thee, I raise myself up toward thee,

I lay hold on thee, I exult in thee, at last I cleave to thee.

(Leclerq et al. 1982:310)

Another important innovation in Bernard's writing is his belief in distinct *developmental stages* that unfold naturally, with the aid of self-knowledge. Again, in the following century Saint Francis and Dante continued these themes, taking up the three-part Platonic soul and the emphasis on positive inner qualities that unfold in a regular sequence. Nor was the idea of developmental stages the exclusive property of monastic scholars. We read of the lay teacher Blessed Angela of Foligno (1240-1309) whom people travelled great distances to learn spiritual technique from. She taught "three stages of prayer," beginning with a "bodily" stage in which the disciple simply masters the words and the ritual; a "mental" stage, in which one concentrates on the meaning; and a "supernatural" stage, in which "the soul is carried away by God's mercy, and by meditation on Him, as it were beyond the bounds of nature" (Leclerq et al. 1982:312-313).

Taken together, these developments are quite revolutionary. They suggest that man has intrinsic qualities that, with the guidance of God and experienced instruction, unfold in a linear sequence leading toward an ideal state. They anticipate both the rationalist and the romantic approaches still found at the core of developmental theory. The rationalist line was soon to find its greatest medieval spokesman in Thomas Aquinas, and the romantic line in Meister Eckhart with his notion of the "divine spark" in every human soul.

Rationalism: Aquinas and the Empiricists

The exuberant religiosity that brought forth the crusades and the building of the great cathedrals in the twelfth and thirteenth centuries was accompanied by a vigorous intellectual growth, and Paris was the center of that growth. In the twelfth century Peter Abelard taught at Paris, and among his famous pupils were the popular theologian Peter Lombard, Thomas a Becket's eminent secretary, John of Salisbury, and the Roman revolutionary hero Arnold of Brescia. A century later came Albert the Great, Bonaventure, the Franciscans' "Subtle Doctor," Duns Scotus, the revival of Islamic philosophy led by Siger de Brabant, and, of course, Thomas Aquinas. By the end of the thirteenth century Paris had a faculty of over five hundred, and its students, drawn from all over Europe, were too numerous to keep track of.

But I remark on these facts only to show that the great psychologist of the age, Aquinas, was part of a thriving tradition of study and debate. If this were not so, it would be difficult to understand how anything as bold and new as his ideas about the mind could have withstood the conservatism of his era. In chapter 4 I discussed the controversy over classical scholarship that enlivened Paris at the time of Aquinas, and the key role played by him and by his teacher, Albert. It is a tribute to the power of Aquinas's intellect that Greek learning not only survived this controversy but advanced considerably as a staple of Christian teaching. The only major feature that distinguishes his thought from that of the seventeenth century is his retention of God's grace as a pivotal principle of development. Let us look closely at his complex ideas and their impact on later thought.

References to the development of the soul occur in several of Aquinas's works, but the main source of his psychology is the encyclopedic *Summa Theologica*. He allied himself most closely with Aristotle on most issues, but he also drew on Pseudo-Dionysius and Plato. The most radical principle of his psychology is the addition of a capacity for wisdom that is not directly controlled by God. Besides the usual "infused virtues," which are instilled in man by God, Thomistic man is naturally endowed with virtues that he can develop by the exercise of will, through practice, and that also lead toward spiritual perfection. These natural virtues are subdivided into the intellectual (understanding, science, wisdom, art, and prudence) and the moral (more prudence, justice, fortitude, and temperance). They are perfected by experience, subject to the intellect or will, and useful in leading a productive, easy, and virtuous life.

At a higher moral level, to be attained by the perfection of at least some of the natural virtues, lies a level of moral capacity more familiar to the medieval scholar: the level of the "infused virtues," subdivided into the theological (faith, hope, and charity) and the infused moral (same as the natural-moral, but directed toward the search for God, rather than toward the search for a good life). These virtues are received by the mind through the gift of divine grace, and are useful in the attainment of supernatural life and merit. Above the level of the infused virtues lies yet another level, that of "gifts of the holy ghost." This level is mystical, and derives from the teachings of Dionysius discussed in chapter 4, its object being union with God himself.

THE VIRTUES ACCORDING TO AQUINAS

	Natural Virtues	Infused Virtues
KINDS	**Intellectual** Understanding Science Wisdom Art Prudence	**Theological** Faith Hope Charity
	Moral Prudence Justice Fortitude Temperance	**Infused Moral** Prudence Justice Fortitude Temperance
CAUSE	Nature; experience; repetition	Infused by God with sanctifying grace
OBJECT	Truth of reason and reasonable good; complete natural life	Means to union with God; perfection of man for supernatural life and merit

(Adapted from Brennan 1941:91)

The natural virtues, according to Aquinas, reside in the body, not in the soul; they grow as they are exercised, often with the external help of guides. They grow, in other words, through habitual practice, and they atrophy through neglect. Growth can take the form of *extent*—increase in the kinds and numbers of situations in which virtuous habits are shown—or of *intensity*—the degree to which such habits approach ultimate truth or beauty. Acts that equal or surpass a habit in intensity contribute to the growth of that habit; those that are beneath it actually reduce it. Moreover, although it is possible for a man to develop certain virtues and neglect others, the development of the higher virtues depends on the perfection of the lower ones; and perfection depends on the balanced development of the whole person. Human virtue as a whole, then, is "an ordered disposition of the soul," an internally balanced and clear-headed person, well adapted to his environment.

A major problem in Aquinas's psychology is the relationship between the natural virtues on one hand, and the infused or supernatural virtues on the other. He taught that the intellect is somehow able, by means of divine guidance, to be aware of its own limitations, and to set these aside, so that the will finds itself at the service of the supernatural. Although it is difficult for the twentieth-century mind to follow such reasoning, I find it strangely similar to the writings of the great modern physicists—Paoli, Planck, Heisenberg, Einstein—on the logic of discovery in physics and mathematics.

Most of Aquinas's psychology is based on Aristotle's work, although one can also detect Platonic elements, such as the growth of virtue through its generalization from a single object to an entire class; and the idea of *levels* of truth that are reached in a stepwise sequence. But more interesting than the source of these concepts is their resemblance to the psychology of the Enlightenment—particularly that of the British empiricists, and most particularly that of Thomas Hobbes.

The key principles that link Aquinas and Hobbes are the physical locus of the habits, their gounding in behavior, their hierarchical progression, their increase through repetition at the same or greater intensity, and their function of increasing internal order and external adaptation. Together, these ingredients begin to suggest modern empirical, environmentalist concepts of development, of the behaviorist variety. One begins to visualize man as a sensitive organism, building up experience of himself and the world through experience in order to become ever more complex, more integrated, and better able to cope with his complex environment. I shall return to this linkage in the next chapter.

There is yet another sense in which Aquinas's psychology appears to anticipate modern thought, this one even more sophisticated than early empiricism: In proposing that virtue is a composite of acquired and infused traits, his psychology already deals intelligently with the thorny problem of whether behavior results from environmental effects on an infinitely malleable organism, or from the unfolding of innate biological tendencies. Aquinas proposed a solution to the nature/nurture controversy, a problem that still grips academic psychology.

Great as Aquinas's influence has been, we must remember he was not the only major Aristotelian psychologist of his time. In fact, his work fanned the flames of a debate over the limitations of human reason, and it was his famous younger contemporaries Duns Scotus (1266-1308) and William of Ockham (d. 1349) who built upon Aristotelian principles a radical empiricism, and drove a wedge between philosophy and theology. All three—Aquinas, Scotus, and Ockham—founded schools of thought that thrived throughout the Renaissance.

John Duns Scotus was born, as his name implies, in Scotland. He entered the Order of Friars Minor in 1278, and was ordained a priest in 1291. He taught at the universities of Oxford, Paris (where he received the doctorate of divinity in 1305), and finally Cologne, where he died. In all his thought, he was intensely concerned with the question of how the human mind can know ultimate truths; he therefore speculated closely on the particular sources of particular kinds of human knowledge. His speculations led him to the conclusion that all knowledge comes from sense experience. Contrary to Aquinas, then, theological truths must be revealed by God, and cannot be achieved by the intellect, even with divine help. He proposed that the mind is a "blank slate" (*tabula nuda*) at birth, and that it acquires general truths through the exercise of the intellect—whose prime function is to know "being as being"—upon the material of the senses— whose function is to know things-as-themselves. We cannot arrive at certain fundamental truths about God and his creation, however, because our intellects are simply not up to it—a punishment for original sin.

Scotus thereby went a step toward the Nonconscious, Lawful Universe, by holding that the structure of human knowledge and the structure of the universal consciousness do not necessarily correspond, and that the former is an unreliable guide in the search for the latter. However, he did not go so far as to say that divine reason is wholly opaque to rational thought. That step was reserved for Ockham.

William of Ockham, an English-born Franciscan who taught at Oxford and Paris in the early fourteenth century, is generally considered the last of the great medieval philosophers. As the founder of nominalism, he was, like Scotus, an empiricist. In addition to seconding Scotus's belief in the sensory basis of human knowledge, he contributed to psychology a convincing argument that there is *no* necessary correspondence between human and divine thought, and that the search for a rational theology is hopeless. This did not dim his enthusiasm for theology, of course, as it did that of the deists of later times, but it helped to provide a philosophical footing for the English school of psychology, and therefore for the sciences of man in their modern form.

It would be a mistake to think of the medieval history of developmental psychology as a linear progression from a shamanic emphasis on trance to a rationalist empiricism. Most of the exquisite arguments brought forth by the scholastic doctors remained minor influences on the religious life and belief of the masses, and for every new idea there were a host of counterarguments from more conservative minds. Rather, I have tried to continue in this chapter three ideas that might help us understand the modern history of maturation theory: First, there is a discernable association among social organization, way of life, and belief, including belief about human nature. The need for a church organization, with a stable hierarchy and a ready supply of dedicated adherents, was closely linked in the early Middle Ages to the concepts of scriptural authority and spiritual gradualism. As the church grew in power and prestige, and the relative security imposed by its rule led to the growth of an intellectual elite, that order began to give way to classical scholarship.

Second, the new concepts themselves affect the direction of social history. The meditationist psychology stimulated the development of the monasteries, which in turn helped the spread and consolidation of Christianity and, with it, literacy, and indirectly contributed to travel and trade. All these things stimulated the rise of the universities and, thereby, pagan learning as well.

Third, literacy and a tradition of scholarship proceed in a symbiotic relationship with the transcendental concept of the cosmos. The idea of a spiritual elite gives rise to the ideal of the Vita Contemplativa, which inspires philosophic thought. The accumulation of beautiful philosophic works that results provides a fund of raw materials upon which further cycles of the process draw. The psychologies of the Enlightenment and the romantic rebellion differed profoundly from those of the Middle Ages; but they took the form they did because of the monastic tradition and the specific ideas of Augustine, Dionysius, Saint Bernard, Meister Eckhart, Aquinas, Scotus, Ockham and other medieval thinkers.

9. *Precritical Versus Postcritical Psychology*

In chapter 1, I listed the main questions of developmental psychology. I noted that the search for self-understanding is always faced with the problems of diversity and change, and that these problems lead naturally to the search for order. The search for order, however, immediately stubs its toe on the problem of subjectivity. Orderly ideas that appear conclusive to one mind are highly questionable to another; the problem of diversity and change among sense experiences is simply complicated by the diversity and change of human viewpoints.

The Greek method of dealing with this problem, the method adopted by the scholastics, was to search out basic principles upon which all men agree—principles like the superiority of pleasure over suffering, love over hate, and life over death—and to progress from these by intuition and logic to deduce infallible conclusions about the details of nature, including, of course, human nature. This made sense as long as one held to the belief that the cosmos is conscious, and that the human soul is also a product of this consciousness and therefore capable of knowing it intuitively.

But the discovery of scientific methods of study and reporting that took shape in the Renaissance suggested ways of improving these ideas. Experiment and verification could produce powerful consensus among thinkers where introspection and scholasticism could not; and consensus reduced the feeling of uncertainty attending discovery (even when the uncertainty was justified, unfortunately).

We have seen how the decay of medieval institutions and the rediscovery of the human intellect began, in about the thirteenth century, to rekindle interest in nature and the world of the senses. We have seen how the progressive discovery of the so-called laws of nature led increasingly to the metaphor of a machine in interpreting the cosmos. By the middle of the seventeenth century, Harvey had understood the circulation of the blood, thereby greatly advancing the machine metaphor for the human body as well. It was inevitable that the human mind should not escape this fate for long; but the idea of the conscious universe was still strong, and it posed an obstacle. If the mind was merely a machine, how could it communicate with the cosmos? One either had to adopt the ancient proposition that consciousness was innate in the mind, or to admit that the cosmos was an enigma, or reduce everything to the meaningless actions of cogs and levers.

Compare René Descartes's attempt at a mechanical psychology in 1650 with Hobbes's attempt in 1651. Descartes tried to account for all the functions of the mind on the basis of the movements of spirits in the blood, nerves, and sense organs. He knew something about physiology, and was doing quite well until he got to the problem of the *will*, that old causal agent lurking behind the primal billiard ball, cue in hand. As we could have guessed from having tasted his theory of knowledge, Descartes stopped short of an empiricist answer. The will, he concluded, is the autonomous function of the soul, which resides in a little gland in the middle of the brain. Although the contents of our thoughts, Descartes concluded, arise from external stimulation, consciousness is ultimately orchestrated by the executive soul, whose function is innate. It is the ultimate "I" of "I think, therefore I am"—a holdover from the Conscious Universe, and the fountainhead of the *bete noir* of modern holistic psychology, the mind/body dichotomy.

Hobbes was bolder at challenging the Conscious Universe. All thought, he declared, could be traced to the physical action of nature on the sense organs and its processing in the machinelike brain. Nor did the will present a problem in Hobbes's view. He resurrected Aristotle's dictum, repeated by the Thomists, the Scotists, and the nominalists, that men learn by experience what gives pleasure and what reduces it. They conceive an attraction to the former and an aversion to the latter. These are called appetites and aversions. Sometimes it is difficult to tell what complex action will best satisfy the appetites, so men (and animals) "deliberate" what action to take; hence the quote from Hobbes we met in chapter 5: "In deliberation, the last appetite, or aversion, immediately adhering to the action, or to the omission thereof, is what we call the 'will'" (Hobbes 1651:343-344). Next question?

The distinction between Descartes's and Hobbes's views of the mind is vast in its consequences. Descartes was still entrenched in the Platonic viewpoint we now call rationalism; he believed that the path to the understanding of ultimate principles lay in introspection, a belief that is closely related to the teleological conception of the universe which he inherited. If Truth and Beauty are the possessions of a conscious universe, man's ability to grasp them must stem from an inherent correspondence between our minds and the cosmic consciousness. The observation of consciousness itself, it follows, should reveal the path to ultimate under-standing. Hobbes, on the other hand, was a thoroughgoing empiricist of the nominalist type, who eschewed metaphysics and insisted that Truth was to be found *solely* in the observation of the sensible world. In the absence of a theory of the evolution of the brain, this idea focused attention strictly on the functioning of the sense organs, and on observable behavior and its consequences. The mind was conceived as Duns Scotus and Ockham had conceived it: a machine that began life as a blank slate (Hobbes preferred the term *tabula rasa*), receiving impressions from its environment and building these into understandings, appetites, aversions, and character traits.

Hobbes was not the first Enlightenment empiricist, but he was the first one who was interested in the mind enough to write a systematic psychology. His writings suggested an empirical way of studying human mental functioning; as such, they provided a great stimulus to scientific psychology, for a very simple reason. Since individual minds function differently, introspection as a method is not verifiable; it is nearly impossible to reach agreement on the facts among independent introspec-tors. Observation, of course, is a different story. Given that there are differences in sensory functioning, it is still possible for a number of observers to record observable events, compare notes, and arrive at a consensus about what happened. And this is just the effect that Hobbes's ideas had on Enligtenment thinking about the mind.

Hobbes was interested in the development of the mind, not just in its fully developed functioning. His theory of development was based on the notion that all complex thoughts, desires, and traits develop as a result of associations between simple sensory stimuli. This viewpoint, still a strong element in modern psychological thought, has been dubbed *association-ism*. We need not spend much time on Hobbes's version of associationism; we will get a feeling for it as we examine its plentiful effects on developmental theory later on. But as a theory it represented a tremendous leap toward an empirical psychology, because it held that the environment acts *mechanically*, or as Hobbes said, it "presseth the organ proper to each sense; which presure . . . by the mediation of the nerves and other strings and membranes of the body continue[s] inwards to the brain and heart" (Hobbes 1651:311). There is nothing in the environment that corresponds to our consciousness of it.

Notice how strikingly different this conception is from either the preliterate notion of the conscious, anthropomorphic universe, or the classical notion of transcendental knowledge through teleology. If the universe were conscious, it would be quite impossible for us to understand that consciousness apart from its explicit messages to our senses. If there are ultimate truths, it is quite impossible for us to know them, except by deducing them from the associations of our perceptions. In effect, associationism is not only the philosophic ground of empiricist psychology, it is the ground of empiricist science as a whole. The whole structure of science rests on a theory of developmental psychology.

It is ironic, then, that while empiricism produced enormous triumphs of understanding and application in the physical sciences, it failed to do so in the field of human behavior. In the late twentieth century, two hundred years after the careful studies of Tiedemann and Tetens, a hundred years after the encylopedic summaries of William James and Herbert Spencer, our success rate in the prediction of significant behavior is...well, insignificant. We have failed to eliminate or even reduce the quantity of destructive activity and emotional suffering in the world. There even seems to be steadily less and less argreement about the laws of the human mind and personality.

Looking at the problem from the vantage point of the search for moral excellence, we can discern three basic types of modern psychologists. First, we have the postcritical psychologists, those who have accepted the limitations of empirical knowledge demonstrated by Kant, and sought to preserve the ancient questions about value and purpose in human life, at the cost of relinquishing the vision of a unified mental science corresponding to the science of physics. The postcritical psychologists are those who agree with the words of Erich Fromm: "Psychology...became a science lacking its main subject matter, the soul; it was concerned with mechanisms, reaction formations, instincts, but not with the most specific human phenomena: love, reason, conscience, values" (Fromm 1950:6).

Second, there are those of whom Fromm speaks, those I call the precritical psychologists, who have embraced the positivist search for certainty, in the process excluding from their search any question as complex and subjective as the quality of moral excellence. For these psychologists, replication and prediction are the only sure steps to success. Ruth Wylie provides a good example in her summary of research on a profound and hopelessly subjective element of human experience, the self: "The basic constructs as defined in the writings of the self concept theorists frequently seem to point to no clear empirical referents." (1974:8).

The third type consists of a few brave individuals who have struggled to synthesize the spiritual quest and the search for certainty through scientific method. I will save them for chapter 11, in which I return to the issue of the soul in modern psychology. Here, let us pursue the division these synthesizers have struggled to bridge.

Two Types of Intellect

In the 1650s, about the time Hobbes published the *Leviathan*, the brilliant young French mathematician Blaise Pascal wrote about the two distinct types of intellect found among learned men—what he called the mathematical and the intuitive minds.

> Mathematicians who are only mathematicians have exact minds, provided all things are explained to them by means of definitions and axioms; otherwise they are inaccurate and insufferable, for they are only right when the principles are quite clear. And men of intuition who are only intuitive cannot have patience to reach to first principles of things speculative and conceptual, which they have never seen in the world, and which are altogether out of the common. (Pascal 1650:10)

Pascal's two types of intellect correspond fairly well to the instinctive inclinations of our two types of modern psychologist. The precriticals of course represent Pascal's "mathematicians"; the postcriticals, his "intuitives." The precriticals, who are sometimes called "reductivists" (Maslow 1951), "tough-minded" (James 1898), or "uniformists" (Wrong 1961) are scholars who believe in the ultimate value of precise description and measurement, and who make the pursuit of these things a major goal of their work.

The precriticals of the extreme sort are unwilling to accept as conclusive or even provisionally useful any statement about human behavior that is not based on the sort of evidence that is generally accepted in the physical sciences. On the whole, precriticals are empiricists (they believe knowledge is obtained by the study of things as they present themselves to the senses) and positivists (they believe that observations approach truth to the extent that they lead to accurate prediction). Accordingly, they believe that science progresses by the gradual accumulation of reliable (that is, verifiable), precise information, and the search among this information for invariant patterns, or "laws." Accordingly, precritical scientism leads to the careful dissection of complex structures (behavior patterns, social groups, organs, organisms) into small units, which can be closely observed under controlled circumstances. "Controlled" might mean either the ideal environment of the experimental laboratory, or the use of large populations whose relevant characteristics (age, sex, etc.) are known, and can be "controlled for" in the sense that their statistical associations with outcome measures can be shown. An example of the first type would be Skinnerian behaviorist research, where animals are used to develop models of behavior, using simple, measurable differences in stimulation between experimental and control groups of genetically near-identical animals in near-identical environments. A rather extreme example of the latter type would be almost any article from the "Social and Behavioral Science" section of the *Journal of Gerontology:* the matching characteristics of experimental and control samples are carefully observed, the validity and reliability of the questions given are painstakingly established, but there is rarely any discussion of the relationship between the variables being measured on one hand, and their role in the total lifestyles, personalities, social relations, or previous experience of the subjects on the other hand.

The precritical is well aware of the difficulty of applying his findings to complex social problems, much less to questions of man's ultimate destiny, but he feels there is no better way to proceed than the slow, careful accumulation of reliable evidence. He finds the concepts used by more "humanistic" psychologists distressingly vague, and notes that their use rarely leads to a definitive test of their validity, let alone a widely accepted model of how the mind works. Rather, theories based on intuitive analyses of ad hoc observations of complex behaviors simply spawn endless variant theories, each equally as untestable as its parents. In a rare attempt to address the topic of *wisdom* in lifespan developmental studies, Clayton and Birren conclude that the absence of fruitful results on the topic stems from a lack of "specific research questions amenable to empirical analysis" (1980:125). Likewise Bloom despairs of the possibility of applying psychology to the study of social betterment at all, until characteristics of superior individuals "can be restated in more specific and operational terms and as such can be observed and systematically measured" (1964:228).

Postcritical psychologists, whom others have called "holists" (Maslow 1951), "ideographic" (Allport 1961) "tenderminded" (James 1898), or "organismists" (Goldstein 1939), believe that the important questions of psychology are to be pursued along roads other than that taken by the physical sciences. They have sought solutions to questions of personal and social health, wisdom, and compassion, and have found human nature as a whole too subtle, varied, and capricious for the piecemeal methods of positivist inquiry. For the postcriticals, the key to understanding human behavior lies in the discovery of linkages, or patterns, relating the many complex habits, appetites, experiences, perceptions, desires, demands, capacities, resources, assumptions and feelings that together determine the relationships of individuals to their environment. The view has rarely been stated as clearly as it was by Alfred Adler in 1927:

> The single manifestations of the psychic life must never be regarded
> as entities sufficient unto themselves. It was learned that we could
> gain an understanding of these single manifestations only when we
> considered them as partial aspects of an indivisible whole. (1927:5-6)

The postcritical finds it difficult to apply the precise findings of the precritical in such a way that the result is useful. He finds that "real life" is usually so different from the laboratory that conclusions drawn from the one find little application in the other. He finds in his encounters with actual people that apparent similarities of opinion or behavior often mask enormous differences in intent or meaning, and apparent differences are often understood by his subjects themselves to be insignificant. This leads him to be sceptical of statistical associations.

Accordingly, the postcritical psychologist is often at a loss to find precise measurements by which to demonstrate his findings; but he is disturbed less by this than by what he regards as the sterility of Scientism. Most postcriticals tend toward philosophical rationalism (insight is often as reliable as perception) and pragmatism (there are various correct answers to any question of fact, each with its own utility).

Whereas the precritical looks to the perfection of instruments for observation and recording in his urge to advance psychology, then, the postcritical insists that in doing so the precritical has lost sight of any real values that might make psychology worthwhile; he is looking in the wrong place, like the drunk who searches under the lamp post for the key he lost somewhere else. Such arguments are common in intellectual history, and not all of them are important. But if psychology is to remain relevant to the great questions of mankind's past and future, it will make a great deal of difference where this argument leads. With this in mind, let us look more closely at the persistence of critique in the face of the Hobbesian machine.

The Growth of Experimentalism

Experimental psychology is now a large and diverse enterprise. There are 745 pages of text in the 1957 edition of Boring's famous book on the history of the field (Boring 1957), which is itself of course a brief summary of the hundred-odd years of work it covers. These next few pages, then, are meant more as a stimulus than as an explanation. I shall confine myself to a broad overview of the relationships between philosophical ideas about the human mind on one hand, and the growing influence of experimental science on the other.

What this brief discussion shows, I think, is that the current division between postcritical and precritical views of the mind evolved gradually, becoming clear only after the experimental method had existed long enough to demonstrate its inadequacy as a philosophic tool. In the eighteenth and nineteenth centuries, there was a growing belief, both on the part of the empiricist advocates of "mechanical man" and on the part of their holistic and romantic antagonists, that the experimental method could settle their fundamental differences. The history of experimental psychology is a history that illustrates well how a dominant intellectual conviction or zeitgeist—in this case, faith in a particular kind of analytic procedure as a source of knowledge—leads to inappropriate applications of its consequences and muddles the very arguments whose solution it is supposed to supply. From where we now stand intellectually, then, early experimental psychology offers a series of astounding paradoxes.

The mood for experimental psychology was set, as we have seen, in the seventeenth century with the idea of the mind as a machine. Although Descartes and Hobbes disagreed profoundly on the nature of consciousness, they did agree that certain aspects of experience, especially perception, could be studied as parts of the physical world, a position that was echoed by Locke, Hume, Mills, and others right down to modern times. This is ordinarily referred to as the origin of empiricist psychology, and it seems to have been independently discovered in France, where a physician in the service of the Duc de Gramont by the name of Julien Offrey de La Mettrie published it a hundred years after Hobbes. La Mettrie had fallen ill on a military expedition, and had noticed that his thought processes grew muddled in proportion to his bodily suffering. The conviction "came to him with the force of a conversion that thought is after all nothing but the result of the mechanical action of the brain and the nervous system" (Boring 1957:213). Publication of this revelation in French apparently affected strongly the nervous systems of other French philosophers (notably Condillac and Cabanis), for they found themselves repeating it.

Germany, however, had developed a kind of immunity to the empiricist fever. We saw in chapter 6 how romantic notions of an inborn destiny burning in the human soul had led psychologists like C. G. Carus, von Schubert and Schopenhauer to propose a holistic psychology that resisted mechanical analogies. Kant strengthened this trend with his doctrine of innate ideas. Against the Hobbesian proposition that all thought originates in sense perception, Kant insisted that certain ideas are *not* deducible from experience at all, but must be innate in the mind.

This German resistance to empiricism should have led (we are now inclined to think) to a holistic, introspective method of psychological science. But to our modern fascination, just the opposite happened. It was in romantic Germany, not in empiricist France or England, that experimental psychology began.

Why this happened is difficult to say, but it certainly had something to do with the rebellion of the German middle class against the snobbish artificiality of the nobility in the late eighteenth and early nineteenth century. The nobility at that time had developed courtly manners to an extreme degree that isolated them from the middle-class practical world of science and commerce. Their styles of behavior and speaking became self-consciously baroque to the extent that they seemed almost devoid of practical content. They even considered the German language unfit for cultured discourse, and preferred to write in French.

Central to this artificial refinement was a positive disdain for practical knowledge. Writing of the situation, Elias says, "In countries with a courtly culture, the technical term and everything that betrays the specialist is a stylistic blemish" (1978:36). The very things that the middle classes valued, then—practical education, exact knowledge, technical expertise, even nationalistic pride in their language and folk customs—marked them as coarse in the eyes of the aristocracy.

The reaction of the upper middle class was rebellion. The scholar became a heroic figure *to the extent* that he showed a depth of understanding based on detailed study. Against the empty formalism of aristocratic *civilite*, German intellectuals posed the concept of *Kultur*, meaning exact knowledge of the world, as well as of great ideas.

German psychology, then, was founded on this middle-class pride in precision and specialized knowledge. Hermann von Helmholtz in physics and Johannes Muller in physiology, for example, were precise technicians and prolific writers, helping to establish a tradition of German scientific scholarship early in the nineteenth century. Their concepts were deeply affected by the holism of German philosophy, but they drove home their holistic concepts with the tools of scientific precision. Let us look more closely at the odd results.

Kant's doctrine that certain ideas are innate in the mind and must be studied introspectively or not at all inspired Johann Freidrich Herbart (1776-1841) in an attempt to rescue psychology from the jaws of empiricist philosophy. To do so in the academic climate of the time, Herbart felt compelled to declare the study of the mind to be a science (*Wissenschaft*), properly based on exact observation.

However, Herbart had an unusual view of what science was. He eschewed experimentation, which he correctly observed requires the division of thought into discrete units, and declared that the mind is unitary. Thought processes, which he understood to be largely unconscious operations based on Kantian givens and sense data, Herbart felt could be inferred through observation. The conscious ideas and sensations that result from these unconscious operations, however, could be observed systematically. Herbart called these conscious results *apperception*, and thereby introduced a concept that proved extremely useful to later experimentalists. The idea that introspection will reveal the results of systematic unconscious processes that are fundamentally the same in all minds allowed the researcher to infer from his own thoughts and feelings, and from the words of his experimental subjects, those crucial mental operations that his experiments could not explain, and for which he could not think of an appropriate method of observation. Fechner, Helmholtz, and Wundt later used apperception as a kind of "black box" which allowed them to construct plausible theories out of the puzzling results of experiments on perception and sensation.

The great physicist Helmholtz (1821-1894), for example, used the concept of "unconscious inference" to account for such peculiarities as the fact that sense data on the size of visual objects and the positions of the eyes in viewing them are translated unconsciously into the perception of distance. The first real experimental psychologist, Wilhelm Wundt (1832-1920) expanded on the notion of apperception by adding other mental inputs, such as "feeling," which he believed contributed to experience through an unconscious "psychological compounding."

Gustav Theodor Fechner (1801-1887) was perhaps experimentalism's least probable ancestor of all. He set out to prove Leibnitz's antiempiricist theory that the universe is actually made up of consciousness, and the problem is not to explain Mind, but the opposite: to explain why things appear to our senses as material. If Body is really Mind in disguise, Fechner reasoned, there ought to be an exact correspondence between mental imagery and bodily energy; he set out to prove that this was in fact the case. In the process he devised fairly accurate ways of measuring these correspondences. Changes in the subjective sensations of the brightness of lights or the heaviness of objects, for example, could be correlated with objective measurements of these qualities.

Fechner had committed a mistake that is still being committed regularly in the behavioral sciences today: He thought that proving an association (or as we would say, a correlation) between phenomena was equivalent to proving a causal theory. Of course the two are not the same at all. Fechner's techniques were soon used by his German colleagues Helmholtz and Wundt to prove the empiricist idea that Mind can be reduced to Body, exactly the opposite of Fechner's theory. In fact these techniques are used with the same philosophic bias in precritical experimental psychology today.

We will have more to say about Wilhelm Wundt (1832-1920) in chapter 10 where we look at the evolution of functional theory. Wundt had a tremendous impact on the experimental psychology of the late nineteenth and early twentieth centuries, probably for three reasons. First, he was a prodigious writer, and attempted to systematize everything that was known about the human mind in his time. Second, his period of greatest productivity followed closely on the publication of Darwin's *Origin of the Species*, a time when a fervent faith in precritical natural science combined with a vast curiosity about man as a biological specimen. Third, and perhaps most significant, Wundt made a clean break with romanticism. He held that psychology is the study of immediate experience, and that its method is experimental. Period. The program of psychology is to: (1) analyze experience into its component elements; (2) determine the manner of interconnection of these elements; and (3) elucidate the laws of their interconnection. Here was a program that promised to avoid the metaphysical battles of early theorizing, and to put psychology on a path like the paths of physics and biology, one of gradual accumulation toward comprehensive understanding.

Wundt founded a psychological laboratory at Liepzig in 1879—one of the first academic institutions of its kind. In it were trained the first generation of American experimentalists, including among others G. Stanley Hall and James McKeen Cattell. Experimentalism had matured to the point where it could now be confidently replicated in laboratories throughout the Western world. What happened to it after this diaspora, particularly in America, we shall take up again in the next chapter.

Meanwhile, what of critique? To understand the fate of the postcritical perspective in academic psychology, we must retrace our steps and look again at holistic understanding—a function that necessarily fell to the healers.

The Doctor and the Machine

I noted in chapter 5 that the view of madness that prevailed in Western society until the end of the Renaissance was inherited from the preliterate past. Madness was believed to be caused by the interference of conscious forces beyond the control of the individual, except in cases of witchcraft, where personal responsibility was thought to be involved. In the seventeenth century all this changed. With the ascension of the Lawful, Nonconscious Universe, madness became a disease of the reason, and as such a matter of shame and a blot on society's name. Madhouses were built; empiricist science was called in. Almost immediately, diverging views of insanity and its treatment took shape: one was based on the active use of a personal relationship between the healer and the patient (postcritical method); the other was based on the search for an impersonal organic pathology (precritical method). The postcritical approach grew out of an old tradition. The Moors had established highly humane institutions for the mad in Spain as early as the fourteenth century, and this tradition was even carried by the Spanish to the New World as early as 1566 (Mora 1967). Also in the sixteenth century, during the plague of witchcraft trials that raged across Europe and the New World, Johann Weyer attributed the behavior of some witches to mental illness, and devised a form of treatment that showed many parallels to modern psychotherapy (Mora 1967:51). The Enlightenment eclipsed the efforts Weyer had begun, and it was not until a physician at the Hôpital Général in Paris, Philippe Pinel, tried taking the chains off the inmates of the mad wards in 1793 that psychotherapy made a serious reappearance; and even then it was never fully integrated with biological theories of insanity.

Pinel was followed by William Tuke, who established a Quaker community for the insane in York at the turn of the eighteenth century. Pinel and Tuke presented themselves as benign but highly authoritarian figures who stressed the effects of environment on the psyche, and sought to restore sanity through strict discipline and moral influence. They established a new medical type, in fact, that was to last throughout the nineteenth century—the "medical superintendent" of the mental hospital—a figure who was, however well meaning, "without paraphernalia, more a thaumaturge than a scientist . . . who represented paternal authority, traditional values, and punitive judgment" (Mora 1967:63). The parallel to the modern nursing home director as a social type is striking.

One of the great figures of this time was the American revolutionary politician and neuroanatomist Benjamin Rush. Rush held to the dominant precritical view of the late eighteenth century that mental illness is primarily physical in origin (he attributed it to disorders of the vascular system of the brain), but he did not let this prevent him from taking an active interest in the thought and speech itself of the patients at Philadelphia Hospital. Rather, he stressed the importance of listening carefully to the patient, and in *joining* the patient's perceptual and cognitive world as far as one could in treating him. He appears to have been the first physician who adopted "the view that the organic genesis of a symptom does not interfere with the fact that the same symptom remains subject to the physiologic and psychologic laws presiding over the appearance of the symptoms at large" (Riese 1967:121). On the other hand, Rush made no attempt to integrate his empiricist anatomical theories and his holistic psychological techniques. Like John Milton, Rush was a microcosm of his time, and embodied its paradoxes.

That Rush was typical in his precritical theories of mental illness we can see from the leading medical texts of that day. William Cullen, for example, a respected physician of the period, published in 1791 a popular theory that all mental disease resulted from states of "excitement and collapse" in the fluids of the brain. About the same time, Franz Joseph Gall established the pseudoscience of phrenology, which enjoyed great popularity in psychiatry right up until the time of Freud. Gall was an energetic researcher of the then-popular school of "empiricist medicine." He simply made a point of examining the heads of everyone he could find who had any kind of noteworthy mental trait—from madmen to geniuses—and correlating his measurements of skull formations with the traits in question. His findings suggested, of course, that the bumps on the head and the proclivities inside it were closely matched; the idea led to anatomical searches for local sites of mental traits within the anatomy of the brain.

Early attempts to apply precritical approaches to real social problems now strike us as immature. The physiological theorists joined forces with the Victorian moralists in the middle of the nineteenth century, to prove the anatomical linkage between sexuality and madness. O. S. Fowler, a popular follower of Gall's theories, gives us a good example in his *Animativeness, Or Evils and Remedies of Excessive and Perverted Sexuality,* published in 1865. Here Fowler presents the mind as a stratified system of passions, much like a layered geological formation, with destructive and base "animativeness" in the lower reaches, and, as one progresses upward, the ensuing layers of "veneration," "conjugality," and "paternal love." The development of the higher centers depended upon—what else?—the suppression of "animativeness." One sees a hint of Freud's *id, superego*, and *ego* here, to be sure.

Physiological research continues today as an important tradition in psychiatry. That it is essentially a precritical tradition in the sense I am using here is shown by its reliance on the dis-integration of its subject matter.

> It was the use and misuse of the experimental method which promoted in the second half of the nineteenth century the rise and growth of the doctrine of cerebral localization. Both anatomic and experimental researches aim at the decomposition of the organism, a decomposition in space, as in dissection, a decomposition in time, as in experimentation...The method in both anatomic and experimental investigations is the same, i.e., the *analytic* method. (Riese 1967:87)

Although physiological study was, during the nineteenth century, the dominant *medical* tradition in the study of madness, it was by no means without rivals. In fact, it was less effective and less popular in the *treatment* of mental suffering than its main rival, the holistic approach to the patient's psychological state: psychotherapy.

We have noted that Pinel, Tuke, and Rush in the late eighteenth century reintroduced Weyer's two-hundred-year-old treatment of the whole person into psychiatric medicine, but they did so largely without systematic methods or theories. About the same time, a technique of treatment began to develop that, while anathema to the precritical tradition of the medical profession, was increasingly systematic, and much more successful. I am referring to the uses of hypnotism, catharsis, and suggestion, which began in earnest with the discoveries of Franz Anton Mesmer in Vienna in 1775, and culminated with the work of Breuer and Freud in the 1890s. It is a fascinating story, liberally sprinkled with dramatic cures as well as with feuds among the leading practitioners (Mesmer and Puysegur, Charcot and Bernheim, Freud and Adler). The details are not essential here, only the effects of what came to be known as dynamic psychotherapy on the field of personality psychology as a whole.

The psychotherapeutic tradition established beyond doubt that mentally ill people could often be helped through the manipulation of their thoughts and feelings, without reference to their bodies as such. It was this grappling with the totally idiosyncratic experience of the person, and with his or her totally idiosyncratic way of thinking, talking, and perceiving, that produced results, not the isolation of specific anatomical anomalies, as in the neurological sciences. It required the use of the therapist's own unique experience, in an intuitive way, to search not for precision, but for the grasp of complex and subtle patterns. It was a form of philosophic critique (cf. Habermas 1973).

Since the postcritical study of mental illness chose the patient's *whole* consciousness as its object, as opposed to his reflexes, sensations, and judgements, the degree of precision attained by empiricist techniques has been difficult if not impossible to reach. The psychotherapist was forced to look outside the circle of accepted scientific thought for models of his intellectual task. He had to trust his ability to grasp his patients' consciousness directly, and he returned to the introspective method of Plato. He had to trust his predictions, without the evidence called for in the experimental method, and he turned to the teleology of Plato, Aristotle, and the German romantics. In his famous paper on infantile sexuality, Freud sought to pacify the biologists with a footnote: "The use of teleological forms of thought in biological explanations can hardly be avoided" (Freud 1910:588).

Such ways of thinking were difficult for the precritical physicians to absorb. On the whole, they overreacted to the postcritical approach to treatment, even barring its study from the medical curriculum. They denounced the use of hypnotism as quackery in spite of its results, and most researchers paid no attention to it at all. The study of the mind was split into two hostile camps, and in spite of many brilliant efforts to reconcile these camps, the rift is still very much alive. Wrote Zilbourg in his *History of Medical Psychology*, "The whole course of the history of medical psychology is punctuated by the medical man's struggle to rise above the prejudices of all ages in order to identify himself with the psychological realities of his patients" (1941:524). The prejudices of precritical, scientistic medicine itself posed the most serious challenge in that struggle.

Critique and Symbolic Relativism

Implied in any holistic approach to the understanding of human behavior is the concept of relativism, the idea that it is the relationship of acts, thoughts, feelings, and surroundings to one another that determines their significance, apart from any inherent meanings that may hold constant for various people in various situations. We have seen how this attitude developed as a natural result of the practical problem of understanding the experience of mental patients. A mental patient or anyone else experiences his world as an interrelated whole unlike the whole experienced by others, and we distort his experience the minute we dissect it into analytic bits for comparison with that of other people. Just as the subjectiveness of holistic ideas inteferes with their scientific communication and replication, so the holistic quality of subjective experience interferes with its understanding via precise analysis. If the holistic is subjective, the subjective is also holistic.

Once the analytic method of science had taken firm hold, philosophy could not ignore this problem for long. Bishop George Berkeley noted in 1710 that, the prevailing empiricism notwithstanding, we experience the world indirectly, through structures that are imposed by our language. Goethe took up the idea again in 1800, as did Fritz Mauthner and Hans Vaihinger in 1900 (Janik and Toulmin 1973: Vaihinger 1925). It was a challenge that the scientists could avoid as long as they were making obvious and useful progress, but such was not the case in the studies of man.

Psychiatry had shown that attempts to cope with alien ways of thought had to deal with this process of interpreting reality, and that the principle of mechanical associations of ideas proposed by Hobbes was not very helpful as a guide. The associative process seemed to be largely unconscious, and largely nonrational. In the late nineteenth century, psychiatry was joined by a new science with exactly the same problem: anthropology. Just as neurotic patients entertained ideas and undertook tasks that seemed self-defeating from a strictly rational point of view, so "primitive" people followed customs whose value seemed inaccessible to a Darwinian or any other materially functional point of view.

A number of evolutionist and historicist theories developed in anthropology in the late 1800s, but none of these seemed to account for the cultural facts that began to accumulate in the notebooks and journals of the new science. Human behaviors were not distributed like genetic characteristics, spreading from a high frequency center to a periphery where they merged with other traits from other centers. They were not clearly related to environmental pressures, since many distinct ways of life were likely to develop under similar ecological conditions. They were amazingly stable under some conditions, resembling biological structures, and flexible under other conditions. Moreover, the administration of colonial empires full of unfamiliar cultures gave practical importance to theories of culture, as attempts to civilize the natives frequently met with disastrous results.

An important advance on this problem was made beginning in the 1880s, when a young German physicist and geographer, Franz Boas, turned to the study of culture. From the beginning, Boas took the view that primitive cultures made sense in their own right, independently of whatever functional significance their component ideas and skills might have. Taking the romantic point of view, he refused to dissect cultures into their component behaviors for comparison with others, and sought the subtle and complex sense of *pattern* that seemed to knit each way of life into a satisfying whole. His method was simply to describe, with as little theoretical structure as possible, and in as great detail as time would allow, every facet of the language, thought, behavior, history, material output and environmental conditions of each group. It was, to borrow the psychiatric term, case study, and with it Boas was able to develop convincing analyses, showing how themes like competitiveness, or hierarchy, or basic concepts of masculinity and femininity, structured many aspects of a given way of life, from economic behavior to art, language, kinship and religion. With this outlook, Boas founded American academic anthropology and trained its first generation of scholars—Margaret Mead, Ruth Benedict, Robert Lowie, Alfred Kroeber, Edward Sapir, Ralph Linton, and many others—a fellowship later dubbed the Relativist School.

Psychiatry, Anthropology, and Human Development

There have been important contributions to the advance of critique in developmental psychology aside from those of psychiatry and anthropology: William James and John Dewey with their Pragmatism; Martin Heidegger and Edmund Husserl with their Phenomenology; Soren Kierkegaard, Jean-Paul Sartre, Paul Tillich, and others with their Existentialism have pressed for the study of subjective experience, and for the acceptance of criteria other than empirical verification for the evaluation of psychological research. Critical philosophy has continued to develop, and now includes many outstanding twentieth-century scholars such as Cassirer, Langer, the later Wittgenstein, Foucault and the Hermeneutic school of Habermas, Prosch, and Polanyi. I have included psychiatry and anthropology (and I include descriptive sociology here) in the historical discussion of developmental theory, because scholars in these fields are active in writing and teaching it. The easy blending of ideas from these fields is seen in the work of both psychiatrists and descriptive social scientists who have addressed developmental issues. Erik Erikson studied the Sioux and the Yurok and wrote biographies of East Indians (Gandhi) and Russians (Maxim Gorky). Psychologists Erich Fromm and Michael Maccoby spent many years in rural Morelos to capture the cultural dimension of personality development. Sharon Kaufman, Robert Coles, and David Plath have all combined dynamic case analysis with the cultural dimension to produce holistic accounts of lifespan development processes.

Critique and Social Psychology

Meanwhile another inroad was being made on precritical empiricism from a different source. The new biological theories of behavior left little room for the functioning of the imagination in the human psyche, fixated as they were on measurable environmental stimuli and their measurable behavioral responses. Around the turn of the century two eminent psychologists in the precritical tradition, William James and John Dewey, began to question the assumption that imagination could be ignored. From their research, they learned that the individual develops a mental picture of the stimulus situation, and it is to this picture that he responds when presented with a similar stimulus; otherwise it would be difficult to explain learning at all. James and Dewey developed the idea of *parallelism*, the idea that the activity of the nervous system is represented in the mind of the individual. Dewey, who was working at the University of Michigan in the 1880s, met the sociologist Charles H. Cooley, and the two men exchanged ideas. Later Dewey went to the University of Chicago (1894-1904), where he met and influenced psychologist George Herbert Mead, and sociologists W. I. Thomas and Ellsworth Faris.

Dewey's colleagues, working from the model of parallelism, developed the concept of *self-consciousness* as a key social construct. They held that people routinely develop a picture of themselves in the course of growing up in a society, and that their social behavior is the result of the way they seek to present this self to others. Since the self-concept is sensitive to what others say and do, any understanding of the person requires close attention to the interactions between people in real social situations, and to how each actor understands the significance of this interaction in terms of his self-concept.

Mead, Faris, and others began in the 1910s to attack the prevailing notions of human instinct in the psychological literature. Their self-concept is a holistic idea, because it focuses on the way people combine perceptions into complex pictures, and on how they adjust these pictures to make sense of complex social processes. It is a relativistic idea, because it shows how behavior results from the ad hoc understandings that are generated in social situations. Accordingly, the method of this group, who called their idea "social psychology," was largely ethnographic—the detailed description of real social processes, together with interviews to elicit the meaning of these processes for the actors involved. But the most important contribution of social psychology to the postcritical perspective lies in its portrayal of the fundamental causes of human action. If the individual is self-conscious, the social psychologists reasoned, he can and does react to his own behavior as well as to his environment. He is capable of autonomous self-determination. This basic position on determinism creates a great gulf between the view of maturity reflected in the work of this tradition on one hand, and that of the precritical psychologists on the other. In the hands of the Chicago school there developed the basis of a psychology that was not only postcritical, in the sense that it avoided the naïve empiricism of the Enlightenment, but was also postromantic, in the sense that it avoided teleological notions of development toward an innate ideal. Here post-Kantian philosophy and the science of human nature began to see eye to eye. This perspective of self-consciousness, now generally called "symbolic interaction," gradually joined forces with relativist anthropology and with holistic psychotherapeutic perspectives in the United States, and together they have helped to produce the current resurgence of critique as a theoretical perspective.

The Rise of Critique

In the 1980s many developmental psychologists are turning away from precritical scientism toward a more autonomous, self-directed view of human behavior, and at the same time necessarily to a more relativistic and holistic view of maturity (Gergen 1980). There appear to be several reasons for this shift. In addition to the romantic tradition, kept alive in psychotherapy, anthropology, and symbolic interactionism, two determinants of the trend are especially important : (1) the need for a model of mental health that goes beyond mere absence of disease; and (2) the increasingly obvious failure of positivist science to produce workable models of the human psychological lifespan. I will deal with (1) in chapter 11, where I take up the problem of restoring the soul to developmental psychology; and I will return to (2) in chapter 10, when I take up the question of causal models. Here let me point to the growing number of important theorists outside the predominantly holistic traditions of psychoanalysis and humanistic psychology who are outspokenly critical of precritical science.

The emerging trend can be seen clearly in Rudner's widely quoted *Philosophy of Social Science*, published in 1966, and Brewster Smith's *Social Psychology and Human Values*, published in 1969. There, the view of man as actively engaged in the construction of his own personality and environment is combined with the growing evidence from research that this creativity produces an almost infinite variety of developmental trajectories. These themes are taken up again in the seminal work of Klaus Riegel (1975), Robert White (1976), Norma Haan (1977), and Kenneth Gergen (1980). In this view, any attempt to devise a model of maturity cannot be based solely on empirical evidence, but must also involve conscious value judgements on the part of the scientist. In Rudner's words, "To refuse to pay attention to the value decisions which must be made, to make them intuitively, unconsciously, or haphazardly, is to leave an essential aspect of the scientific method out of control" (1966:6).

Are Two Kinds of Psychology Necessary?

Pascal's analysis of the mathematical and intuitive styles implied that they are both imperfect approaches to a fully developed intellect; true knowledge combines the best features of both. If this is true, it would appear that psychology can look forward to a future when the controversy between empiricism and critique is solved through the achievement of a general theory of the mind. Such an achievement would require the elimination of disagreement by way of a truly objective method, and at that a method which reliably produces practical self-understanding. Whether or not this is in fact possible has everything to do with the way we function as social and behavioral scientists.

The attitude of precritical psychologists seems to be that critique will go away if they ignore it, and they can get on with the upbringing of a mature positivist psychology. They point to the increasingly complex and subtle problems solved by the natural sciences, with increasingly important practical results. They direct attention to the relative youth of psychology as a discipline, and to the great increase in the complexity and thoroughness of nomothetic studies made possible by the advent of computers. They point to the increasing sophistication of biological models of the brain and behavior, and the resulting success of genetic mapping and chemotherapy for the diagnosis and treatment of psychiatric disorders. They remind us of the relative effectiveness of modern advertising and propaganda as a result of psychological research.

The postcritical psychologist, of course, rejects this view. He is more impressed by our inability to reduce crime, insanity, war, and unproductiveness than by our ability to manage public opinion. He points to the failure of one theory after another to generate effective social programs, or even to continue for long as an attractive avenue of research. He is often struck by the fact that we are trying to understand the mind by means of the mind, and that our understanding is limited by the mind's ability to grasp, even with the help of computers, the implications of what it is telling itself. Perhaps most important of all, he will remind us that the physical sciences proceed on the basis of an epistemology that is totally incompatible with the subject matter of psychology: the Lawful, Nonconscious Universe. The very thing upon which progress in physical science depends—the elimination of subjectivity—at its best robs psychology of an important piece of its subject matter. At worst, it divorces the science of human behavior from the very questions whose solutions led to the invention of science itself: the nature of the universe and man's place in it. In chapter 14 I will consider what kind of progress is possible in the sciences of man.

Now we have seen how maturation as an observable process split off from the philosohic inquiry into maturity as a recognizable state based on ethical and cosmological beliefs. But we have already noted the impossibility of studying development without some kind of model of an end state: no maturity, no maturation. The precriticals had to redefine the phenomenon in order to study it. And so they did, with the concept of *adjustment*, to which we now turn.

10. Functionalism:
Nature Versus Nurture

Since the very idea of maturation is impossible without some notion of maturity, the philosophic quest for man's place in the universe could not be and was not derailed by the discovery of scientific method. But for the precriticals it was shunted onto a siding until the main train should come through—the quest for agreement on the nature of the universe itself. The new hope of these men was that the answers to ethical questions would reveal themselves once mankind knew all that could be known with certainty. If natural laws could be found that would explain to the satisfaction of rational men the varieties of human behavior and experience, the questions of ultimate purposes might be halfway solved.

Turning, then, to the problem of diversity, post-Enlightenment thought found the machine analogy irresistible. Differences in the appearance and operation of rationally designed machines can be explained in almost every case by reference to the functions assigned to them by their designers, to the properties of materials and the state of craftsmanship available for their construction. So in nature, the study of diversity always produces evidence of simple laws. Function dictates form. Moving closer to the study of maturation, the same laws seem to apply to stability and change. Tall, straight pines do not grow on windswept coasts, nor short, crooked ones in deep inland forests, but each conforms to the law of its environment. Again, function dictates form.

Functionalism in Hobbes: Nurture, not Nature

In functionalism, then, lies a principle of maturation more promising than pure speculation; it was the principle Hobbes adopted in the *Leviathan*. Just as the pine "learns" to shed the wind or reach for the sun by associating minutiae of pressure, light, and warmth with increments of growth, so the human mind links ideas and behavior to minutiae of pleasure and discomfort. Hobbes's generation knew little about biology, but they had the rudiments of a functional psychology in Aquinas's and Scotus's Aristotelian teachings on the educational process, a psychology in which the mind was depicted as a passive vessel. Hobbes, moreover, was an educator, and this metaphor probably appealed to him for that reason. He undoubtedly knew how to teach complex ideas through the association of simple images. Later, as biological knowledge developed, the issue of genetic versus environmental function would become a central one in developmental psychology, but for Hobbes, there was little to choose from the "nature" side of the controversy. For him, maturation was a matter of adaptation to environment.

We have seen that Hobbes's effect on the psychology of his time was profound. Associationism continued to produce research throughout the next two centuries. The great empiricist philosophers, John Locke, David Hume, and Jeremy Bentham, adopted it outright. The first true empirical studies of child development, by Dietrich Tiedemann in 1787 and by F. A. Carus in 1808, were based upon it. Willhelm Wundt, the founder of experimental psychology, was an associationist; and it was Wundt's work that inspired the first American psychologists (Boring 1957:392, 507). Nor did the basic idea lose credit when biological science was introduced into the study of maturation. Associationism's impact on Freud, Herbert Spencer, and William James was extensive; it formed a basis for the behaviorist school of modern psychology.

Associationism appeared at a time when biology and physiology were just emerging as fields of inquiry, and it took practically nothing from, and offered even less to, these fields. It suggested that the differences between man and man—even between men and animals—in mental functioning were merely matters of degree, not quality. It paid no heed to humoral theory, one of the leading biological theories of the time, or indeed to any theory of the relationship between the body and the mind. When Hobbes attempted a taxonomy of the branches of knowledge, he eliminated the life sciences altogether.

In order to understand the success of associationism, then, we must remember that there was as yet no biological theory of the functions of the brain. In fact, there was no functional theory of biology that could account for the existence of the brain. For this, psychology had to wait for a series of discoveries that culminated in the all-time greatest achievement in biology:

Darwin's *Origin of the Species*. In the meantime, biologists sought to account for all kinds of behavior almost indiscriminately by invoking the concept of "instinct," which was just another way of asserting the importance of their science by denying that the behavior in question was learned (Eisley 1961:346 ff.). In the absence of a functional theory, this smacked of teleology, and could not satisfy a good empiricist.

Enter Nature: Biological Theories of Development

The theory of natural selection was the end-product of a long and difficult series of discoveries involving dozens of exceptional thinkers in several branches of science. Before Darwin could formulate his ideas—and impress the scientific world with them—the world had to accept three monumental new ideas: the age of the earth, the basic mutability and interrelatedness of biological forms, and the key role of *chance* in natural history. The French naturalist Georges Louis Leclerk, better known as the Comte de Buffon, sketched the broad outlines of the theory of evolution a century before *The Origin of the Species*, but no one (perhaps not even Buffon himself) took it seriously.

First, there was the problem of the earth's age. Before James Hutton raised the question of the earth's antiquity with his new geological methods in 1795, the Bible was the only serious source on geological time, and Creation was usually dated a couple of thousand years before Christ. Nor did Hutton's methods succeed in shaking this idea until Sir Charles Lyell published the *Principles of Geology* in 1834, showing how geological age could be read in the rocks of the English countryside, and producing the inescapable conclusion that the earth was many millions of years old.

Next, there was the problem of biological form and function. The natural history of the Bible held that all living species were created in their present forms, according to the whim of their creator. The functional and historical interrelatedness of the living world could not emerge until a classification system was found that adequately described the functional similarities and differences of species. This was accomplished by the indefatigable Swede Carl von Linne, known to the world by his latinized name, Carolus Linnaeus, in 180 works spanning several decades. His *Systema Naturae*, published in 1735, contains what are still the basic taxonomic structures of biology. Linnaeus understood to an amazing extent the functions of biological structures, and he classified living forms according to degrees of similarity in the way they seemed to have solved the most basic problems of existence. His success led the embryologist C. F. Wolff to suggest in about 1760 a convincing substitute for teleology in accounting for the ontogenetic development of living forms: the increasing differentiation and increasing functional integration of organic structures— the developmental principle most biologists go by today.

But before the implications of Linnaeus's taxonomy could be grasped, evolutionary change itself had to be demonstrated; this task was pushed forward by scores of amateur fossil collectors in the eighteenth and nineteenth centuries, and led by men like Baron Cuvier, who demonstrated extinction in 1812, and William Smith, who invented the stratigraphic method of showing evolutionary sequences in 1818.

So firmly entrenched was the classical dedication to the idea of a conscious universe, however, that all these discoveries together shook the faith of only a few. "So what if evolution occurs?" the academic community replied. "God planned it that way!" This idea, called progressivism, held the lead in scientific circles until the 1830s. The missing piece needed to convince scholars of the usefulness of evolution as a concept was some idea of the *function* of evolutionary change. Until it could be shown that such change followed natural and predictable laws, the existence of phylogenetic change was a fact of little use to biology.

The key to this problem came from an economist, Thomas Robert Malthus. In 1798, Malthus published *An Essay on the Principle of Population*, containing the famous law that population, which increases geometrically, will always place pressure on the resources in the environment, which increase arithmetically. Under the circumstances, said Malthus, nature favors the strong at the expense of the weak. It took but a little imagination to think of applying this principle to evolution. Selective breeding of plants and animals had been practiced consciously for centuries. The remaining problem was to discover the *mechanism* by which selection took place. In 1803 Lamarck reverted to teleology, and suggested that species change by *striving* toward evolutionary improvement. Lyell suggested in the *Principles of Geology* that the appearance and disappearance of fossil forms might be evidence of a "struggle for existence." But it took the painstaking observations of a great naturalist to document the ways in which species actually adapt to their environments, and thereby to convince the world that biological form always (well, almost always) follows function. And this was the role of Darwin's great work, the capstone of a century of inquiry. There remained only the knotty problem of explaining the *persistence* of biological traits over long time spans, and the mechanism of their change. The former was solved by Gregor Mendel's peas, whose genetic antics appeared in print six years after *The Origin of the Species*, and the latter was solved (in part) by Hugo de Vries's mutating primroses in 1901.

Natural selection as an idea brought order to an immense corpus of data: the functional similarities and differences of biological forms; the distribution of species and their geographical variations; the functions of specific biological structures; the fossil record; and population dynamics, to name a few. It gave new direction to the study of anatomy, physiology, biochemistry, and embryology by revealing the plan that had given rise to the structures and processes studied by these sciences. Life could now be interpreted functionally, with some degree of confidence. Take an elementary fact like the existence of two sexes, for example. Without the theory of natural selection, it is difficult to see how the parsing out and recombining of genetic material throughout a breeding population, and therefore how sex itself, has any relevance to survival. Why not dispense with those troublesome creatures, the males?

The effect of the theory of natural selection on psychology was equally great. The nervous system had evolved gradually from a rudimentary organ to the complex brain of man, not through the guidance of a teleological principle; not as the receptacle of some transcendental wisdom, but through exactly the same process that had produced the difference between the bat's webbed fingers, or the horse's hooves, and the prehensile human hand—in response to environmental pressure, in support of a characteristic way of life, at the service of the organism's survival. Far from being the seat of God's plan evoked in many an Enlightenment phrase (like Alexander Pope's "the God within the mind"), the brain was the obedient servant of our digestive and reproductive anatomy! No longer could passion and reason be listed as contending functions in the old sense, since the new biology displayed *all* the brain's functions as serving the same basic ends. Differences between species in brain anatomy and functioning could be understood in terms of their ways of life; and to some extent, the opposite was also true:

Differences in behavior showed differences in inherited characteristics.

Nature, not nurture.

Although the new biological functionalism did not sweep environmental theories away, it deeply and permanently affected our view of human psychological diversity. The eighteenth-century concept of "instinct" was revived, given a genetic basis, and applied to every conceivable kind of behavior. Several serious genetic theories of character evolved, such as those of Kretschmer (1931) and Sheldon (1942). Says Faris, "The apparent success of the instinct theory in explaining animal behavior seemed to promise that the same mechanisms would provide the key to human actions. The dominant psychological tradition toward the end of the nineteenth century was one of detailed physiological study of the individual, with virtually no interest in his social relations" (1967:89). The new biology gave rise to the new field of anthropology in the 1880s, and led the first anthropologists to propose a linear sequence of cultural evolution to account for differences of behavior among living human groups.

Among the most dramatic influences of the theory of evolution on developmental psychology were the seminal works of Freud and of G. Stanley Hall. Freud got the idea of the retention of "primitive" infantile thought contents and associations from the evolutionary principle of the conservation of structures. His concept of the organization and development of the brain is derived from so-called recapitulation theory, that is, that the ontogenetic development of the organism repeats its phylogenetic evolution—an idea first put forward by Grohman in 1824. His notion of the role of the instincts is clearly derived from evolutionary functionalism, and his view of the person/society relationship as basically conflict-ridden derives from the Darwinian picture of nature.

Hall, the eclectic, impulsive founder of American academic psychology, went even further. To him, as to many of his generation, Western civilization seemed to be emerging from centuries of moody violence onto a high plateau of self-discipline and progress, and the analogy of this progression to the maturation of the individual Victorian character seemed clear. His famous work, *Adolescence* (1904), published before the Great War shattered the historical side of the illusion, developed the idea of recapitulation into a basis of lifespan psychology and historical interpretation. So central was this doctrine to Hall's thinking, in fact, that the man himself, with all his genius, was dragged down into relative obscurity with it when it fell from academic grace.

But in America one of the most far-reaching effects of Darwinian biology on the field of human psychology was to prove man's animal origins, and open to the field the study of animal behavior. If the human brain was just a fancy animal brain after all, direct inferences from animal physiology and behavior ought to enlighten us on the subject of its structure and function. English acquaintances of Darwin like John Romanes (1848-1894) began to publish comparative studies of animal and human psychology as early as the 1880s, and the practice soon spread to America through the work of Jacques Loeb, beginning in 1891, Edward Lee Thorndike in 1898, and Herbert Spencer Jennings in 1899. In Russia, of course, Pavlov began his famous experiments with dogs inthe 1890s, and V.M. Bekhterev continued along these lines a decade later (Boring 1957).

More Cogs and Levers: Homeostasis and Drive Theory

Natural selection theory gave impetus to the growing hope that mental laws could be discovered that would allow the full understanding, even prediction, of human thought and emotion. We now understood, or thought we did, the biological tasks to which every brain in the animal kingdom had equally been put; it remained only to find out how these brains went about their job of satisfying the body's needs. A likely place to look for functional models was, of course, the other organ systems of the body. As knowledge of these developed in the nineteenth century, it became clear that the body was an integrated, self-regulating system; changes in the external or internal environment brought about adjustments that resulted in something like a steady state. If light was increased, the pupil contracted to let less in; if the muscles were exerted, the heart and lungs worked harder to supply them with oxygen-rich blood; if temperature fell, the capillaries contracted to conserve body heat.

In the middle of the eighteenth century, Pierre-Louis Mareau de Maupertuis (1698-1759) had noticed the tendency of organisms to conserve resources, and had named it "the principle of least action." He may have been aided by the speculations of the Ionian philosophers, some of whom had been fond of describing the universe as a balanced system of contending forces. At any rate, Claude Bernard developed the idea fully as a biological principle in 1865, calling it the "steady state" principle. It was probably Walter Cannon in 1939 who coined the now-familiar term homeostasis for the same thing.

Was it possible that the brain also functioned to minimize the disruption of an ideal organic state? Is it in fact a machine that assigns survival significance to incoming stimuli and activates responses that will keep stress levels at a minimum? It is difficult to say who first introduced the question into psychology. Ellenberger (1970:277) notes that Friedrich Nietzsche developed the idea in the 1880s, and concludes that there is "no question of Nietzsche's influence on the ideas of Freud" (ibid.). By 1963, Butler and Rice could say that "for thirty years it has been a dominant belief in American psychology...that behavior is...primarily or secondarily based on drive reduction" (Butler and Rice 1963:79), and as late as 1977, Norma Haan saw little change in the field of ego psychology: "Most prior investigations of ego are dependent, whether this is recognized or not, upon Freudian and behavioristic notions of achieved states resident within the person and activated by drive" (1977:19). Stimuli, in other words, act as "irritants," resulting in action favoring the reduction of the irritation.

Two things about drive theory are of interest to us here. First, it focuses attention not on innate differences between individuals, but on their innate similarities. Differences are attributed to characteristic levels of sensitivity, intelligence, and the effects of different environments on conditioned responses. Drive theory sets limits on the supposed plasticity of the organism. Second, drive theory is ideally suited for experimental research, being based on closely observed minutiae of behavior. It becomes unwieldy as an explanatory concept when applied to the understanding of character or character development, because there one is dealing with complex sequences of behavior that cannot easily be broken down into discrete, quantifiable units.

Nevertheless, drive theory has some important uses for those who would explain human behavior. Based as it is on the idea of homeostasis, with its analogues in chemistry, botany, zoology, mechanics and engineering, it brings, as Menninger says, "wondrous things into the fold of science, and point[s] beyond the strictures of its own field" (1963:83). It helps to account for a great deal of apparently irrational and nonfunctional behavior, for example, the common failure of heart attack victims to recognize their own illness and deal with it. Since it assumes that operant drives need not be conscious (and in fact usually are not), the theory can be evoked without reference to the subject's post hoc explanations of his acts.

In short, drive theory is useful as a way of explaining irrational behavior, as well as similarities of behavior among individuals. It therefore forms one important basis for theories of mental health. As an example, consider the newly popular idea of "stress" as a source of illness and maladjustment. According to the stress model, people develop in the course of their lives skills for coping with such everyday problems as finding friends and lovers, making a living, raising children, conserving their energy, avoiding strife, and satisfying their ideals. These coping skills might involve the energetic search for rational solutions, or the use of interpersonal skills to recruit help, or the habit of running away when things get out of hand, or psychological tactics like simply ignoring problems. If the environment changes significantly, or if the person himself changes, often the skills he has learned no longer work to solve his problems, and he becomes vulnerable to depression, anxiety, and illness. This theory is based on a homeostatic model of the person/environment relationship. It assumes that each of us normally has a set of needs or drives that require satisfaction (needs such as security, self-esteem, intimacy, and so on); and that our personalities function to see that we get these needs met *with a minimum of discomfort*. It assumes that each of us has an anxiety tolerance level, and that once this is exceeded, coping mechanisms are automatically triggered to bring us back to an emotional equilibrium.

Functionalism in America: Nature AND Nurture

It was in twentieth-century America that the nature/nurture controversy came to a head and eventually produced a rich variety of attempts at reconciliation. Throughout the nineteenth century, there were continental and English scholars and physicians interested in *practical* knowledge of the mind, but for the most part the methods and ways of thinking of such service-oriented theorists were antipositivistic—critical or romantic. The scientists of mental phenomena, principally Wundt at Leipzig and his colleagues, were less interested in function than in the structure of experience. Like the chemists and physicists they so admired, they sought with painstaking care to identify the primary units of their science—sensation, perception, attention, desire—and to establish firmly the exact relationships among these elements. It was the fusion of this experimental attitude with the desire for practical answers—in short, functionalism—that characterized the early years of psychology in America. We cannot understand the American history of developmental ideas without some clarity about this enormously important fact.

Edward Boring, America's foremost historian of psychology, struggled to understand his countrymen's passion for functional theories of behavior. The early Americans had learned their science from Wundt, but immediately turned their back on Wundt's goals of precise description in favor of utility. Why? Boring concluded that it came from a combination of Darwinism and the values of the frontier. "America's success-philosophy, based on individual opportunity and ambition," he wrote, "is responsible for shirt-sleeves democracy...for pragmatism...and functionalism of all kinds, within psychology and without" (1957:507).

I agree. And I would also draw attention to another fact about early American psychology that the modern student is likely to overlook: It started small. Nearly everyone with a professional interest in the topic knew nearly everyone else and they all influenced each other. William James founded the first American psychological laboratory at Harvard in the 1870s, and G. Stanley Hall got the first American doctorate in the new science there in 1878. Many other famous psychologists—among them John Dewey, George Herbert Mead, James R. Angell, E. B. Titchener, Edward Thorndike, and Robert Woodworth—studied under James, and they in turn trained most of the outstanding people of the next generation. Meanwhile Hall founded the American Psychological Association in 1887, and the first English-language journal in the field. E. C. Sanford, who got his degree under Hall at Johns Hopkins in 1888, had a flair for the lab work which bored Hall to distraction. Sanford trained both Terman and Gesell.

> At one time it seemed as if the majority of American psychologists had been associated with Hall earlier at Hopkins or at Clark . . . . In 1890, just before the wave of laboratory founding had reached its height, there were probably not more than ten psychological laboratories in America, and at least four of these, beside Hopkins itself, had begun life under the direction of a pupil of Hall's at Hopkins. (Boring, 1957:524)

In the hands of these men the pace of research on human behavior accelerated dramatically, and theory grew increasingly complex and sophisticated. The basic principles of functional causality laid down by nature-theorist Darwin became almost unquestioned background in most of this research. To be sure, nurture theorist Hobbes had a great modern disciple in the German experimentalist Wundt. Wundt's ideas in turn stimulated generations of American behaviorists like John Watson, E. L. Thorndike, B. F. Skinner, Clark Hull, and Edward Tolman; Hobbes himself would have cheered the words of Thorndike in 1913: "It is possible to get any response of which a learner is capable associated with any situation to which he is sensitive" (quoted in Schiamburg 1985:20). But on the whole, Darwinian functionalism held the high ground in the early years of American functional psychology.

Modern developmental research took an early interest, predictably enough, in child development. In the early 1900s, the leading names in the field were the biologically oriented "maturationists," G. Stanley Hall, Lewis Terman, and Arnold Gesell. In their studies of children, they were looking mainly for the unfolding of genetic potentials within the organism.

The interest of Hall and his contemporaries in childhood and adolescence was closely related to the social conditions of their time. Industry was expanding rapidly, and with it new forms of organization and management were being explored in all fields of life—government, the military, work, public health, and education. The idea of a scientifically engineered society, in which human potentials were cultivated like hothouse flowers on a huge scale, had come into its own. The education of successful competitors for the best jobs of tomorrow became a national obsession. As a result, educators and parents alike wanted to know more about the development of children's intelligence and ability. Biological theories were popular, not only because they fit the Darwinian mold, but because, like preliterate notions of oedipal fate, they provided a handy rationalization for the failures—the ones who did not respond to the new techniques of social engineering.

Focusing as they necessarily did on the universal aspects of behavior at the expense of the idiosyncratic, biological theories also had the advantage of lending themselves to mass-production techniques of social engineering. As a result of the great waves of immigration from Europe in the late nineteenth and early twentieth centuries, America was beginning to resemble an ethnic crazy quilt, and a theory of education was needed that could justify treating all children the same. If abilities unfolded with the same biological predictability in all humans, it would appear safe to ignore the experience and upbringing of the child as the system strove to outfit him for participation in American life.

But the combination of experimental method and biological functionalism contained within it some paradoxes. For one thing, it was difficult to document biological regularities in human development, since babies could not be raised in laboratories. Recapitulation theory was especially difficult to test experimentally, since it was obviously impossible to reconstruct the history of the species for observation purposes. Under the circumstances, anyone who shone forth as a great theorist at the turn of the twentieth century was bound to find himself caught in these paradoxes, as we can clearly see if we look at the life of America's leading psychologist of the time, G. Stanley Hall.

In the 1870s, Hall went to Liepzig and studied under Wundt. He came back to the United States and began lecturing on child development at

Harvard in the 1880s. His lectures were a great success, and he soon began using the term "genetic psychology" to refer to the biologically based field of developmental studies. Hall disliked laboratory work, preferring to rely on insight and wide reading in developing his ideas; but he was so good at this that even in an intellectual world gripped by the vision of natural-science precision he was soon the leading theorist in the field. His book *Adolescence*, published in 1904, was built squarely on the quicksand of recapitulation theory; but it came out "at a time when psychology was supposed to be about to unlock the door to scientific education" (Boring 1957:522), and it was a huge success nevertheless.

Encouraged, Hall turned his intuitive powers elsewhere. He took an early interest in psychoanalysis and helped introduce it to America. He studied sexuality, digestion, theology, and, in his old age . . . old age itself, all with the same far-reaching speculativeness. "He himself admitted," says Boring, "that his intellectual life might be seen as a series of 'crazes'" (1957:518). It is a rare academician who can range so widely over his field of study and still leave a lasting impression upon history, but Hall's intellect was astounding:

> G. Stanley Hall was the acknowledged genius of the group at Clark. Although the term genius is often overused, we can safely apply it to his intellect. True genius may be regarded as a creative developmental thrust of the human action system into the unknown. He embodied such thrusts. He had, in addition, an empathic propensity to revive within himself the thought processes and the feelings of other thinkers. This same projective trait enabled him to penetrate the mental life of children, of defectives, of primitive peoples, of animals, of extinct stages of evolution. What if he could not verify his prolific suggestive thrusts, what if he seemed unsystematic and self-contradictory, what if he exaggerated the doctrine of recapitulation—he nevertheless was a naturalist Darwin of the mind, whose outlook embraced the total phylum, and lifted psychology above the sterilities of excessive analysis and pedantry. (Gesell 1952:126-127)

Yet, for all his success, Hall's fame would prove fragile, and at some level he himself knew it. In his autobiography he confessed, "The dominantly sad note of my life may be designated by one word . . . isolation" (Gesell 1952:127). Hall was an anachronism, a brilliant nineteenth-century philosopher adrift in the scientific twentieth century.

Halls' students, at least the ones we remember, were better adapted to the new climate. They were just as committed to the American version of Utopia, but they not only founded laboratories, they worked in them, tirelessly and intelligently. Such a student was Lewis Terman, the father of the Sanford-Binet "IQ" test, a man who believed that modern society was wasting its genius, and that the waste of genius "was shameful, a tragic loss to society of its most valuable resource. He conceived of social progress as dependent on how rapidly, and with what economy, intellectual giants... could reach their maximum development and produce their great ideas" (Sears 1957:778). Terman believed intelligence was biologically determined, and he set out to prove it. In the process he contributed to an important set of research techniques in developmental psychology—the study of individuals over long periods of time. In 1921 Terman and his colleagues at Stanford began their famous "gifted children" study, one of the first major longitudinal projects in the psychological study of development. Some of the subjects are still being interviewed and tested today.

About the same time that Terman began his work on intelligence, Arnold Gesell founded the Clinic of Child Development at Yale University. Born in the Mississippi River frontier town of Alma, Wisconsin in 1880, Gesell was evidently an impressionable young man when he came under Hall's influence at Clark at the turn of the century. Soon Gesell was convinced of the power of evolutionary theory in developmental psychology, and in 1915 he completed his doctor of medicine degree at Yale, to better understand the physiological bases of behavior. Gesell invented new techniques for the precise study of children. He used photography to "freeze" complex behaviors, so that their details could be carefully scrutinized and compared (a technique that influenced many later scholars, including anthropologists Margaret Mead and Gregory Bateson in the 1930s). Probably the most important contribution of Gesell's work to developmental psychology was the identification of fairly distinct changes in behavior, in fixed order, with similar timing in all normal children. These observations echoed the notion of distinct behavioral *stages* proposed earlier by Freud, Hall, and others; but Gesell's stages were derived by means of highly replicable experiments, not from the combination of mnemonic reconstruction and creative imagination. They advanced the cause, not only of biologism, but of the empiricist approach to psychology in general.

As matchmakers in the wedding of experimental method and functional theory, Gesell and his like-minded colleagues established the pedigree of American psychology. Their work seemed to promise great practical advances in education and social betterment. The promise attracted public attention, and public attention meant—as it always does in America—money and prestige. In 1925 the charitable foundations of the Rockefellers and Carnegies began to give money to Gesell's laboratory at Yale. Soon the popularity of developmental research had spread throughout the country, and in the next decade, child research centers were established at Case Western Reserve University, at Columbia, at the Universities of Iowa, Minnesota and California, at the Fels Institute in Ohio, and at the Merrill Palmer School in Detroit (Berndt and Ziegler 1985).

As a theory, then, maturation at first seemed to soothe with scientific certitude the practical perplexities of educators and reformers. But the ointment contained the fly of fatalism—what is biologically given cannot be improved by human intervention—and a more optimistic theory was needed, a theory that could somehow combine the prestige of biologism and the strain toward social progress. The time was ripe for Freudian thought.

Psychoanalysis was instantly popular in America. Within five years of the founding of Gesell's laboratory, his ideas were under severe criticism even at Yale from the psychoanalytic contingent. His careful experimental method and deterministic beliefs were enshrined in the limited circle of pediatric medicine (the American Board of Pediatrics added "Growth and Development" to its board exams in 1935), but they had little lasting impact on developmental psychology (Ames 1961). In fact, few of the studies of child development undertaken anywhere in the 1930s held any immediate application to the practice of childrearing, or to educational reform (Berndt and Ziegler 1985:133). Maturation theory of course takes account of the sensitivity of the individual to his environment, but it gives clear priority to biological processes as causes in the sequencing of developmental changes in the life cycle.

Maturation theory has lost much of its earlier following, but it has contributed in modern psychology a measure of respectability to the concept of *stages*—changes that unfold in all individuals, in a predictable sequence, and with predictable timing. It has also left an indelible stamp on our concept of maturity itself. The idea that behavior is hereditary often leads us to speculate that developmental peculiarities like impulsiveness, minority gender preference, or unusual mental abilities are inherited. Interestingly, we seem more willing to assume a genetic basis in the case of genius than in that of failure. We Americans prefer to think that those worse off than ourselves deserve what they get, while those better off may not deserve what they have.

Within the biologically functionalist tradition as it evolved in the early twentieth century, however, we find a group of important viewpoints that are more sensitive to the interactions of organism and environment, and that have contributed to the current "dialectic" concepts of function I shall discuss in a moment. Here, I am referring to drive theory, social learning theory, and cognitive development theory.

Modern drive theory uses experimental and naturalistic findings from maturation theory and behaviorist research to build a model that shows the interactions of innate tendencies (for example, hunger, sexuality, aggression, and the need for stimulation) with experience. In contrast to either classical maturation theory or behaviorism, drive theory proposes that the individual is a goal-directed, self-regulating system, and that the understanding of behavior depends on the discovery of its goals. Its best-known proponents are John Dollard, Neal Miller, Donald Fiske, and Salvatore Maddi.

Like psychoanalysis, drive theory is often criticized by the more holistic developmental psychologists for being biologically reductionist. It cannot explain self-sacrifice in the interest of symbolic goals (for example, self-expression or political ideology) or altruistic aims. This criticism is better leveled at the premodern forerunners of drive theory than at its modern proponents. Through such ideas as the drive for "meaning" or "cognitive closure," and the drive to match internal arousal with external stimulation, drive theorists can account fairly convincingly even for things like self-actualization. The following example serves to illustrate the balance of biological and environmental input in drive theory, and its sophistication in handling complex developmental processes:

> The research on early radical visual deprivation, isolation, and later mild deprivation, indicates that stimulation is a critical necessity if the mammalian organism is to be truly adaptive to varied environments. This research also indicates that an optimally stimulated organism is in touch with its environment in an exquisitely delicate way. Its interaction with its environment is, in effect, motivating, since it is the activation mechanisms (in accordance with which activation levels rise, subside, and match in ways that render stimuli attractive, unattractive, adverse, or uninteresting) that govern the organism's transactions with its surround. (Butler and Rice 1963:92-93)

The picture Butler and Rice paint is essentially one of an organism biologically "tuned in" to subtle qualities of its surroundings, and ready—even eager—to process information about those qualities in ways that affect its future behavior.

If drive theory focuses on the internal states of the organism under various stimulus conditions, social learning theory focuses still more on the interaction of organism and environment. Social learning research is really the study of imitative and vicarious learning experience, pioneered by Albert Bandura. Bandura studied under some of the leading behaviorists at the University of Iowa (especially Kenneth Spence) before joining the faculty at Stanford, and was also influenced by learning theorists Neal Miller and Robert Sears. He also borrowed from Freud, in this case the key concept of *identification* with behavior models, the imitation of whom produces new traits (Scroggs 1985). His model of learning introduced complex ideas about mechanisms of attention, memory, inhibition, and motor skill mastery that are standard for all humans, and therefore presumably biological.

A third attempt at synthesis of biological and experiential observations through analytic research methods is represented by the work of the Swiss biologist Jean Piaget and his followers, the so-called structuralists. Piaget designed a variety of intriguing experiments to show how the thought of children evolves though a linear series of stages, from simple "sensori-motor intelligence" (highly reminiscent of the associationist model of Hobbes) through stages of increasing symbolization (akin to psychoanalytic concepts of internalization) and logic to a "formal operations" stage, in which the individual can intellectually dismantle and recombine the elements of his experience to produce creative and "objective" results. The stagefulness of Piaget's concept was clearly derived from biology (and in fact was fully developed before he did any experiments to test it) (Kaye 1980), but he saw experience as the raw material that elicits and shapes the developmental sequence.

Piagetian theory has influenced studies of the adult lifespan chiefly through the work of Lawrence Kohlberg and Jane Loevinger. Kohlberg applied Piaget's stages of cognitive development to the idea of interpersonal relationships, and proposed a parallel set of stages of "moral development." Loevinger developed a set of techniques for measuring ego development, based on Piaget and Kohlberg, that are used in social-psychological studies of levels of maturity. In chapter 11, we shall take a closer look at Kohlberg's model of the maturation process.

The New Biologism: Teleology Reborn

So far we have been looking at environmental and biological determinism primarily as attempts to apply a precritical philosophy to the study of human development; indeed, it was positivism that guided most developmental research from the middle of the seventeenth to the middle of the twentieth centuries. But, as I mentioned at the end of the last chapter, the precritical attitude began to lose its deadlock on this branch of psychology about forty years ago. As a result, biologically informed concepts of man's basic nature have begun to widen, and now include attention to the importance of values and symbols. This new biologism sees man as less *driven* by the interaction of unfolding genetic principles, and more *pulled* by a new kind of *telos*: the individual's own vision of perfection.

As we saw, the romantics and their philosophic descendents in psychology, including the psychoanalysts, never really abandoned the idea of innate developmental goals; it was largely through psychoanalysis that the new biologism entered psychology. As Kohut (1985) reminds us, the early psychoanalysts were concerned mainly with disease, and their models of the psyche therefore lacked development on the subject of extraordinary virtues and abilities. But as Freud's basic notions entered the mainstream of developmental theory, the new theorists began to press against this limitation.

In 1939 Heinz Hartmann made a major contribution to the study of positive maturity with his idea that the ego was not solely a structure for mediating and resolving conflicts between the instinct life and the demands of social reality, but that it included its own energy—a creative and playful

energy, which nonetheless served the development of the mature personality. Hartmann called this function the "conflict free ego sphere." In 1942,
Ives Hendrick took the idea a step further when he reported studies of
child development that seemed to show an increase in creative activity
attending the satisfaction of basic drives. Hendrick proposed an "instinct to
master" as a drive in itself. Along similar lines, Kurt Goldstein coined the
term "self-actualization" in 1940, thereby carrying forward the romantic
notion of an inborn guide toward full maturity, and in turn inspiring
Abraham Maslow (1951) and Marie Jahoda (1958). Shortly thereafter, these
ideas were further developed by Robert White (1963) under the rubric
"effectance." The concept of self-conscious striving toward maturity was
taken up in the 1960s and early 1970s by David Gutmann (1974), M.
Brewster Smith (1969), Heinz Kohut (1985), Norma Haan (1977) and
many others.

As a theory of maturation, the new biologism seems to have two
distinct advantages over the old positivist theories. First it restores, at least
to some extent, the concept of conscious choice to the study of development. In doing so, it frees the theorist to make open moral choices in the
specification of developmental goals. It leads naturally to a concept of
maturity that is more complex and more inspiring than mere wellness.

This need for a more refined notion of maturity was, as we shall see in
the next chapter, the original inspiration for the new biologism. However,
as research findings on actual life histories began to accumulate in the
1960s and 1970s, a second advantage of the new perspective also became
clear: It makes sense out of the more and more obvious diversity of actual
life histories. Even given the fact that culture, wealth, intelligence, physique, sex, social class, and historical era all constrain the choices open to
the individual at key points in his life, it turns out to be still quite
impossible to integrate into a single theory the huge variety of resulting
lifestyles. For the new biological functionalists, it was a matter of demonstrating their own point by adapting creatively to the facts, or conceding
the field to the environmentalists, who meanwhile were far from idle.

The New Environmentalism: Diversity and Dialectic

Whereas biological theories aim at the explanation of human similarities, environmental theories are better suited to account for diversity. The
discovery through research of such great diversity in development, then,
would not have been much of a problem for the environmentalists had
they not been wedded to a precritical view of knowledge. Since the
environment of man is kept on something of an even keel by natural laws,
it is not so difficult for the environmentalist to explain uniformity in
human behavior without departing from his precritical stand. Consequently,
from Hobbes forward, environmentalism tended to remain philosophically

positivistic. The refusal of detailed and sophisticated studies of the life cycle to yield predictive patterns was frustrating to the positivist strain toward the validation of theory. As Benjamin Bloom noted, "Much of what has been termed individual variation might be explained in terms of environmental variation" (1964:9), but there were still few relevant measures of the environment.

To understand the reaction in the 1970s and 1980s of the environmentalists to these developments, we have to digress a bit. In the United States of the 1940s a combination of factors led to a great increase of public interest in mental health and illness. First, there was the widespread acceptance of psychoanalytic theory in the 1930s, which lent impetus to the professionalization of mental health care. Second, there was the greatly increased presence of government in the management of social failure as a result of the Depression and the New Deal (Folta and Schatzman 1968). Third, there was the war, with its many psychological casualties and its warning that modern society might not be as sane as we thought. The Mental Health Act of 1946 established the National Institute of Mental Health, which in the next twenty years spent $550 million on mental health research and $545 million on the training of mental health professionals.

In the 1940s and 1950s, then, even before detailed research had progressed to the point where precritical developmental theory was in serious trouble, the burgeoning mental health professions were feeling an acute need for a clearer definition of their goal—mental health. In 1950 a Midcentury White House Conference on Children and Young People was held, during which the eminent social psychologist Marie Jahoda presented a paper on "positive mental health." Drawing on the work of Hartmann, Goldstein, Maslow, and others, she contributed a seminal work that helped substantially to carry forward the new biologism (Jahoda 1950). Her ideas were expanded and circulated in 1958, when she was commissioned by the Joint Commission on Mental Health and Illness to write a book on the topic (Jahoda 1958).

At the same time Jahoda furthered the new biologism, however, she pointed out the need for a *relativistic and pluralistic* definition of the topic, which would take into account the varied life circumstances and abilities of potential clients. As a precritical researcher, she felt that this would simplify the problem of validating theoretical predictions, as well as render the work of the mental health professional more humane and more effective.

That Jahoda's work was decisive in shaping later definitions of mental health there is no doubt. She is so credited, for example, by Gordon Allport, Robert White, and Norma Haan. Among social psychologists, it is important that her relativistic idea was clarified and expanded by M. Brewster Smith. Smith, who is known for his interest in the cultural dimension of human variability, proposed the notion of "optima" as opposed to a single absolute scale of functioning (Smith 1969).

However, environmental relativism could not simply be absorbed willy-nilly into precritical developmental psychology, because it could not lead to the cumulative approximation of certainty. What was needed was an overarching theoretical frame of reference by which to judge the adequacy of these new situation-bound interpretations. In the mid-1980s, a lively debate continues on the topic of how to integrate the relativistic idea into developmental theory, and important contributions have been made via the dialectic model of Klaus Riegel (1975) and the philosophic pragmatism of Kenneth Gergen (1980) and others. But we can already see the impact of relativism on many major theorists, including the recent work of Robert White (1976) and Norma Haan (1977), who agree that maturation tends, not toward a single end, but toward multiple adaptations to multiple environments, through multiple paths.

Functionalism in Developmental Psychology

The recent history of developmental psychology, then, shows the unfolding of two contrasting sets of ideas in answer to the basic questions of the cause of developmental change and human diversity. The environmentalist developed earlier, largely due to the influence of the late medieval scholastics, combined with the scarcity of biological knowledge in the seventeenth century, when Hobbes proposed it. As the theory of evolution took shape, it suggested causal interrelations between biological structures and behaviors, and led to the biologistic view of development. I have gone into the historical process in detail for two reasons.

First, these two views of the basic questions still form one of the major dimensions along which theories of personality development can be ranked. Robert Havighurst referred to this dimension in 1973, when he divided twentieth-century theories into "tabula rasa" types and "organismic" types (Havighurst 1973:7). Henry Murray had earlier made the same distinction, naming the two types "peripheralist" and "centralist." The former, he said, emphasize the "physical patterns of overt behavior, the combination of simple reflexes to form complex behaviors, and the influence of the physical environment." The latter "stress the directions or ends of behavior, underlying instinctual forces, and inherited dispositions" (Murray 1938:10. Quoted in Frenkel-Brunswick 1974:37). The distinction is, of course, one of emphasis, not one of absoluteness. No modern psychologist would claim that personality can be fully accounted for without reference to both genetics and environment.

The second reason for close attention to the nature/nurture controversy has to do with its importance in understanding the uses of developmental theory. Tracing the history of the two views, we have seen how they functioned at various periods. Like all theories of the mind, biologism and environmentalism must simultaneously try to solve two very different kinds of problems: the problem of scientific rigor, and the problem of social utility. In Europe, where cultural notions of scholarship in the nineteenth century placed academic psychology in a remote room of the ivory tower, questions of rigor took precedence. Practical utility was primarily a problem for philosophers and physicians, and we have seen in chapter 9 how this split developed. Coupled with increasingly sophisticated physiological knowledge, associationist nurture theories produced good laboratory work. It is interesting that the first Darwinian theorists, Freud and Hall, were not lab men in the traditional mold.

The American interest in psychology developed soon after Darwin's sweeping revision of the biological sciences, or it almost certainly would have been a nurturist psychology. As it was, early developmental theory in America was a kind of chimera, a paradoxical mixture of fatalistic nature theory and the antifatalistic drive to answer social questions. This was one species that was doomed almost at birth. There is little wonder that psychoanalysis, which added enough nurture theory to make biological functionalism socially relevant, took such a strong hold in America.

But even psychoanalysis was too fatalistic for a society dedicated to remaking itself. In the 1940s, the reintroduction of teleology by way of the concept of "positive health," and in the 1970s the attempt to build dialectical models that walk a tightrope between biology and environment, have given modern academic developmental psychology its own peculiar flavor.

These last two chapters have traced two of the important effects of the Enlightenment on views of maturity. The hope of a surer method than logical introspection in the search for first principles led to a splitting of analytic, precritical science from critical philosophy. The split has ended up strengthening critique, since the growing sophistication of analytic techniques has revealed with ever-brighter clarity the inherent limitations of any precritical method to illuminate the original questions.

Meanwhile the questions themselves—the meaning of man's existence and the means to make the most of it—were put on hold while the scientists sought agreement on what was certain. That quest, the quest for functional laws of human nature, has also come full circle. The new dialectic theories of the person-environment relationship are better suited than their predecessors to the refined techniques of precritical science. But the tarnishing of positivism itself has left in question the gains of such sophistication. Whatever we have learned from functionalism, it has been oddly irrelevant to the basic questions, as we shall shortly see. As Brewster Smith put it,

For most of us, the two sources to which everyone once looked for what were then regarded as "absolute" values—Tradition and Theology—speak only equivocally if at all. We are still suffering from the crisis of personal and social readjustment occasioned by this loss. (1969:184)

PART III

Studies in
Self-Conscious Psychology

11. Paths of the Soul:
Love, Reason, Conflict

Studies in Self-Conscious Psychology

The last ten chapters have reviewed the history of maturity as an ideal (chapters 2 through 6) and maturation as a process (chapters 7 through 10). Rather than an exhaustive history of developmental psychology, this has been an overview, intended to give basic information one can use to help situate one's own favorite developmental and social ideas and problems in their cultural and historical setting. In this chapter and the next two, I shall offer some examples of this exercise from my own thought.

The present chapter seeks to bring some order to developmental theory by tracing patterns of intellectual affinity and distinction among some ancient thinkers (Plato, Aristotle, Hobbes) and some modern ones (Kohlberg, Gilligan, Freud, Erikson, Maslow, Kohut). Among other things, the exercise helps to expose and explain the weaknesses in some of modern psychology's best-known ideas.

Chapter 12 approaches a perennial psychological problem of great importance to society—the causes and effects of altruism and aggression—through the lenses of culture and history. While there is much that fades from view when this approach is taken (individual differences, for one thing) the exercise brings into focus some unnoticed relationships—for example, among economy, values, aggressiveness, and self-esteem.

Chapter 13 uses the history of psychology to try a fresh approach to a threadbare conundrum: How do the conditions of contemporary society impede moral maturation? I have used Plato's four-stage theory, an ancient set of ideas that has diffused unnoticed throughout Western thinking on the subject of maturity. The result of this exercise is a clearer idea, I think, of the internal contradictions of our American belief system, and the suffering that results from these contradictions.

Chapter 14 sets forth my personal philosophy of social science.

Paths of the Soul

We have spent some time viewing at close range the advent of the Nonconscious, Lawful Universe and how it transformed ideas about the role of man in the cosmos—first through the concept of maturity itself, then through concepts of the maturation process. Now it is time to step back and look again at the history of maturity from a broader angle, in search of larger organizing themes. The diversity of modern views is great, and the task is not easy; yet I think we can see some points of agreement among our contemporaries about what maturity is, and some strong historical threads leading to a handful of dominant ideas about the path of its achievement.

First, what are the common ingredients of maturity found in the rich literature of modern developmental science? I doubt the answers will surprise anyone. First, I distinguish two levels of traits frequently listed: a level of *basic values* necessary for normal healthy functioning, and a list of *superior or seldom-reached* values which serve as desiderata for courses of individual or social improvement. Among the *basic values*, the most frequently mentioned are: (1) a realistic view of oneself and the world—a minimum of fantasy, distortion (including gross rigidity), or solipsistic thinking; (2) social competence—the ability to get along reasonably well with other people, and to get one's needs met through the adequate performance of social roles; and (3) self-control—the ability to manage impulses so that they do not interfere with long term goals. These are the traits without which anyone in modern society—or perhaps any society—would be seriously maladjusted.

The list of *superior values* is larger, and the degree of agreement among scholars about it is smaller. I will not mention all the candidates for the list, which include humor, genitality, energy, and productivity, among other things. With a little trimming and stretching, I can characterize the most popular traits, held by a majority of the best-known theorists, under four headings. In order of popularity they are: (1) *altruism*—warmth, concern, responsibility, gratitude, fairness, and love; (2) *integration*—a complex idea, referring to the harmony of elements in the personality, like feelings, desires and goals, habits, beliefs, and behaviors. Integration includes honesty, self-acceptance, inner calm. It may or may not include self-knowledge or insight, but I consider it the main goal of these traits; (3) *autonomy*—self-assurance and self-respect resulting in freedom from undue dependence upon the opinions and desires of others; and (4) *ethical consistency*—having a set of principles and living by them. If we think of the personalities we have known in our lives, we will recognize that people with an abundance of these traits are rather hard to find, and that many of us are able to achieve a tolerable level of social adjustment—perhaps even "success" or popularity—with few of such qualities at our disposal.

As I said, agreement on this list is not universal, and I might add that there are striking differences among scholars in the matter of emphasis. One can discern, for example, a group of psychologists and psychiatrists, mostly with psychoanalytic backgrounds, for whom the question of integration is central; for another group, mostly social psychologists, it is unimportant or even missing as a criterion of health. The former group includes Ernest Jones, Brewster Smith, Heinz Kohut, Marie Jahoda, Abraham Maslow, Erik Erikson, Carl Jung, and Carol Gilligan. The latter group includes Jack Block, Robert White, Leon Saul, and Lawrence Kohlberg.

Other patterns that clump or divide theorists are not difficult to find, but explaining them would take a detailed study of modern thought beyond the scope of this book, which is mainly concerned with larger historical issues. Let us then return to those issues once more and ask: What are some of the persistent, deep-lying themes or assumptions beneath the modern theories about the origins of such mature traits, and how do these assumptions affect the theories? Without trying to encompass the entire field of developmental studies, I have chosen three themes that I think have distinct major consequences for the way we think about the unfolding of moral development. I call these the path of love, the path of reason, and the path of conflict.

The first two traditions are undoubtedly ancient, probably more ancient than writing itself, but each reached an expression of brilliant clarity at the hands of its Greek master—Plato for love, Aristotle for reason. These two traditions are often in harmony, but their points of difference are of critical importance. The path of conflict arose, predictably enough, from the loss of that sense of harmony between man and cosmos guaranteed by the Conscious, Lawful Universe—the loss that led to the great conflict theories of life—Malthus, Schoepenhauer, Marx, Darwin, Freud. It is as different from its predecessors as machinery is from muscle.

The Path of Love: From Plato to Gilligan

We are already familiar with the outlines of the approach to maturity I call the path of feeling. It is the path set down in Plato's *Symposium*, where the stages of maturity are reached through the extension of love to a series of objects, each of which is loftier than its predecessors. It is taken up again by Christ, whose doctrine employs love to push back the limits of aggression and free the individual from the bonds of tribal society. It is taken up again in the Middle Ages by Saint Bernard, by the Franciscans, and by Dante. In modern developmental psychology, it has found spokespersons in Charlotte Bühler and Carol Gilligan. As its name implies, the path of feeling differs from other theories of maturity in that it puts the emphasis not on intellect or on social constraint as paths to development, but on an awareness of feelings to reveal to the individual a private emotional attachment to suprapersonal values.

In our discussion of *The Symposium* we saw how Plato charted the expansion of love from self-centeredness, through erotic attachment and the competitive love of valor, to the love of absolutes. We can see this as a simultaneous widening of the sphere of altruism and of ethical autonomy if we look for the referents of the virtues that appear at each stage. In the materialist stage, obviously only self-satisfaction is sought. The individual is dependent upon those who give or withhold the means of his satisfaction, and susceptible to inner conflict and ethical inconsistency under the pressure of conflicting demands.

In the erotic stage, the referents are the self and the individual loved other. Again, altruism has expanded beyond the self, but the same contradictions and constraints that once applied to the self now apply to the dyad.

In the stage of honor, the referent is one's own society. Through war and politics, the lover of honor seeks to promote the well being of his city, now and for as long as his deeds bear fruit in history. He is now above the conflicting demands of kin and community, and immune to his earlier dependencies upon the life and comforts of the flesh. There is now harmony between his public actions and his private thoughts.

In the stage of philosophy, the lover of wisdom expands his altruistic goal to the edification of all mankind, forever. With his eyes turned toward cosmic affairs, he is no longer dependent upon the opinions of men at all; it is the integrity and consistency of his life and thought themselves that take the center of his attention.

This expansion of the frame of reference is a main point of Platonic philosophy, as can be seen dramatically in several of Plato's other works. In the allegory of the cave, the philosopher is shown liberating the average man from an appalling slavery to custom and opinion. In *The Republic*, Plato explains the importance of philosophy in enlarging human peace and prosperity. But one of the most eloquent arguments for the basis of these virtues in the cultivation of personal feeling, is *The Crito*.

In *The Crito*, Plato explains the necessity of Socrates's death. Socrates cannot renounce his philosophy out of pity for his friends, because to do so would be to choose rational utility over felt truth. To go against his feeling would trivialize his entire life, which had been a search for intuitive certainty. That that certainty transcends syllogistic logic—that it is *deonto-logical,* as opposed to *utilitarian*—is summed up in Socrates's essentially illogical defense: it is better to suffer an injustice than to commit one; it is better to behave consistently than inconsistently; it is better to hear one's inner voice than the voice of society.

There is another sense, too, in which close attention to the aim of maturity recommends the path of feeling. Every human being lives, to a great extent, in his or her desires and fears. It is our sensitivity to these that makes both self-knowledge and interpersonal empathy possible.

> Individuation of subjective contents through personal choice is the essential condition of recognition and knowledge of other individuals *qua* individuals. In his exploration of alternative possible ends of life, what identifies the ideal that is innately the person's own is the upsurge of love as aspiration to enhanced value. This love identifies that which the individual fundamentally lacks and which constitutes his fulfillment . . . . This love is eros, Plato's *tiktein en tō kalō* in its genetically original manifestation as self-love. (Norton 1976:291)

In one's developmental progress toward humanism and integration, then, the earlier stages of love are not lost, but form the basis of self-understanding and of mutual understanding among all men. This point will reemerge when we turn to the modern debate over the nature of moral maturity—the Gilligan/Kohlberg debate.

The teachings of Christ stand out as the next innovation in the path of love. He added the concepts of forgiveness—the awareness and acceptance and one's own and others' imperfections (Arendt 1958), and charity—the idea that empathy with the pain of others is itself a goal of self-understanding. It is emotional identification with the figure of Christ himself that liberates the individual from the rational self-interest of social conformity. With these improvements, the path of love has come down to us basically unchanged, but often eclipsed in ethics and psychology by the paths of reason and conflict. The Enlightenment favored these other paths, and produced the intellectualist and legalist ethics of utilitarianism that still dominate most of our modern institutions.

In the last few years the feminist movement has infused the path of love with new life, especially in the works of Carol Gilligan. This new work sensitizes us to the long-standing association between the wisdom of emotion and feminine gender, going all the way back to the Greeks. Although Plato could scarcely be called a feminist, he attributes his theory of moral development to a woman, Diotema. In the Middle Ages, the feminine side of spirituality is thoroughly explored in Dante's *Divine Comedy,* where the poet is guided toward divine grace first by his earthly beloved, Beatrice, and finally by the Virgin Mary. In the outstanding Renaissance work on the path of love, Erasmus's *Praise of Folly*, again the artful narrator is a woman—Stultitia, or Dame Folly. In the modern period, Carl Jung gives the feminine principal, the *anima*, its own set of imagery, and places it at the center of the male maturation process.

The Path of Reason: Aristotle to Early Kohlberg

Although Aristotle proposes three stages of life in the *Rhetoric* (youth, manhood, and old age), in the *Nicomacean Ethics* he treats moral life as a single stage (cf. Norton 1976:67, note). He does not appear to have had any particular quarrel with the stages set forth in *The Symposium*, however. Likewise, Aristotle followed his teacher in his division of the soul into an appetitive and a rational part. Where the two philosophers parted company was on the role of emotion and intellect in the achievement of moral maturity. Where Plato clearly saw the individual guided toward Truth by an inner emotional gyroscope, Aristotle considered that feelings were not to be trusted. In the *Nicomacean Ethics*, he carefully distinguishes between "desire," a function of the passions, and "choice," a function of the reason, and shows that virtue and friendship must be based upon the latter. He divides the rational soul into a "contemplative" part, whose function is knowledge, and a "calculative" part, whose function is virtue. He notes that both functions grow through discipline, first the discipline that is imposed by wiser guides, and then through self-discipline, guided by rational calculation.

The supreme good, for Aristotle, was more practical than spiritual. It was not a personal vision of eternal truth itself, but the "happiness," meaning inner harmony and poise, that resulted from true principles. Altruism was a matter of maximizing happiness among men through the calculated effects of rational choices. Integration, autonomy and consistency were to be achieved through both the avoidance and the intellectual suppression of strong emotion.

There you have the path of intellect. Since we can know through observation of the world what produces happiness and what impedes it, and since the function of the intellect is to sift and analyze such causal information, the intellect is the surest source of maturity. Where intellect and feeling conflict, the latter must be suppressed through self-discipline.

In our wanderings through the history of maturity we have crossed and recrossed the path of reason. Aquinas was an Aristotelian, and is credited (or blamed, depending on your point of view) with the intellectual tenor of the Enlightenment. Although this might be true, Aquinas's later turning toward mysticism also helped to build the antirationalist German romantic rebellion. At any rate, the birth of empiricist science in the seventeenth century was certainly aided by the Aristotelian tradition of attention to sense data, and the ethics spawned by empiricism were clearly also in the intellectualist tradition. Although Hobbes was certainly an empiricist, his radical deism links him most closely with the path of conflict, not Aristotelian ethics. It was the synthesis of Aristotle and Hobbes that led, by way of Locke, Kant, Bentham and Mill, to the modern concept of democracy, and its ideal personality type, the ethically autonomous man of humane good sense.

It was inevitable that science should have joined forces with Aristotelian ethics. As we discussed in chapter 9, the essential subjectivity of emotion, and the essential objectivity of science, rendered Platonic thought, and with it many of the important issues of philosophy, more or less inaccessible to scientific circles. It was not until the hopeless subjectivity of physics had become clear that a scientist of Alfred North Whitehead's stature could be heard deploring the fact that science and philosophy had parted company almost completly (Whitehead 1926).

Much of belles lettres and philosophy were caught up in the new positivist mood. Alexander Pope's 1734 treatise, *An Essay on Man*, a summary of Enlightenment ethics, paid homage to the essential Aristotelian themes: Passion and reason are contending forces in the mind of man; happiness is the highest good; happiness is achieved through self-discipline; self-discipline leads to altruism, integration (Pope did not care much for autonomy) and the improvement of society. Forty-two years later, Thomas Jefferson could speak for Americans in the *Declaration of Independence* that "it is their duty to throw off" a government that infringes upon their "inalienable rights," including "life, liberty, and the pursuit of happiness"; and to establish a system of rule "in such form as to them shall seem most likely to effect their safety and happiness." Perhaps stimulated by the moral-intellectual task to which Jefferson had set the world, thirteen years later the English ethicist Jeremy Bentham published his *Principles of Morals and Legislation*, an arithmetic for the calculation of these utilitarian values.

Here was an interesting paradox. Although happiness would seem to be, or at least involve, an emotional state, empiricism would dictate that emotions themselves should be excluded from the method of its calculation. Psychology, to the extent that it followed the natural sciences, could study altruistic behavior as objectively calculated by utilitarian models, but could approach neither the motivation that led to it, nor its subjective effects on those involved. The psychological argument that separated the Platonists and the Aristotelians could not be touched by positivst psychology. Luckily, however, all psychology is not positivist. As we saw in chapters 9 and 10, relativism has gained a respectable place in the science of the mind, and in recent years the debate between feeling and intellect has been again hotly joined.

Kohlberg as Aristotle, Gilligan as Plato

The theory that moral maturity is the result of a disciplined, adult intellect, then, is a natural legacy of positivist psychology. It is an idea that can be found in a great deal of social science, from the works of Herbert Spencer to Robert Bellah. But perhaps the most articulate spokesman of this point of view has been Lawrence Kohlberg.

Building on Swiss biologist Jean Piaget's work on cognitive development in children, Kohlberg studied the moral outlook of sixty-four boys over a period of twenty years. At his Harvard offices, Kohlberg developed in the 1960s a method for researching the way people make moral decisions. He would put to his subjects a series of moral dilemmas. From their solutions, and the justifications they gave, he could derive their "theory of morality," which he could then rate according to a hierarchical model of moral maturity that follows Piaget's stages of cognitive development:

Kohlberg's Stages of Moral Development

Preconventional Thought
At this stage, the person is self-centeredly concerned about the punishment or reward that will follow from an action.

STAGE ONE
Punishment/Obedience: Sense of justice self-centered. Avoidance of pain, deference to power. Hobbesian.

STAGE TWO
Instrumental/Relativist: Deeds valued in terms of what people think of them, or of what they will bring in reward.

Conventional Thought
At this stage, the person is somewhat altruistically concerned about what his group values. Conformity and loyalty are valued.

STAGE THREE
"Good boy/nice girl" orientation: Acts judged in terms of getting important others' approval. Conformity accepted as natural and right. Intention considered important.

STAGE FOUR
"Law and order" orientation: Acts that maintain overall order and authority are good. Duty and respect important. Most adults are at this level most of the time.

Postconventional Thought
Person makes an attempt to define moral principles for him/herself.

STAGE FIVE
"Social contract" orientation: Welfare of the majority (Utilitarianism) is the goal. Rules must be negotiated to that end. Freedom to make contracts important, freely made contracts are binding, not arbitrary rules.

STAGE SIX
"Universal/ethical" orientation: Universal, self-chosen ethical principles like logical consistency, universality, and elegance important. Individual conscience a guide to higher moral reasoning. Aristotle's Just Man.

According to Kohlberg's concept, biological development sets lower limits on the age at which each successive level of moral development *can* be reached, but does not guarantee that a new level *will* be reached when the individual is biologically ready for it. For the higher levels of moral maturity, the individual must be trained in complex analytic thinking. It is the objectivity and universality of the solution that proves its maturity, since, in his view, moral questions are "resolvable on purely logical or rational grounds" (Kohlberg 1973:202). Kohlberg found that few people achieved State Five in young adulthood unless they had attended college.

Carol Gilligan worked with Kohlberg at Harvard in the early 1970s. In a series of extensive studies spanning a decade now, she has compared the moral reasoning of men and women—something that Kohlberg did not do systematically. In her studies, Gilligan found some serious difficulties with Kohlberg's way of rating moral development. For one thing she found, not surprisingly, that women place a higher value on feelings than men do. For another thing she found that they are hesitant to make hypothetical moral judgements, because by definition they cannot be present in real social settings to look after the outcomes of such disembodied decisions. Women are more particularistic, and feel more personally involved in the human consequences of their choices. In short, her subjects felt "a responsibility to discern and alleviate the 'real and recognizable trouble' of this world" (Gilligan 1977:511), and were less interested in generalizable ethical laws. Moreover, they were guided in their moral decisions more by their own feelings of inner harmony or turmoil that resulted than by the logical consistency of the decisions themselves.

As a result of these tendencies, Gilligan's female subjects rated lower on moral development than men, according to Kohlberg's method. This did not seem right, since many of the women were handling complex moral questions in a highly intelligent and altruistic way. The theory needed to be rewritten, she concluded, so that the progressive separation of the individual from specific, real interpersonal connections was not necessarily seen as moral maturation. Respect for the abstract rights of others is good, but at least equally good is an empathic joining of others' goals.

It is an old argument, and a serious one. That it has taken many forms in many eras, we have seen from our discussion of the paths of feeling and intellect. The following poem by Wallace Stevens (1923) argues it another way:

HOMUNCULUS ET LA BELLE ÉTOILE

In the sea, Biscayne, there prinks
The young emerald, evening star,
Good light for drunkards, poets, widows,
And ladies soon to be married.

By this light the salty fishes
Arch in the sea like tree-branches,
Going in many directions
Up and down.

This light conducts
The thoughts of drunkards, the feelings
Of widows and trembling ladies,
The movements of fishes.

How pleasant an existence it is
That this emerald charms philosophers,
Until they become thoughtlessly willing
To bathe their hearts in later moonlight,

Knowing that they can bring back thought
In the night that is still to be silent,
Reflecting this thing and that,
Before they sleep!

It is better that, as scholars,
They should think hard in the dark cuffs
Of voluminous cloaks,
And shave their heads and bodies.

It might be that their mistress
Is no gaunt fugitive phantom.
She might be, after all, a wanton,
Abundantly beautiful, eager,

Fecund,

From whose being by starlight, on sea-coast,

The innermost good of their seeking

Might come in the simplest of speech.

It is a good light, then, for those

That know the ultimate Plato,

Tranquilizing with this jewel

The torments of confusion.

That Kohlberg's position is essentially Aristotelian, and Gilligan's essentially Platonic, can be shown in a number of ways. Kohlberg's model follows the Aristotelian notion that virtue begins with externally compelled practice, and moves toward internal self-discipline and logic. Both Kohlberg and Aristotle focus on the utilitarian calculation of effects, and both regard feeling as essentially in conflict with, and inferior to, rationality. Both have what Copleston (1962:89) calls an "aesthetic" sense of justice, wherein the pursuit of happiness and beauty is diametrically opposed to suffering.

Gilligan's emphasis on feeling, on the other hand, echoes Plato's notion that emotional identification with the other, grounded in self-love, is the fundament of character. Her nonrational sense of obligation, and her insistence on the union of virtue and suffering, find parallels in *The Crito*: The rational calculation of moral effects breaks down when one *loves*, whether the object of one's love is mortal or eternal. Finally, there is the fact that Plato's authority on the subject of moral development is Diotema, a woman.

The story has an important footnote, however. Although Kohlberg's most famous work was published in the 1960s, and it was this work that Gilligan addressed in her book, Kohlberg seems to have shifted in the direction of Platonism late in his career. In a 1973 paper, for example, he recognized the importance of feelings in moral development. In order to develop principled moral reasoning (Stage Five), he noticed that a child "must undergo...experiences that lead him to transform his modes of judgement" and that "often, the experiences that promote such change have a fairly strong emotional component." Apparently, he concluded, "It is...the emotion that triggers and accompanies the rethinking" (1973:193), and principled thought itself is not merely cognitive, but includes an ability to "see a basis for commitment" (195). This leads Kohlberg to contemplate the psychodynamic concept of moral development put forward by Erik Erikson, and to suggest, "Both structural [that is, Piagetian] and functional [that is, psychodynamic] stage theory hold that there is a parallel between the development of the self and orientations to the world, but cognitive and moral stages stress the world-pole, and functional stages stress the self-pole....An integrated theory of social and moral stages would attempt to combine the two perspectives" (201).

Finally, Kohlberg concludes that there might be a seventh stage of development, similar to the psychodynamic stage Erikson called "integrity." Since this stage cannot be arrived at logically, Kohlberg refuses to call it "moral," but includes it as a possible "religious" stage. In a striking passage, Kohlberg speculates on the kind of research that would explore this stage, and we see the nomothetic scientist contemplating the virtues of holistic description: "Our concept of [Stage Seven] must rest more on the psychological testimony of lives than upon structural analysis" (204).

The Path of Conflict: Hobbes to Freud

As we have seen, both the path of feeling and the path of intellect were originally based on the metaphysical assumption of an Absolute Good. For both Plato and Aristotle, the Good was the ultimate purpose of the Conscious, Transcendent Universe. Once this assumption is dispensed with, both positions lose a certain logical footing. As Bronowski has pointed out (1979), it was only an illogical fondness for moral absolutes in early industrial England that saved utilitarian democracy in that country. Utilitariansim, after all, rests upon the Aristotelian conviction that all sane men must ultimately come to similar conclusions and negotiate their desires with one another. Marxism, with its assumption of Darwinian struggle, is a much more empirically sound philosophy, closer to Hobbesian pyschology. In Hobbes's Nonconscious, Lawful Universe, views of maturity either had to be justified on grounds of discoverable natural law or excluded from scientific and philosophical debate. Hence, Hobbes's theory of the "social contract": No one really likes being altruistic; it is simply necessary for survival. "The passions that incline men to peace," Hobbes wrote, "are fear of death, desire of such things as are necessary to commodious living, and a hope by their industry to obtain them. And reason suggesteth convenient articles of peace, upon which men may be drawn to agreement. These articles are they which otherwise are called the Laws of Nature" (1948 [1651]:390).

Knowing little about primitive society, and nothing about man's evolutionary past, Hobbes was merely guessing about human life under "natural" conditions, whatever that might mean. Without our modern knowledge of natural selection, he lacked a functional theory of the way human thought and emotions work. Since he lived in a particularly chaotic time and place, generalizing from his own observation was bound to produce a pessimistic conclusion about human nature. That modern psychologists and anthropologists are on the whole less pessimistic results from a better understanding of the functions of altruistic behavior in man's actual evolution and survival.

But most of our optimism stems from the research of the last half century or so, on the ethology of living animals, on the growing fossil record, and on knowledge of modern primitive societies. The first two centuries of discoveries that led to the theory of natural selection and the modern functional view of human nature mostly seemed to confirm Hobbes's pessimistic view. We have dealt with these discoveries in more detail in chapter 10, but let us look briefly at the picture they painted of human maturity up to the time of Freud.

Darwin's view of nature was one we might call ethically pessimistic. I cannot think of a better way to describe the moral basis of a world in which the most biologically fit continuously replace the weaker in a relentless, brutal struggle for survival. This picture was suggested by the development of economics, which demonstrated the effects of competition on modern populations; and by the new science of geology, which revealed an almost endless series of extinctions stretching back to an incalculably ancient time. It was a picture that inspired pessimism not only in Darwin but in many of the great minds of his era. Schopenhauer saw the human condition as a bed of nails, fashioned of conflicting wills. For him human ethical maturity consisted of identification with one another's pain. Marx saw human history as a blind juggernaut driven by struggle for the control of wealth. Ethical beliefs were mere illusions. Altruism existed only as a form of empathy among the oppressed, or as an ideological weapon wielded by the ruling classes in the interest of oppression.

One might expect that the effect of the Nonconscious, Lawful Universe, and the path of conflict that resulted from it as a theory of maturity, would be to promote cynical self-centeredness. Says behaviorist B. F. Skinner, himself a leading proponent of the precritical outlook, "If a person can no longer take credit or be admired for what he does, then he seems to suffer a loss of dignity or worth, and behavior previously reinforced by credit or admiration will undergo extinction" (1971:202). But the change of worldview spearheaded by Hobbes has had subtler effects than the promotion of wholesale pessimism. For one thing, the path of conflict never replaced the paths of love and of reason—the one was very much alive in the romantic tradition, the other in scientific humanism. For another thing, the advance of science and industry was accompanied by a general rise in the levels of both education and opportunity in Western society, and both tendencies stimulated moral debate and introspection. Finally, there was man's relentless search for meaning in the face of despair, and our intuitive recognition of the morally superior people among us. The soul was not dead. Rather, the path of conflict produced a whole array of intricate solutions to the problem of describing and accounting for maturity. We can get a feeling for conflict theories of maturation by looking at some of the leading conflict theorists starting with Freud.

Freud and his ideas are so ingrained in our culture I think I can be brief and informal in describing his basic concept of maturation. The problem of maturation is set by the biological nature of man, which is basically selfish and inclined toward pleasure. Such a creature must somehow live in a society which demands a good deal of the opposite kinds of behavior—altruism and self-sacrifice—and therein lies the tragic conflict of human life. This conflict is managed first in the developing child by the superego, a psychic structure that develops through the repetitive frustration of instinctive drives, and the child's internalization, through identification, of the sources of the frustration—principally parents. The superego then "stands in" for the parent, and punishes the instinctive wish before it is expressed. As the healthy individual matures, however, the function of buffering between social demands and instinctive urges is gradually taken over by the ego. With respect to the external world, the ego interprets and regulates stimuli so that their demands on the individual are manageable; with respect to the internal world, it evaluates the social implications of impulses and permits, delays, or suppresses them accordingly.

In keeping with biological functionalism, then, the mature person is one who is able to do this effectively so that he both gets what he wants and satisfies social demands for performance. Such a person is reasonably happy, energetic, warm, and socially well-adjusted. Few people actually attain this balance of conflicting forces, however, and hence Freud's view quoted earlier, that the majority of us suffer from a mild form of slavery to our baser passions, or to unrealistic expectations of ourselves—in other words, we are victims of the "collective neurosis," if we are lucky enough to be sane at all. The path from this state of normal impairment toward ideal maturity lies through self-understanding, a process in which the repressed traces of denied instincts, and the circumstances of their denial, are brought to light. By facing these old conflicts and making them part of our conscious selves, we rob them of their power to confuse us and deflect our energies from mature projects.

Conflict Theory After Freud

In this model, we see the values of self-knowledge and autonomy, whose importance is recognized in most ancient and modern models of maturity, but it is difficult to find traces of true altruism or ethical commitment in the Freudian formula. These latter values, it seems, could result only from compromises among the conflicting wills of basically egocentric individuals. But the deep structure of our beliefs about maturity could not long tolerate such an oversight. As Freud's sympathetic biographer Reiff says, "Freud never understood the ethics of self-sacrifice. The omission leaves his human doctrine a little cold, and capable of the most sinister applications" (1959:55-56; quoted in Haan 1977:78). Attempts among Freud's followers to repair the flaw began rather early, as can be seen from a lecture that Ernest Jones gave to the British Psychoanalytic Society in 1936 on the criteria of success in treatment. Jones made two essential points in favor of classical views of maturity. First, he noted that while the self-centered neurotic might be capable of great energy, his energy is of a recognizably different quality than that of the fully mature person. In the latter, energy "radiates through the whole personality in a harmonious fashion" (Jones 1948:380), presumably with equal ease whether the task faced by such a healthy person is an altruistic one or a self-centered one.

Second, Jones distinguished between the infantile, punishing conscience of the superego, and what he called the "conscious ego-conscience." The latter "is a compound of love for an ideal and self-condemnation when that ideal is departed from" (212) and grows out of the superego through "infusions of love" once the superego has lost its hostile character (presumably through analysis) (214).

In classic psychoanalytic theory, there would be no need to propose a teleological progression toward an ideal mature state here. Jones's "infusions of love" would result from the projection of an idealized self onto an alter ego or an idea, which is then loved narcissistically. However, there are two images in the Jones formulation that bear a haunting resemblance to the teleological romantic image of an innate *daemon* or "authentic self"— the image of the personality as a harmonious, resonant whole, and the image of a loved ideal, toward which one strives with one's whole being. And although the language is very different from that of either Kohlberg or Gilligan, the actual distinction in views has begun to blur.

These images of altruism, integrity, and autonomous ethical commitment appear again and again within the path-of-conflict tradition, and I shall deal with three distinct expressions of them: the "identity dynamics" of Erik Erikson, the "self psychology" of Heinz Kohut, and the "self-actualization" of Abraham Maslow.

Erikson

Erik H. Erikson was exposed to psychoanalytic theory in 1927, when he went from his native Karlsruhe to teach at Anna Freud's Burlingham School in Vienna. He was then twenty-five. In 1933 he moved to the United States, where he worked at Harvard, Yale, and the University of California before publishing *Childhood and Society* in 1950. As the title of this now-famous treatise on personality development implies, Erikson was interested in the ways in which social norms interact with biological drives to produce the characteristic strengths and weaknesses of individuals. He constructed from his clinical experience and naturalistic observations of child behavior a set of eight developmental stages, triggered by biologically determined life events. Each event brought a change in the growing person's characteristic mode of relating to his or her environment, and therefore raised new disturbances in the delicate equilibrium between drives and social adjustment. Each disturbance might be mastered through the development of new skills and attitudes, or it might not. In the latter case, certain important aspects of character development would be arrested at the crucial stage, and adequate solutions to later developmental problems would not materialize. The stages (and their biosocial "triggers") are as follows: (1) trust versus mistrust (oral stage); (2) autonomy versus shame and doubt (bowel and bladder control); (3) initiative versus guilt (locomotion); (4) industry versus inferiority (latency); (5) identity versus role confusion (puberty); (6) intimacy versus isolation (full physical maturity); (7) generativity versus stagnation (social maturity); and (8) integrity versus despair (physical decline).

Aside from his wonderfully lucid writing style, Erikson was a seminal thinker for several reasons. Although his causal theory was, like Freud's, fundamentally biological and, as such, a true product of Enlightenment empiricism, he paid closer attention than had classical psychoanalysts to the fact that developmental events take place within a set of cultural and familial traditions, and the style of personality that emerges from them is heavily influenced by those traditions. Erikson also perceived the severe threat to mental health posed by the weakening of such collective habits and beliefs. Second, he extended the theoretically "formative" period of personality from early childhood where it had been corraled by the Freudians, into late maturity; his theory therefore found ready use in the study of normal adult character, an interest that was rapidly growing in popularity at the time. His view of character was thus more plastic and more *culturally relativistic* than his predecessors', in the sense that he saw maturation as a lifelong dialectical process involving the biological person and the environment. As a result, Eriksonian theory could be applied to the study of individual and cultural differences with greater ease and assurance than could classical psychoanalysis. In this, he showed connections to the "new biologism" discussed in chapter 10.

Moreover, Erikson's view was fundamentally optimistic about human nature. He thought of man as a deeply social being, in whom altruistic values lie close, at least, to biological needs. This view was, as we have seen, more in keeping with the classical paths of love and reason as a tool for understanding maturity. For example, he placed the concept of the *self* at the center of his analysis. The need for a coherent, consistent self-concept, which could only be fulfilled in a coherent and supportive social milieu, was for him fundamental. In this sense, Erikson represented a step away from the crude determinism of early psychoanalysis. The concept of self-consciousness, which, as I mentioned earlier, was developed first by the social psychologists James and Dewey, views man as essentially purposeful in a conscious way—as essentially *proactive*. Such fundamental characteristics of a theory are of immense significance when it comes to their application in self-understanding and therapy. Erikson subtly restored an important element of the classical views of maturity.

Kohut

If Erikson represents a compromise between the pure conflict model of Freud and the proactive teleology of nonpositivist maturation models, Heinz Kohut represents another major step along this path. Kohut was born in Vienna in 1913 and received his medical degree from the University of Vienna in 1938. He joined the faculty of the Department of Psychiatry at the University of Chicago in 1947, where he continued to teach until his death in 1981.

As a psychotherapist with a psychoanalytic background, Kohut had been sensitive to the psychological currents which had torn his native Austria during his youthful years—the terrible years of the Nazi ascent and the war. He became a keen student of history and of the relationship of character to cultural milieu. As such, he studied the transformations of character that accompanied Nazism—not only the mass abdication of responsibility, not only the banal reaction to evil, but also the heroic self-transformations of the resistors. As a result of these studies, Kohut was impressed by two aspects of personality development that had not been studied in detail by his predecessors. These were: (1) narcissism—the individual's tremendous sensitivity to any limits placed upon his drive to experience personal power and ethical perfection; and (2) the central importance of a matrix of empathic relationships between the individual and others in his close social milieu. It was the breakdown of this matrix throughout German society, he felt, that led to the mass neurosis of the Hitler years. On the basis of these observations he developed his "self psychology."

Kohut found in healthy as well as neurotic people "a yearning that does not relate to the attainment of pleasurable discharge of drive-wishes, but to the compelling urge to realize the deep-rooted design of the nuclear self" (1985:49). He concluded that this nuclear self is of very early origin, and not a derivative of the drives, but rather the opposite—drives are "secondary phenomena," "disintegration products following the breakup" of the early feelings of power and perfection attending the infantile sense of self (1985:74). They result from failures of empathy, failures of the developing individual and his close others to accurately recognize and respond supportively to one another's mental and emotional states. A brief summary, then, of Kohut's developmental scheme is as follows:

The individual is born with a complex, primary "self"—a cognitive-affective structure experienced as powerful and perfect and sustained by a "matrix of empathic selfobjects." As he learns to distinguish between his own person and others, this primary self gives way to a "grandiose self," made up of the individual's central ambitions and self-assertions, and an "idealized parent imago," made up of his central values, projected on the parent and then reintrojected in the form of an image of perfection. This in turn gives rise to an autonomous structure at all levels of personality functioning, called the "nuclear self": "that unconscious, preconscious, and conscious sector of the id, ego, and superego which contains not only the individual's most enduring values and ideals, but also his most deeply anchored goals, purposes, and ambitions" (1985:10-11). This structure is itself a central motive in all the individual's major decisions, and functions independently of his other needs and drives. In mature people, "wisdom" is finally reached in middle life, when the individual learns to accept his own finitude, and transfers his feelings of power and perfection to "a suprapersonal and timeless existence," in which he is an ardent participant (1985:119).

By locating basic values and ideals in the self, and making the mental structure of the self independent of the body both in origin and in operation, it would seem that Kohut in effect restores the higher functions of spiritual life to the position of philosophic supremacy they held prior to the Hobbesian revolution; but this is not quite true. The quality of spiritual life, according to Kohut, is regulated by the empathic relationships among all members of a society. Individual development is an intricate dialectic between the continuously changing self of the individual and his empathic relations with others. The sum total of these relationships make up "culture." "A healthy self... is continuously sustained... by ongoing psychological work that provides the cohesion and vigor of its changing yet continuous structure within a matrix of selfobjects who are in empathic contact with its changing needs. The sum total of the results of this work... we call 'culture'" (1985:84). Causality in maturation is thereby removed from the brutish forces of nature where Hobbes had consigned it, but it is not restored to the status of an immanent *telos*. Rather, causality is handed over to the elusive and impossibly complex whims of history. In this sense it is representative of the dialectical relativism of the mid-1900s—the new environmentalism. Kohut was a pioneer on the track opened by other socially conscious analysts like Erikson, freeing the self from biological determinism and relativising the concept of maturity. But as a pioneer on the path of conflict, he seems to have begun his quest with an unquestioned (and perhaps largely legitimate) belief that in the interpretation of behavior, the struggle for survival is the appropriate basic motif. Ethical values accordingly serve individual goals. He saw the "empathic matrix" of society as a byproduct of the biological dependency of the child, therefore always susceptible to suppression, distortion, and failure.

Conflict-Free Biology? Maslow

In Gilligan and Kohlberg, in Jones, Erikson, and Kohut we see examples, I believe, of an old, central, and continuous philosophic effort in Western developmental psychology—an effort to reconcile the techniques and assumptions of Darwinian functionalism with the more ancient and deeper assumptions of innate ethical values. In chapter 10 we discussed similar contributions to this effort, contributions from Kurt Goldstein, Heinz Hartmann, Marie Jahoda, and Brewster Smith. Of course other names are also important—Alfred Adler, Pitirim Sorokin, Kurt Lewin, Ashley Montagu, Erich Fromm, Carl Rogers...So far, though, all our examples have come at this magnificent problem with clear scientific convictions, in search of compatible ethical applications. We need to round out our discussion of this theme with a different kind of example— someone who, although already highly regarded as a scientist, began his quest with greater clarity on the ethical side, and sought openly to bring science into harmony with belief.

Abraham Maslow's entire approach to psychology resulted from an effort to develop a scientific ethics. As Scroggs says, "The clue to Maslow's personality theory—the concept that deserves to be called his *key idea*, is his conviction that a scientifically verifiable code of ethics could be derived from a psychological study of the essence of human nature" (1985:273). This was a passion and a belief, by the way, that Maslow shared with his senior colleague, friend, and ethnic kinsman, Pitirim Sorokin.

Maslow was born the son of poor Russian immigrants in New York in 1908, the only Jewish child in a tough neighborhood. Through the experience of frightful ethnic discrimination, Maslow seems to have become a highly autonomous person. He rebelled against his parents' choice of profession (law), defied them by moving to Wisconsin and marrying his childhood sweetheart while still an undergraduate, and then rejected the teachers he had greatly admired earlier, behaviorists Watson and Harlow (Scroggs 1985). He must have come to see his own life as a process of continuous revolution, directed from within, against powerful life experiences. The key experience of his professional life was a decision made quite consciously and deliberately as the result of a personal ethical crisis precipitated by a historic event: the bombing of Pearl Harbor by the Japanese in December 1941. Maslow decided he would devote his entire professional energy and intelligence to the promotion of world peace.

Trained as a behaviorist, Maslow set out to use scientifically impeccable techniques to prove that altruism, creativity, and autonomy are innate biological drives, and that they unfold naturally when conditions are favorable. Through a combination of experimental research and detailed observations of highly moral individuals (the latter a technique his friend Sorokin also used), Maslow developed a stage theory of maturation based on four basic needs over and above sheer physical survival: (1) security, (2) love, (3) self-esteem, and (4) self-actualization. In his view, the satisfaction of each need led to the arousal of the next one, so he referred to the whole group of needs as a *hierarchy*.

In the Enlightenment tradition of Locke and Rousseau, then, Maslow saw human nature as basically good. The presence of evil in human affairs is to be accounted for by the frustration of the basic needs of one individual or group by the selfish actions of another, an injustice that grows out of our ignorance of our own basic nature.

The conclusions of Maslow's research are not so different, then, from those of Erikson, Kohut, and other path-of-conflict theorists. His contribution to the theory of maturity shares with theirs the conviction that ethical idealism expresses a fundamental need of every human being, that this need typically faces many obstacles to fulfillment because of human ignorance and injustice, and that it therefore can be fulfilled only in a social climate of unusual empathy and love. Like Erikson's epigenetic development of integrity, the Maslovian hierarchy is also a biologically functionalist, unilinear stage theory. Like Kohut, who studied the key experience of the "nuclear self," Maslow was deeply interested in the personal experience of ethical certainty—what he called the "peak experience." And if the final product of each of these developmental theorists is compared in its broad outlines with the models of maturity proposed by Plato and Aristotle, the comparison shows a surprising correspondence in all but the mechanism: natural law versus innate wisdom.

Nor is Maslow unique in his vision of the purpose of psychology itself. In making his science the servant of ethical insight, he is in agreement with the words of John Dewey that "psychology is the method of philosophy."

What lessons can we draw, then, from the repeated reemergence of familiar ethical principles, whether one is drawn by the naturalist's curiosity or driven by the philosopher's intuition; and whether one follows the path of love, or reason, or conflict? To answer the question, perhaps we have to ask another one: Why do these principles seem to make so little difference in our everyday lives?

The answer, I think, lies in the fact which Ortega y Gasset (1960) calls, "the strange adventure that befalls truths"; namely, that while truths themselves are always true, their truth *for someone* depends on that someone's perception of their relevance to his culture-bound and history-bound experience. In the next three chapters, let us look at how these dual constraints of culture and history affect our access to supracultural and supratemporal truths, and what we can do about it.

12. *History and the Interpersonal: Altruism and Aggression*

The Problem: Culture, History, and Maturity

Maturity, to the extent that it refers to behavior and not to mere physical development, is a social concept. It is a way of classifying acts and attitudes that involve others. As societies change, their historically derived systems of meaning, including ideas such as maturity, often fail to keep pace with the life experiences of their members. Here let us illustrate this with an example of the way in which industrialization has produced confusion in our attempts to manage interpersonal relations. At this point, we must change our focus. Until now, we have been looking at ideas of maturity from the vantage point of modern psychology. We have been standing *inside* the present, looking out. Now we must step outside of psychology altogether in order to see it in relation to our lives. As a task that gathers within its limits nearly all of social science in one way or another, this is much too large for an encyclopedic treatment, and we must be content with an illustration. I can think of no better illustration than the management of altruism and aggression.

The very words altruism and aggression are loaded with emotion, with value judgement. Our earliest memories are likely to be tinged with feelings of pride for having made others happy, or having protected our interests (or those of someone close to us) aggressively from some injustice. Among these positive feelings are also pangs of shame or guilt for having failed to be friendly or competitive at the right moment. These are social feelings. It is impossible to imagine having them in the absence of personal relationships; it is equally impossible to imagine such relationships without altruism or aggression. The terms describe the basic emotional polarity of social involvement—their absence signifies indifference.

Maturity implies the ability to recognize and execute the socially proper degree of these traits, in the proper way, at the proper time. We can scarcely understand any group's concept of maturity without understanding what it implies about the quality of personal relationships. In this chapter, then, we shall try to expand our understanding of the cultural embeddedness of maturity by looking closely at its ties to altruism and aggression. We shall examine the biological and psychological roots of interpersonal feelings, the ways in which they are handled in various societies and eras, and some moral theories about them. We shall look at altruism and aggression in modern American concepts of maturity, and at how the structure of our lives has led us to these concepts.

Bases of Altruism and Aggression: Biology and Society

The place of aggression and altruism in the basic nature of man is a topic that has fascinated us since the beginnings of philosophy. Hobbes's view of primitive man's "nasty, meane, poor, brutish, and short" life was countered a century later by Rousseau's "noble savage," a concept that fell in turn to the Darwinian picture of a universal struggle for survival. Between 1890 and 1896, the great Russian anarchist philosopher Prince Petr Kropotkin wrote eight essays seeking to prove that mutual support among animals is an equal principal in nature to aggression (Montagu 1950), and in our own time we have the Hobbesian champion Robert Ardrey (*The Territorial Imperative*) and his antagonist Ashley Montagu. So engaging has the battle been that whole scientific societies are devoted to it. A recent bibliography on aggressive behavior (Crabtree and Moyer 1977) lists 3,856 publications on the subject. Obviously we are not going to settle the question here, but we can at least do a little ground clearing.

In trying to write about altruism and aggression in a clear and comprehensible way, I am necessarily faced with a problem that both proves my point (that these are social concepts) and increases my labor: Without a specific social situation as a starting point, it is very difficult to define the terms themselves. Supposing, for example, I say: By "altruism" I mean any behavior by a human being that is intended to benefit other human beings, whether that aim is the ultimate purpose of the behavior, or merely a means to some other purpose. Already you can see a difficulty. What is meant by "benefit?" Who determines "intent?" The same sorts of problems are evident if I say: By "aggression" I mean any behavior in which a human being either (1) seeks his own or his group's advantage with the awareness that his behavior will, or might, deprive other human beings of some satisfaction or benefit they might otherwise have (I call this "competitiveness"); or (2) seeks to inflict suffering in order to gratify his own or his group's desire for power or revenge. Again, it is up to the group to define "awareness," "satisfaction," and so on. Still, we must have some definitions, and we will use those I have just given, with the added clause: as these acts are defined by the rules of the society in which they take place.

For millions of years, man and his ancestors have lived in social groups. With the single exception of the orangutan, there is no such thing as a solitary primate. All social life requires at least sporadic cooperation, as in defense against enemies, mating, and the raising of young. All social life requires competition, as in mate selection, territorial defense, and the struggle for scarce resources. In large-brained mammals, such behaviors are learned, and they are complex. Man shares many aspects of group behavior, such as hierarchical social organization and territoriality, with monkeys and apes, but he also differs from these primate relatives.

For one thing, man is a systematic carnivore, and meat-eating means sharing food. Monkeys and apes will share food only when they are satiated, but wolves, tigers, and humans will feed one another (within strict limits) even when there is not enough to go around. For another thing, infant humans take an unusually long time to reach a self-sufficient state of development, especially in a harsh, primitive environment, and they must be looked after for many years or they will not survive. Man has language, which means a much more complex set of relationships in social groups than is possible for "dumb" animals. Man's survival is based on the mastery of skills that are learned through repetitive close observation and imitation. The hunting of large game, which probably occupied man and his direct ancestors for a few million years, is based on closely coordinated group effort, and on the use of large territories, which must be protected from competing groups.

Already one can see the dilemma posed by human social nature. All these features of the human style of adaptation, and other features as well, mean that humans must master complex behavior of both altruistic and aggressive varieties in order to survive. First, we must be biologically equipped to handle this complexity, which means not only intellectual skills, but emotional ones as well.

> Another important characteristic separating man from the nonhuman primates is his relatively greater control of his emotions—rage in particular. Dr. Jane Goodall's excellent data on chimpanzees show, for example, that big male chimpanzees frequently go into

uncontrollable rages, and the same is true of monkeys. A group of apes or monkeys could not sit around for an hour or so listening to someone talk. One would surely get mad at another, and the group would shortly be in chaos. (Washburn 1971:29)

Second, society must channel emotion so that it appears when needed. While some forms of aggression are valued in all human societies, with a few exceptions (noted in chapter 2), all societies also place a high value on adult personalities that are, in balance, altruistic. The problem, for the society and for the individual, becomes how to regulate emotions associated with aggression, and how to link altruistic behavior with feelings of satisfaction, so that group life can proceed smoothly.

Discussions of the social control of aggression have, like biological theories, occupied some of the best minds of anthropology for many decades. Without trying to summarize the whole topic, I can offer an illustration of it that applies to a great deal of human social life, and that makes some of the key problems clearer.

The paradoxical social need for altruism and aggression leads to a system of rules for allocating these behaviors to specific situations. One such system of rules is called by anthropologists "segmentary opposition." Segmentary opposition regulates competitive activity in many societies, but it was best described by the British anthropologist E. E. Evans-Pritchard in his study of the Nuer of East Africa in the 1930s (Evans-Pritchard 1940). He found that the Nuer organized themselves according to an elaborate system of territorial segments for the control of grazing rights. In the frequent conflicts over territory, the segment system determined who would side with whom.

> Each segment is itself segmented, and there is opposition between its parts. The members of any segment unite for war against adjacent segments of the same order, and unite with these adjacent segments against larger sections. Nuer themselves state this structural principle clearly in the expression of their political values. They say that if the Leng tertiary section of the Lou tribe fights the Nyarkwac tertiary section—and in fact there has been a long feud between them—the villages which compose each section will combine to fight; but if there is a quarrel between the Nyarkwac tertiary section and the Rumjok secondary section . . . Leng and Nyarkwac will unite against their common enemy Rumjok. (Evans-Pritchard 1940:142-143)

That this principle also operates in urban industrial societies like our own, there is no doubt. When I was doing field work among Americans of Japanese descent, I found that the Japanese-American Democrats and Republicans would work together to campaign for a mayor from their own ethnic group, but would bitterly oppose each other over every other name on the ballot. Likewise you might have a running feud with your Uncle George, but you will find yourself defending him against criticism from your brother-in-law. A good interplanetary invasion, while it lasted, would certainly bring an end to international strife.

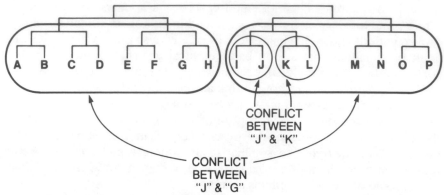

Figure 1: Segmentary Opposition

I use the example of segmentary opposition because it illustrates well the susceptibility of altruism and aggression to social rules. A Nuer who refused to fight *anybody* would be as much a misfit as one who refused to cooperate with anybody; but whom to love and hate, and when, is a matter ideally regulated by cultural fiat first, and personal feeling only in the observance. Maturity, then, means the ability to carry out the cultural directives effectively and with equanimity, the hoped-for result being the good of society. This is the human social definition of altruism.

"Maturity" as Social Control

Given man's competitive-aggressive tendencies, then, a major effort must be made in any successful social system to enforce the peace and reward altruism. We have seen how the Nuer lineage system functions to keep competition within limits; now we turn to the idea of maturity itself, as a social tool for the management of aggression.

Few societies without agriculture or industry are able to produce or store much of an economic surplus, and this was probably true, as I said earlier, for all of our distant ancestors. Most such simple societies lack major social class differences, and strive to limit competition to the acquisition of power and prestige through nonmaterial means, or through the exchange of what limited goods are left over when survival needs are met, or through acts of aggression on "outsiders," however that category is defined. In most such societies, competitiveness may be cultivated, but it is limited to well-defined rituals—marriage negotiations, warfare, games, orgiastic rites—in which the value of altruism is greatly modified or excluded. In some such societies aggressive competitiveness is considered more desirable in some developmental stages and sex roles than others (see Burton and Kirk 1979). Postpubertal male "warriors," middle-aged female traders, and shamans and sorcerers of both sexes are common examples.

In such cases, people in these stages are often considered *predominantly* aggressive, and are subject to powerful external controls, supernatural or otherwise. Extraordinary success at competitive activities tends to be regarded as a mark of supernatural power, and can be dangerous to its possessor. The successful individual risks accusations of misusing his magical powers via witchcraft. He risks incurring the envy of someone whose power is even greater than his own. Given such dangers of competitive roles, transitions to and from these roles are carefully marked by ritual.

In simple societies, the developmental problems surrounding aggressiveness are: (1) to confine aggressive impulses to the rituals and stages prescribed; and (2) to muster sufficient aggressiveness to perform well in those stages and rituals. As I mentioned in chapter 2, those who fail in the former sense are likely to be considered vehicles of supernatural malevolence (for example, witches) and those who fail in the second sense, to be victims of such malevolence (spirit possession, soul loss, witchcraft, etc.). Failures of both types may be designated to special social roles, including roles as healers of the developmental disorders of others.

Remember that time in primitive societies is seen as cyclical, so that each life repeats the culturally given pattern (sometimes literally, through the reincarnation of direct ancestors). At any rate, it is expected that the individual knows by intimate observation just what is demanded of him at each life stage, and that his failure to conform is due neither to ignorance nor to incompetence, but rather to external forces or deliberate malevolence. The deviant person tends to be seen either as completely innocent or as a dangerous malcreant who must be destroyed. Idiosyncrasy is common and expected. But where rules of altruism and aggression are concerned, it needs to be minimized.

As we have seen, the development of literacy, city life and trade changed this primitive situation in several important ways. The accumulation of wealth and knowledge that led to social class differences, slavery, and the Conscious, Transcendent Universe greatly enlarged the scale of heroic competition, and led to new forms of aggression and new social attitudes about it. But for the ordinary person, altruism was still the dominant theme of maturity, and competitive aggression was still confined either to restricted occupational groups like those of the warrior or scholar (the latter conceived as a verbal warrior), or to restricted activities like games and trade fairs.

This can be seen in the exclusion of trade *in the sense of competitive activity* from the legitimate status system in many ancient and medieval societies (Polanyi 1962). We saw that merchants were excluded from citizenship in the Greek polis, and that commercial competition was practically illegal in the Middle Ages, economic bargaining having been largely confined to markets and fairs—ritual settings marked off from normal life by boundaries of time and place—these settings having been characterized as places of license and evil. It is instructive that John Bunyan chose the image of a fair—Vanity Fair—to depict the city of the devil in his seventeenth-century moral parable, *Pilgrim's Progress*. In a moment we shall discuss how the industrial revolution changed this attitude.

Maturation, then, in the premodern world was a process of mastering a succession of traditional social roles, each with its own expectations about altruism and aggression. In nearly all societies, the truly mature person was rarely aggressive, and when he or she was, it was a prescribed form of aggression, directed at a prescribed target, and limited to prescribed settings and times. But as most accounts of preindustrial societies show, this ideal was rarely achieved in practice. On the whole, gossip, ridicule, and outright physical aggression are so characteristic of people everywhere that the defense of altruism has been a major task of philosophy from the beginning. As Hobbes wrote, "Men have no pleasure, but on the contrary a great deal of grief in keeping company where there is no power to overawe them all. For every man looketh that his companion should value him at the same rate that he sets upon himself" (1651:388). In chapter 11 I reviewed that philosophical quest. But now, let us inquire how modern life has transformed the social patterning of altruism and aggression.

Modern Times: The Decline of Ritual

In chapter 6 we saw the beginnings of the relationship between a new view of the universe—the Hobbesian machine—and a new way of life—capitalism. The fact that capitalism required heavy devotion to the calculation of practical outcomes, together with the Enlightenment idea that the mind was not a microcosm of the conscious universe, but a mechanical device for the rational calculation of such outcomes, put a premium on the cultivation of a rational state of mind. In the manner of Aristotle and Aquinas, passion and reason came to be seen in the new mercantile culture as fundamental enemies of one another. The ritual sentiments of awe and inspiration lost ground to the noetic dominion of law and learnedness. The stark puritan church with its sober flock, and the stark puritan schoolroom with its sober student body, became increasingly the symbols of middle-class respectability.

At the same time, the concept of an internally ordered individual began to replace premodern forms of social order. The church had contributed much to the making of the self-controlled citizen, through the ritual of confession (Foucault 1978). Paradoxically, the decline of the church from the fifteenth century on had already given new force to the ordering principles of personal power and military might. Trade agreements, contracts and treaties began to replace age-old rituals of exchange (Polanyi 1962). As ritual was replaced by rational regulation, trade expanded from the market fair into society. As industrialization shook populations loose from their lands, open competition between mutually anonymous individuals became increasingly a way of life. The ritual containment of competition began to disappear.

The implications of this change for personal development were staggering. The temptation to dissemble, lie, and cheat reached such epidemic proportions that the Enlightenment was, like Moliere's *Misanthrope*, preoccupied with the concept of sincerity (Trilling 1971). In such a climate the savageness of nature preached by Hobbes, Malthus and Darwin brought order not only to our view of the cosmos, but to our intuition of modern human society as well.

In the seventeenth and eighteenth centuries, the pace of this change was relatively slow. The society of that era was still predominantly rural, and the bourgeoisie a minority, albeit a boisterous and noisy one. But in the late nineteenth century, something new emerged, especially in America. The pace of social change, the mobility and consequent cultural diversity of populations, the centralization of essential services and restraining institutions, reached such proportions that for the urban middle class the intimate level of society we usually mean by the term "community" had largely disappeared. The best educated, the people by whom and for whom modern cities were invented and have always functioned, ceased to be primarily members of local face-to-face societies, and became instead the products of nationally planned and regulated cultures (cf. Spengler 1928; Redfield and Singer 1954). Since the rituals that were wont to regulate life depended upon the shared emotional experience of like-minded people who live together in communities, this meant the coup de grace of the ritual regulation of competition. It is interesting that even war ceased to be a ritual at the same time. The mechanized wars, from the American Civil War on, were not rituals at all for most of the men involved, since they relied more upon technology than upon human strength or motivation (Smoke 1984).

A correlate of the decline of ritual is the decline of mutual obligation as a principle in regulating social relations. In traditional societies, open competition can be confined because the exchange of goods and services usually takes place between pairs of individuals or among groups whose long-standing relationship is governed by well-known custom. The very word "customer" reflects this relationship. In India, for example, a system of exchange called *jajmani*, based on occupational status ascribed by birth, links customers and providers—and their families—in a controlled series of exchanges that transcends individual lives and fortunes. In Japan, families still keep custom with neighborhood merchants, a practice recognized and reinforced by the exchange of gifts between merchant and customer on feast days.

This difference between traditional and Western (especially American) society has been well analyzed by Norwegian anthropologist Frederik Barth (1972). In most traditional societies, there are many socially recognized performances, or *roles*, whose performance regulates social life. People have a very clear idea what it means to be a tradesman of a certain type, a servant, a teacher, a student, a suitor, a grandmother, and so on. The amount of individuality in the performance of these roles is limited. At the same time, every individual has a large repertoire of roles through which he enacts the full scope of his social personhood. He plays many parts, shifting behaviors (and even beliefs and values) as he shifts parts.

Under such circumstances individuals are usually paired off as role partners, and competition is limited simply because one is not free to change partners or revise the rules. In Western societies, by contrast, such clearly defined roles are much less important. People are relatively free, not only to choose with whom they interact, but to make up the rules as they go along. This kind of behavior is well studied by the symbolic interaction school of American sociology, under such rubrics as "defining the situation" (Thomas 1931), and "presenting the self" (Goffman 1959).

Modern Times: Achievement

Chapter six discussed how upward mobility led to the supression of sexuality and the cult of success. We are now ready to look more closely at the effects of these changes upon altruism and aggression.

First, let us recall the shift from heroism to success, and from dependence upon God and family to moral autonomy. The young male achiever learns early in life that he is in competition with his father and his brothers, and is rewarded for successful aggression even toward them. Such themes are prevalent in fin de siecle literature, from D. H. Lawrence's *Sons and Lovers* to Freud's *Totem and Taboo*. The ritual nature of this competition is to some extent preserved through the institution of school sports, but the young achiever is made to understand that this is mere practice for the real thing, and the real thing is economic achievement, expressed for the time being as schoolwork.

At the same time, the young achiever learns altruism. One is loyal to one's family in dealings with other families; to one's team in contests with other teams, and so on. The principle is that of segmentary opposition. Competitive situations, moreover, are regulated by the principle of equality. No one has the right to limit the other's competitive striving, except by dint of superior ability. Ethnographers of American culture from de Toqueville to Margaret Mead to Robert Bellah and colleagues have noted the tempering effects on American competitive individualism of both Christian and democratic notions of brotherhood (cf. Bellah et al. 1985:28-35).

As he enters adolescence and then adulthood, the settings for competitive striving and altruism change, and the rules become more complex. Dating is a competitive battle of all against all. Work is a complex maze of loyalties and rivalries. Leisure use and consumership are opportunities for competitive self-expression. Because of the decline in ritual and the weakening of role regulation mentioned earlier, every moment of every day the achiever is called upon to decide between altruistic and aggressive values, dictated by the momentary situation. He finds himself confronted with a set of contrasting values that force an endless series of choices on the basis of ongoing circumstances.

In order to clarify the effects of this, I shall contrast Japan, a relatively traditional society with which I am familiar, with the United States.

Japan is now changing rapidly, but when I was there twenty years ago competitive achievement was more limited and ritualized than in America. In career development, for example, every middle-class male faced a series of key rituals in his life, during which the doors of opportunity opened momentarily and then slammed shut again, more or less permanently. Among these rituals were the school entrance examinations. In order to get a good job, a man had to graduate from a good college; which in turn depended on a good college entrance examination; which in turn depended on attending a good high school, and so on. This system resulted in a brutal all-or-nothing drive to pass the examinations that involved the aspirant's whole family and often began in kindergarten. The Japanese called it *shiken jigoku*, "exam hell." Male suicide rates peak in the late teens in Japan.

Meanwhile, open competition for grades was minimized both before and after college entrance; once in a good job, the achiever found competition with workmates similarly kept to a minimum. Progress up the bureaucratic ladder was made in a series of leaps; the victors or the vanquished, or both, were often transferred out of their old work group to keep things easy. Contrast this with the American school, in which students compete openly for approval, and with the American job market and promotion process, where aspirants are frequently pitted against each other with a minimum of rules.

Similarly, in Japanese mate selection, dating is a new phenomenon. Previously the families of a prospective couple engaged in an elaborate and indirect ritual of fact-finding, culminating in a formal *miai*, or viewing of one another by the couple. At this crucial moment, the couple might exercise free choice, and the formality of the ritual assured that the match could be abandoned without loss of face on either side. But to break the process at any other point was extremely difficult. Contrast this with the

American dating game, in which young men and women make and break emotionally charged bonds in an open competitive market. The famous neurotic quality of American adolescence is related to the frequency and severity of risks people must take in the mate selection process.

The comparison of cultures serves to underline the theme of this chapter—that every society must find a way to regulate altruism and aggression, and that every society develops its own solution. We can see quite graphically how the problem of mature behavior differs in these two cultures if we look at the ways in which altruism and aggression are expressed in comparable situations, and where those situations typically occur in the life cycle. For simplicity, let us concentrate upon three kinds of social situations; *hierarchical, egalitarian* and *self-directed*.

In *hierarchical* situations, altruism is expressed in the values of *nurturance* on the part of the superior and *compliance* on the part of the subordinate. The corresponding aggressive values are *control* and *autonomy*. In *egalitarian* relationships, the altruistic values of *cooperation* and *responsibility* are balanced by the aggressive ones of *competition* and *free choice*. Vis-a-vis *the self*, altruism is often expressed through *self-denial*, where aggression permits disinhibition and *self-expression*.

In a traditional society like Japan, most social life is regulated by ascribed social roles, whose performance rules are largely altruistic. Aggressiveness is permitted during ritual "openings" in the social organization, such as the rituals of examination and *miai* I mentioned earlier:

JAPANESE VALUES AND THEIR SOCIAL CONTEXTS

Ascribed Social Roles	**Ritual Openings**
(family, community, church, consumership, work, school, "voluntary" groups, etc.)	(exams, promotions, etc.)
nurturance	control
compliance	autonomy
cooperation	competition
responsibility	free choice
self-denial	self-expression

In the Western open competitive model, by contrast, these same values are distributed among daily activities:

AMERICAN VALUES AND THEIR SOCIAL CONTEXTS

Ascribed Social Roles	Achieved Social Roles
(family, community, church, nation, some work, some voluntary groups)	(school, some work, consumership, leisure use, some voluntary groups, mate selection, etc.)
nurturance	control
compliance	autonomy
cooperation	competition
responsibility	free choice
self-denial	self-expression

In order to manage aggression, then, the American requires a general set of abstract principles that, while allowing him to get ahead, prevent him from interfering with the right of others to do the same. To some extent, he finds that the values of altruism apply to situations in which his membership and status are fixed by society—family, community, church, and nation—and those of aggression apply to situations in which his membership and status are achieved—school, work, marketplace, mate selection, leisure setting. But this cannot, as we have seen, be relied upon as it can be in preindustrial societies, where participation in aggressive/competitive situations is regulated by ritual.

Developmentally, the principles of value choice change from one period of life to another, at least for the male. At the most general level, we can see how the child begins life in the bosom of altruistic settings, whose values he learns by instruction and by example. Before school age, however, he begins to learn the boundaries of this value system. His groups are in competition with other groups, and members of his own groups are even expected to compete increasingly with one another. Formal schooling greatly accelerates the learning of competitive values, which overtake the cooperative ones as the individual steps into the brutally competitive world of the career. Between the ages of five and perhaps forty, his membership in competitive achieved-membership situations increases, and the competitive quality of these situations becomes increasingly serious in its consequences. Those who are unable to internalize and act on the competitive values are developmental failures of the Milquetoast or mama's boy variety.

Middle age brings a gradual increase of commitments to fixed-membership groups again. The individual establishes a family of his own, joins a church, settles in a community, and develops colleagues and friends. The pendulum of altruism/aggression swings back the other way until late life, when one is again heavily dependent upon fixed-membership groups and their altruistic values for survival and comfort. The life cycle might be crudely diagrammed as follows:

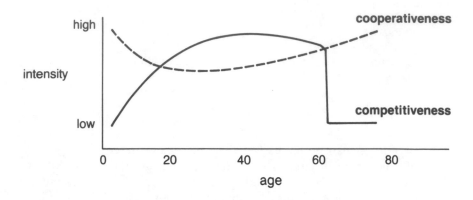

Figure 2: Changes in Social Demands with Age

The trouble for industrial man came, as Freud understood, from the difficulty of integrating motivational opposites in a single character. In contrast to people of earlier eras, when competitiveness was given limited and clearly defined time and space in society and heavy sanctions were brought against the indiscreet use of it, industrial man had to show a daily willingness to compete, as well as to be loyal, and worst of all, to do it with limited supernatural guidance. He constructed himself and his society willy-nilly as he went along, and he did it largely on the strength of his intelligence and energy. Too often the personality's capacity for mutuality, or industry, or both, were victims of the failure to manage these conflicting responsibilities. In chapter 13 I shall return to this dilemma when I raise the question of a workable sense of maturity for our own time.

Moral Maturity in Modern Society

Social life, then, demands the management of altruism and aggression on the part of every individual, and rewards their successful management with the mantle of maturity. Although their management is never simple, in primitive societies the rules are at least less confusing. Aggression is typically confined (in principle at least) to specific life stages, roles, and rituals. As societies become more complex, so does the problem; as the problem becomes more complex, we become dangerously aware of the arbitrariness of our cultural solutions. We have become so self-conscious about this issue in our time that it provides a steady stream of critical self-analysis. In the nineteen-twenties and forties we had the Lynds's *Middletown* study and Margaret Mead's *Keep Your Powder Dry*. In the fifties we had W. H. Whyte's *Organization Man*, Riesman's *Lonely Crowd*, and Goffman's *Presentation of Self*, and in the sixties Jules Henry's *Culture Against Man* and Toffler's *Future Shock*; in the seventies Slater's *Pursuit of Loneliness* and Lasch's *Culture of Narcissism*; and in the eighties Bellah et al's *Habits of the Heart*.

What these studies show is that we have not one view of maturity, but many. Bellah and his colleagues (1985) examined in detail the question of altruism and aggression in modern American society, and found their middle-class subjects torn between conflicting views of self-expression (the thrifty self-reliance of Ben Franklin and Ralph Waldo Emerson and the expressive spontaneity of Walt Whitman) and social responsibility (the utopian collectivism of John Winthrop and the democratic individualism of Thomas Jefferson). In this chapter I have tried to illustrate how cultural patterns of interpersonal behavior regulate the universal principles of altruism and aggression. Although American traditions surrounding the management of cooperation and competition are unique, the problem of their management is a cultural universal. The anxiety and confusion that surround that problem in America today are the result in part of economic and technological changes that have dissolved many of the social assumptions on which our ancient and tenacious concepts of maturity are based. Let us look more closely at the way in which social change produces disharmony between the conditions of life and ideals of maturity.

13. History and the Self:
The Four-Stage Legacy

T he history of maturity will have a different meaning for each of us, depending upon the nature of our personal developmental struggles, and upon the ways in which history has shaped the social demands on us and suggested solutions for meeting those demands. In this sense, history is a living, breathing force in our lives. It is part of our environment; and like every part of our environment, we interact with it. We are products and makers of it. We continuously reexperience it and reinterpret it anew, largely without knowing this. The disciplines of literary art, history, philosophy, and psychology are the tools that literate societies have evolved for the purpose of clarifying and enriching such processes of self-understanding.

Psychology, then, is also a product and a maker of history. It is a set of learned habits of thought, with a past. It addresses a set of history-rich human questions, and it does so with a set of history-rich assumptions about how to ask and answer such questions. Its purpose is to concentrate the best intelligence of our species on the process of self-understanding. An unself-conscious psychology is therefore a mere vestigial organ that survives within the social institutions where it once served a function. As psychology's nature is historical, its self-consciousness must be historical as well.

We have seen in the discussion of altruism and aggression how modernity poses *interpersonal* problems that our historically given concepts have not prepared us for. Let us now look at the process of individual maturation; at the way in which history has taught us to anticipate and evaluate our own competence, and at the dislocations that modernity has wrought in our relationships with ourselves.

Again, we must be content with an example to illustrate a vast and subtle problem. For my illustration I have chosen a set of ideas whose simplicity and power have assured them a prominent place in intellectual history, from Plato to the modern masters of developmental psychology: the four stages of *The Symposium.* I shall reintroduce this set of ideas and its role in history, then use it as a framework through which to view some of the developmental dilemmas of the modern American self.

The Indestructible Four-Stage Legacy

The four stages of maturation set forth in *The Symposium*—self-centeredness, erotic love, honor, and wisdom—may very well be older than Plato, but they are probably no older than complex, stratified society and writing. They imply individual responsibility, self-consciousness, heroism and the exchange of complex ideas as ideals; and they imply transcendent universal principles and linear time. It is clear that these features of early Greek culture are not only very much alive in Western Europe and North America today, but have spread to include both sexes and all social classes.

We saw the reappearance of these four stages during the Middle Ages, in the work of Saint Bernard. Not surprisingly, the great devotee of Franciscan thought Dante Alighieri also applied this bit of Platonist wisdom to his epic tale of personal development, *The Divine Comedy.* There he shows the circles of hell beginning at the outer rim with those angels who were "neither on the side of God nor the devil, but only for themselves." From there one progresses to the circle of those trapped in the second stage, the incontinent lovers; and then through the many errors of the stage of competitive struggle (violence, deceit, greed) to the greatest sin of all, pride, exemplified by Satan himself. The fourth stage, union with the timeless universe of God's will, comes only at the end of Dante's ascent through Paradise, a realm whose successive levels also recapitulate the sequence.

The importance of Dante's treatment of the Platonic stages in modern Christian life is seen in the three major vows of the modern monastic orders—poverty (the overcoming of material selfishness), chastity (the overcoming of erotic desire), and obedience (the overcoming of desire for personal honor). Their impact on modern creative literature can be clearly seen in James Joyce's autobiographical *Portrait of the Artist as a Young Man.* There the author first "achieves" poverty, ironically by default; then overcomes sexual lust; and finally turns his back on ambition—again ironically, as this greatest of sins is represented by the church herself. Joyce passes up an offer to join the priesthood, and is seen at the end setting out to find truth in his own way, through the introspective discipline of his art.

The four-stage theory was largely replaced in the scientific community by associationist theories of development following Hobbes. Being teleological, it made little sense to positivist science. As we have seen, the Aristotelian concept of a rationally guided happiness commanded more philosophical attention in the seventeenth and eighteenth centuries than the Platonic concept of an inherent sense of truth. In fact, this idea is so profoundly alien to the scientific viewpoint, that even when stage theory reemerged into psychology with Freud, a crucial part of Plato's original meaning was left behind. Since the seventeenth century, only a few romantic psychologists like Troxler and von Schubert retained the concept of spiritual enlightenment that forms the basis of Plato's fourth stage. Since Freud, that meaning has been relegated to an esoteric strand of philosophy and literature quite remote from academic psychology. In psychology the fourth stage has been replaced by self-actualization, which bears a superficial resemblance to its ancestor, but is not the same thing at all. The change tells us a great deal about the worldview of modern Western society, and about the role of psychological science in that society. It is a crucial point because, as I began this book by saying, one's idea of the highest stage of maturity defines one's developmental theory as a whole. In changing the definition of stage four, *modern positivist psychology has fundamentally altered the whole idea of maturation intended in the Platonic model.*

Freud's great achievement was the blending of traditions from ancient philosophy, positivist psychology, biology, psychotherapy, and romantic literature, using a language that made sense to his own era. Since physical development was by then known to represent the teleological unfolding of some kind of genetic code, the idea of inherent stages of development could be rescued from the jaws of *tabula rasa* psychology if such stages could be shown to have a biological basis. Freud's resurrection of stage theory accomplished this by connecting the motivational character of each of the first three stages (survival needs, sexual needs, and needs for power) with a physiological function and its associated body zone (orality, genitality, and anality/phallicity). He did not directly address the fourth stage (need for wisdom), but hinted at something like it with his concept of the ego—a psychological structure that was to some extent independent of the body. He also reversed stages two (eros) and three (honor), making genitality a later development than anality/phallicity. I believe this made more sense to Freud because of the prevalence of sexual neuroses in the clients he saw. Since mature sexuality was more difficult to master than competitiveness, it must be higher on the ontogenetic scale. The disagreement between him and Adler, of course, had to do with the relative importance of these two functions/stages; Adler kept the Platonic priority.

Controversial as they were, the enormous popular appeal of Freud's ideas secured them a seminal place in developmental theory. That his use of four stages was one of his most powerful contributions can be seen from the vantage point of the 1980s, for much of his fertile thought has been altered or disregarded by all but the most doctrinaire of his modern followers, while his use of four stages has formed the backbone of a good deal of serious new scholarship.

	STAGE 1	STAGE 2	STAGE 3	STAGE 4
Plato	pre-love	eros	honor	knowledge
St. Bernard	self-love	charity	salvation	grace
Dante	self-centeredness	incontinence	pride	grace
Monasticism	sin	poverty	chastity	obedience
Erikson	stages 1-5	intimacy	generativity	integrity
Bühler	detatchment from childhood	sex needs	social self-realization	self-fulfillment
Maslow	survival	belonging	status/power	self-actualization
Kohlberg	stages 1-2	stage 3	stages 4-5	stage 6

The Four Indestructible Stages

Erik Erikson's eight epigenetic stages represent the elaboration of Platonic stage one into five childhood substages, plus Platonic stages two through four, in their original order, as the adult process of development. Maslow's stages represent a bold revival of the original four, if one simply widens the definition of eros to include social "belonging" in addition to sexual attraction. Maslow and Erikson also change the meaning of the last stage, in the sense that I alluded to earlier. Bühler's eight stages consist of the modern version of the Platonic four, each subdivided into a growth phase and a consolidation phase. Kohlberg's stages of moral development also fit the mold in broad outline. His stages one and two are versions of the prealtruistic stage one of *The Symposium*, but Kohlberg's stage two anticipates his stage three, an early, narcissistic phase of social love. Kohlberg's stages four and five represent phases of the Platonic "honor" orientation, in which the good of society is seen as a moral goal (stage four) and rules are valued that promote competitive striving (stage five). Kohlberg's stage six represents the modernized Platonic stage four.

The Transformation of Stage Four

When I first discovered the parallels between the original Platonic stages and their modern descendents, I was faced with two possible interpretations: either there was a historical connection, or Plato had discovered something so close to a universal empirical regularity that his solution had been independently discovered two and a half millenia later. As I studied the problem, I grew more and more impressed by the evidence for the former interpretation, for two reasons. First, there was ample evidence of Plato's direct influence on later writers. Second, the Platonic thread was anchored to a particular worldview—the Conscious, Transcendent Universe and the Path of Love—and other worldviews had produced other ideas of development.

The reemergence of the Platonic stages in psychology after the scientific world had parted company with the Conscious, Transcendent Universe is hard to explain. The point at which the worldviews of Platonism and science diverge is the point at which one accepts or rejects ethical absolutes. I believe the resurrection of Platonism symbolizes the importance of ethical certainty in human life, but it required a gradual, profound change in the nature of that certainty. The height of maturity for the ancients meant the grasp, however imperfect, of that *ultimate awareness* that underlay and accounted for everything perceivable and deducible. That grasp alone made fundamental purposes clear and pointed the way to the infallible correctness and nobility of thought and action.

As perhaps with all truly revolutionary philosophical developments, the discovery of scientific methods at first led to a flush of enthusiasm for those methods as a new path to the elusive old certainty. People already committed to other paths (for example, revealed religion) were sceptical, and many who took the path of positivism later turned away in disillusion. But while the philosophers—Descartes, Spinoza, Leibniz, Berkeley, Kant, Bentham, and Mill—were struggling to wrest ethical certainty from positivism, science was proving itself useful in the solution of other questions only a little less important: the motions of the spheres, the machinery of the body, the harnessing of energy, the secrets of magnetism and electricity, the chemistry of fire. There was so much to do, one began to forget about ethical questions—or to accept unanalyzed practical solutions to them, as the utilitarians did. Finally, most scientists came to see the public display of ultimate ethical questions as a sign of bad breeding or an unacceptable heresy. It was an attitude that led Ortega y Gassett to look back at the past three centuries and surmise that positivism was a "small town kind of philosophy."

It has also led many modern students of humanity to declare that science itself has become a kind of religion. I agree, as long as we distinguish, as Jacob Needleman (1975) has done, between "religion" as a set of social institutions for standardizing ultimate beliefs on one hand, and Platonic wisdom, or the actual pursuit of ultimate knowledge (what Needleman calls "the path") on the other hand.

There is little to wonder at, then, that the Platonic stages had to be reinterpreted for modern psychology to assimilate them. But before we deal with their transformation, we are faced with the puzzling question of why they were resurrected at all. One reasonable explanation is an anthropological one: the Platonic stages had been around so long that they had become an integral part of our unconscious worldview—a facet of the deep structure of our culture. Ritual behaviors and mythic images are often retained long after their original meaning has been lost.

This might be all the explanation that is needed, but we should keep in mind the human need for ethical certainty, which leads us to recognize that among us there *are* people, few in number, who have achieved a great deal more than the personal comfort and social admiration that attend psychological "health," and have become what human beings are somehow supposed to be. If there are such people, who will explain them to our scientistic civilization, if not the psychologists?

To be sure, there are traditions in psychology that explain away the problem. Ethical certainty is reinterpreted as intolerance for ambiguity, drive for cognitive closure, flight from cognitive dissonance, need to believe in a just world, or simply the cathexis of values. Or the numinous experience that validates belief is dissected physiologically and pharmacologically.

But there are those who take the question seriously, and it is these modern psychologists, I believe, who seek to adapt the Platonic stages to the ends of their science. It is not an easy task, but it has its precedents. It is essentially the task of transforming "the path," however it is conceived, into "religion," however it is organized and taught. It requires the transformation into accepted wisdom of that which can be fully understood only by pursuit of "the path" itself—in this case, the intuitively obvious fact that ethically superior people exist.

The crucial difference between the Platonic and the modern versions of stage four is that the former represents an approach to absolute and eternal truth, whereas the latter doubts that there is such truth that can be known or even approached. Given the positivist position of science, there are three ways of approaching morality: (1) the Aristotelian path of logic, in which aesthetic principles of consistency and generality define a hierarchy of values; (2) the relativistic approach, in which the subjectivity of the individual (or the culture) is accepted for what it is; and (3) the functional approach, in which the "natural" functioning of things is accepted as the ultimate standard of value, as in utilitarianism. All of these approaches to the explanation of morally superior stage four behavior are represented in modern developmental theory.

We have seen, for example, that Kohlberg's theory represents the Aristotelian aesthetic approach. His stage six resembles Platonic stage four insofar as it calls for a questioning of conventional morality, and encourages action that is judged worthy for its own sake, rather than for its effect on some socially approved standard of reference. But Kohlberg's highest stage is simply one in which the individual recognizes aesthetic principles in his moral decision-making that transcend conventional cultural rules—principles like generality and consistency. Such an achievement requires no inner moral gyroscope to guide the individual between opposing but logically equal acts; it requires only a disciplined mind to steer clear of the aesthetically flawed standards of the herd. A Kohlbergian Socrates would not necessarily have taken the hemlock. The real Socrates had to rely on ethical intuition—the universal telos denied by science—to understand the superiority of that choice.

Turning to the treatment of moral superiority in Erikson's work, we see an application of cultural relativism. His eighth stage, integrity, resembles the Platonic ideal in a different way. For Erikson the morally superior person is one who sets an example to others of the essential validity of their cultural ideals. In the process of solving the developmental dilemmas that lead toward integrity, the individual finds those ways of living, those expressions of love, work, and idealism, that fit both the circumstances of his life and the requirements of his society. In the process, one achieves "an accrued assurance of one's ability to find order and meaning" (Erikson 1963:268)—that is, integrity. Here, ethical certainty is the key. But seen from the supraindividual and suprasocial viewpoint of the psychologist, that certainty rests upon an illusion. It represents a noble achievement, the unity of belief and action, but in the absence of absolute values, that achievement is nothing more than maximal adaptation to the microcosm of the social here and now. In his biography of Gandhi, Erikson asks not what ultimate truths such a life reveals, but how it evolved out of the developmental puzzles posed by his culture and his place in human history. Integrity is achieved not by way of "the path," but by the map of society and the compass of biography.

Of the modern descriptions of stage four, Maslow's biologically functionalist one is the most detailed and systematic I have seen. It is based on a direct and intensive study of the phenomenon to be explained: the presence among us of morally superior people. Maslow notes that the self-actualized person *is* more ethical than others, and that such a person seems to have an inherent certainty that guides his moral choices. "A few centuries ago," he muses, "[self-actualizers] would all have been described as men who walk in the path of God, or as godly men" (1951:221).

Concerning the basis of their ethical certainty, however, Maslow seems a bit uncertain. Self-actualizers' codes of ethics "are relatively autonomous and individual rather than conventional" (209), but on the other hand "truly ethical behavior ... is behavior based on fundamentally accepted principles" (210). That these principles are to be evaluated, not in their own right, but in the light of their effects on biological functioning, however, is clear. First, they are revealed to the individual through an innate biological drive "to do what he is fitted for" (91). This need, like the needs for security, belonging, and status, "are in some sense, and to some appreciable degree, constitutional or hereditary in their determination" (141). Second, it is their life-serving function itself that gives them value:

> The gratification of basic needs leads to consequences that may be called variously desirable, good, healthy, self-actualizing. The words desirable and good are used here in a biological rather than in an a priori sense, and are susceptible to operational definition. (142)

Unlike most modern adherents of the four-stage model, Maslow had the courage to study the lives of morally superior people in detail, and to take what they said seriously. Accordingly, he had great difficulty in reconciling these individuals' subjective sense of absolute enlightenment with the prevailing relativism of his science. After grappling with his subjects' reports of frequent experiences of spiritual ecstasy, Maslow concludes, "It is quite important to dissociate [this ecstatic feeling] from any theological or supernatural reference . . . . Because this experience is a natural experience, well within the jurisdiction of science, it is probably better to use Freud's term for it, e.g. [sic] the oceanic feeling" (216). Followers of Freud will recognize this term as one he used to describe a hypothetical preoedipal sense of union between infant and mother, a feeling recaptured later in life through various neurotic or psychotic maneuvers such as extreme sexual submissiveness, suicidal thoughts, and the omnipotence fantasies of schizophrenics (Fenichel 1945).

Of course Maslow was not suggesting that self-actualizing people are crazy. He simply had difficulty finding a concept in psychology that could be applied to their spiritual experience; he ended by choosing a concept usually applied to a state that, while "natural," falls outside the range of normal adult consciousness, and has nothing to do with any order of reality not encompassed by the balustrade of science. His concept necessarily excluded, as any academic psychological concept must, the Platonic notion of a telos.

The Maslovian definition of stage four, then, like all its analogues in twentieth-century developmental science, is fundamentally different from the Platonic ideal to which it bears such a haunting outward resemblance. I have dwelt upon this fact because I think it is probably the central problem in the application of psychology to the modern search for maturity. I shall come back to it shortly.

The Search for Maturity

Throughout this book I have been saying we must have an idea about what maturity is before we can have a theory of how to achieve it. I do not presume to have a definitive answer to the first question, and so I must necessarily be tentative in approaching the second. I have chosen to use the Platonic stages as a practical guide to the search for maturity. I have done so not because I believe them in any literal sense, but because their deep roots in our culture, and their rich associations in our thought, make them exceptionally useful as a tool for self-understanding. Because they appear so early and so often in our civilization, our thinking about maturity is already to some degree structured by them, whether we know this or not. To this extent we find them persuasive; and to the extent that we base our choices on persuasive ideas, they have a certain validity.

In what follows, then, I am going to speak as though the four stages describe a valid developmental sequence in the search for maturity. My hope is that this exercise will suggest some new ways of experiencing our moral relationship to our society and history.

Stage One: Security

In chapter 6 we reviewed briefly the conditions of modern industrial society that bear on ethical definitions of maturity. If there is anything in our way of life that can be called an advantage over earlier times, it is the opportunity, that the majority of us enjoy, of economic wellbeing and freedom from arbitrary threat to life and property. Ours is not just a secure life, but one of comfort, abundance, and an assurance of stability that has rarely been reached by any class in earlier times. True, there are too many in the most advanced societies who are excluded from this large circle of prosperity. True, also, we might well be borrowing our wealth at a rate of interest (the exhaustion and pollution of the planet) that our children may be hard pressed to pay. But for now, for most people, relative prosperity is no illusion. We begin our grownup lives as Plato's "children of poverty and plenty"; that is, lacking the experience that leads to wise autonomous choices, but having the time and energy to begin the search for that experience.

But any serious long-term threat will challenge the pilgrim with distracting demands on his attention; and the nature of our search is shaped by the nature of our special insecurities. Briefly and generally, then, I think the key challenge to security in our time is our unprecedented dependence on events that are remote from us in scale, in understandability, and often in distance as well. This dependence is pervasive in all aspects of our economic and political life. Although we are literally drowning in goods, the things we depend on are produced by a vast, dispersed system of complex institutions about which we know little, and over which we have no control whatsoever. Although we participate ritually in our government, our laws are made in remote places according to arcane formulas, to the extent that we feel bewildered just trying to understand enough to cast a halfway intelligent vote. The education, medical care, and justice that are so crucial to our hopes are wielded by institutions that are often indifferent to our ideals and deaf to our voices. Here I will concentrate on just two aspects of this dependency on the remote, in an effort to illustrate how it might be affecting our search for maturity. These aspects are: (1) the possible end of the world by way of the twin threat of nuclear extinction and ecological suicide, and (2) the insecurity of old age.

1. *The Possible End of the World:* Our dependence on remote systems is most dramatically demonstrated by the proliferation of nuclear weapons in the aresenals of the world powers, and by the dangerous destruction of the earth's life-support system through overpopulation and underregulated commercial activity. These horrors themselves are avoidable; the extent of their threat to our lives is well known, and yet we feel helpless to stop or even vigorously oppose the processes, because we have all but lost the ability to influence the governments and industries that perpetrate them. The insecurity they pose is different from any other ever faced by mankind. Unlike war and pestilence, they threaten not just our communities, but our entire species and perhaps earthly life itself. Unlike mythico-religious visions of Armageddon, they are devoid of any transcendental meaning or vision of rebirth. But how might they be affecting our development?

Stage one of the Platonic quartet is characterized by a focus on one's own needs to the exclusion of others'. In order to break out of this stage, one must first turn one's full attention to a loved other, then learn to apply the altruistic principle of this relationship to human relationships in general. Others must be seen, not as objects for self-gratification, but as themselves. For the first step of this stage it is a minimum condition to believe that one's own biological survival is, for the time being, secure. How secure? A relaxed moment now and then is probably not enough. One must have the sustained interest to engage the other in searching dialogue, to discover fully their separate selfhood.

As Erikson, Maslow, and others have shown, in order to trust and esteem themselves, people in our culture must have faith, justly or not, that they are not dependent on others in a helpless or destructive way; that they are *inter*dependent in a way that is mutually dignifying and rewarding. The sense that we are not free to act on our values, because we depend for our wellbeing on others we neither trust nor admire, robs us of our self-trust and self-admiration. This situation is strikingly similar to the unwanted dependency of adolescence as a stage of modern life, a condition that leads to self-doubt, inner preoccupation, and narcissistic need. It is a situation wherein we find it extremely difficult to love others as themselves, in contrast, that is, to the stage one love of the other as a source of nurturance and support, or as a substitute for self-esteem.

The second step of stage two involves an intrinsic belief in the basic worthiness of others in their full individuality. It is difficult to imagine how this complex completion of the erotic stage can begin without the development of particular relationships. Unwanted dependence on remote and abhorrent institutions represents the modern version of that same condition that disqualified Athenian slaves and women from the pursuit of maturity.

2. *Old Age Insecurity:* Prior to modern times, personal security automatically became, after a few short decades of life, a spiritual matter. Life was short, but death was not the end of consciousness. Long life was desired but not expected, and many people put more energy into achieving a "good death," which meant one that would ensure a prosperous hereafter. This gave a certain practicality to the cultivation of spiritual maturity.

Modern technology has given us the opposite situation. Most of us will live to see eighty, but we will retire from work long before that, and the last two or three decades of our lives (almost as much time as the entire expected span in the seventeenth century) may be materially lean and insecure. Where will we live and who will care for us, once we have lost economic control and physical competence?

In the modern world the solutions to these questions often depend on distressingly remote forces. Livelihood for the retired is set by governments and massive corporations, not by responsible kin. Like income, health and housing are dispensed according to politically determined policies, administered through impersonal bureaucracies. Spirituality in old age might help us endure the indifference of others, but it probably will not solve the material question. Does the sight of increasing numbers of elderly living in idleness, poverty, and obscurity help to remind the young of the basic insecurity of their relationships and indifference of their institutions? Given the difficulty of securing a decent old age through one's own autonomous action, I cannot imagine that it does not, with the same general results we reap from the threat of Armageddon.

Undoubtedly, some people in the twentieth century have achieved Platonic maturity in spite of this distraction, and others will continue to do so. Such an achievement requires the solution of those problems of material insecurity that are characteristic of our time.

Stage Two: Eros

We have seen how the industrial revolution raised the hopes of the middle classes for material success, and how the distortion of sexuality resulted from this. Although our sex lives may still leave much to be desired today, we are better off than our grandparents. Relatively cheap, safe, effective birth control is one reason; the relative decline in importance of hypergamy as a source of upward mobility is another; the loss of community-based social control discussed in chapter 6 is a third; and the waning of religious prohibitions on earthly delights still another. Sexual intimacy between men and women has probably improved a great deal also as a result of a gradual decline in gender stereotyping and in the political and economic oppression of women. These last developments help men see women as fully developed individuals, thereby opening vistas of mutual interest and exploration in close relationships for those who are ready for them.

All of these improvements bear indirectly on the task of Platonic stage two—the discovery of selflessness through erotic love—but the nature of their bearing is as problematic as the relationship between sex and love. That relationship is of course mediated to a large extent by cultural attitudes. Of the many ways in which Western sexual attitudes affect maturation in the twentieth century, I will focus on three which, taken together, present a major challenge to the achievement and maintenance of erotic love: (1) the hedonism that goes with material overproduction; (2) the sexual equality that goes with economic individualism; and (3) the denial of eros in old age.

1. *The New Hedonism*: Riesman (1950) and others (Riesman, Potter, and Watson 1960; Lasch 1979) have documented the shift from an ethic of work and saving to an ethic of pleasure and consumption that we are experiencing today. The change has accompanied the shift in twentieth-century society from a relative scarcity of manufactured goods and services to a relative abundance, achieved by way of increased labor efficiency. The problem of our time is not how to produce what people need and want, but how to create needs and wants for what our industry produces. Debt, once considered the frightening price of failure or a sign of bad character, is now exalted as a sign that one has achieved "credit," a term almost synonymous with economic self-sufficiency and responsibility. Lifestyle, based on one's taste in material goods and leisure pursuits, has to some extent replaced community, profession, and religion as a source of identity. It has become natural and good to gratify one's senses as often and as fully as one can reasonably afford, and the more one can afford, the better, all else being equal.

That this value goes with a reduction of sexual guilt hardly needs to be said. It also goes with an increase in self-esteem attached to sensual pleasure itself, and with a tendency to evaluate experience automatically according to how good it feels. Now, the guiltless enjoyment of sensual pleasure is certainly no hindrance to intimacy; but the undifferentiated and reflexlike avoidance of displeasure is. Any close relationship involves the exchange of demands and expectations, some of which are difficult and unpleasant. More importantly, getting to know someone intimately always involves hurt when illusions are dashed or expectations unfulfilled; and it always involves unpleasant insight into one's own weaknesses. At these junctures, the new hedonism conflicts with the achievement of deep erotic love, and tends either toward a kind of narcissistic isolation, or toward an equally narcissistic promiscuity, the playboy/playgirl mentality character-istic of stage one.

2. *Sexual Equality and Emotional Self-Expression*: The waning of gender stereotypes and the new authority and power of women have given a particular character to the new hedonism that otherwise would probably not have had. Since the decline of ritual and the normalization of competitive striving that followed the Enlightenment (chapter 6), men have been saddled with a burden of emotional self-control that has rendered most of them incompetent to recognize or express their sublter feelings. The result has been that women have had to take over the responsibility of managing not only their own emotional lives, but those of their men as well. As a result, women are on the whole better emotional communicators than men, and not surprisingly (as Gilligan's research suggests) more interested in emotions and more aware of their importance for intimacy and pleasure as well.

The relative strength of the modern woman, then, coupled with the emphasis on personal gratification granted by the new hedonism, has greatly increased the cultural value of emotional self-awareness and sensitivity, at least among the well educated. In some ways our historic present is repeating the twelfth century emergence of civility. In the long run, this is almost surely for the better; for the time being, it is having a disruptive effect on relations between women and men. Women's expecta-tions for emotional communication have risen faster than the average man's abilities in this area. To the extent that both men and women realize the cultural crippling that afflicts men's emotional sensibilities, women can perfect their role as emotional teachers. In Diotema, Socrates's teacher of the four stages, they have history's outstanding model.

3. *The Denial of Eros in Old Age*: Given the limits of material security I mentioned earlier, the extension of the lifespan well beyond the working years represents a real opportunity in modern man's search for maturity. With improved health and educational resources, the retiree is relatively free to learn, to reflect, and to experiment with life. Late life is, after all, the natural time for the achievement of stage four.

To grasp this potential, though, the elderly will have to grapple with the popular social attitude that they have (or should have) outgrown sexual love. It is one thing for a person to come to the well-considered conclusion, as many have, that sex is no longer important for oneself. It is another thing for a person to deny erotic needs out of shame or fear of retribution. For one thing, it is not unusual for stage two to achieve its first full flowering late in life, especially when one's youth was spent in a sexually repressive epoch. For another thing, the later stages of maturity, especially stage four, demand a keen self-awareness that can be built only upon a thorough self-acceptance. One may outgrow the activities of earlier stages as one matures, but it would be a great mistake to regret or reject the self authentically expressed in those activities. Since most people have erotic needs in late life, self-acceptance for most people entails the full recognition and embracing of their sexuality and the discovery of socially acceptable ways of expressing it. When one works with old people, one often sees the association of exceptional character and sexual self-acceptance.

The resolution of stage two, then, is expressed first in the mutual recognition and acceptance of erotic love; then in the perception of those things in all others that makes them desirable. It demands an acceptance of one's own desire and a willingness to suffer for love. It is also nurtured by a harmony of men's and women's expectations of each other; it can be easily disrupted by sudden changes in the cultural norms that regulate such expectations. Modern life puts the resolution of stage two at risk for these reasons, but modern women seem on the whole better equipped than men to lead the search for maturity at this stage.

Stage Three: Honor

The world has come a long way since the principal source of honor and identification with one's community was the murderous ritual of war. The replacement of heroism with the ethic of success (chapters 5 and 6) has indeed been a source of anxiety for modern man, and has inspired the rebellion of romantics from Friedrich Nietzsche to Allen Ginsberg. Whether it has raised or lowered the rate of spiritual maturity in the world is anybody's guess; on the other hand, as it has almost certainly improved life's quality for the average human being. It has led to a mass literacy and mass leisure that still promise the elusive possibility of mass learning. It has begun to include women as equals in the competition for social recognition. It has increased the social distribution of an increased scope of life choices.

But modern social conditions appear out of step with our historically given concept of honor in several ways. First, central to that concept is an enduring community of like-minded people to whom one's actions are highly visible, intelligible, and potentially nontrivial. It is this community that grants or withholds honor; yet it is increasingly difficult for the modern achiever to identify any such community. His work is usually carried on outside his residential community (and is unintelligible and/or trivial to his neighbors, anyway); the faces of his coworkers are likely to change every few years or even oftener, so that they may pay homage to his title without knowing or caring anything about how he got it; and (since people are interchangeable in a bureaucracy) all the while they may be looking for an opportunity to displace him themselves.

Second, the industrial revolution's change from heroism to success as the form of honor shifted the basis of honor from a productivity of "beautiful words and deeds" to a productivity of socially useful goods and services (Arendt 1958). Modern economic history, on the other hand, is a history of mechanization, wherein ten craftsmen are replaced by a mill-worker; ten millworkers by an automated machine; ten plowmen by a tractor; ten tractormen by a combine. Today the largest segment of the working population are white-collar "information processors" (Bell 1973), whose individual productivity is largely unmeasureable, even by efficiency experts. Those who dirty their hands with tangible products are most often interchangeable members of production teams, and we scarcely need mention the millions in industrial societies who are intermittently or permanently without productive work of any kind. It is increasingly difficult to corner honor even by the mastery of socially useful skills, as technological change consigns most of these to the flea market at an increasing pace.

Where, then, is honor to be found? The twentieth century proffers to a few the path of celebrity, to most the path of conspicuous consumption. Of celebrity, Christopher Lasch has written:

> Most Americans would still define success as riches, fame, and power, but their actions show that they have little interest in the substance of these attainments. What a man does matters less than the fact that he has "made it." Whereas fame depends on the performance of notable deeds acclaimed in biography and works of history, celebrity—the reward of those who project a vivid or pleasing exterior or have otherwise attracted attention to themselves—is acclaimed in the news media, in gossip columns, on talk shows, in magazines devoted to "personalities." Accordingly it is evanescent, like news itself, which loses its interest when it loses its novelty. (1979:117)

Of conspicuous consumption—the path of most of us—it is probably fair to say that we often feel drawn to use whatever means we have left over from the struggle for existence to purchase the *appearance* of those who have "made it." Where we live and how we furnish it, what we drive, how we spend our leisure time—these are the aspects of our lives that give us our sense of social worth. They announce to the nameless crowds through which we move that we are socially mature: productive, independent, valued (by someone, somewhere) for what we know or what we do or who we are.

It might be argued that this is no more shameful than the Greek longing for esteem bought with beautiful words and deeds, since both betray a dependence on conventional and therefore ephemeral values. But I think there is an important difference between Platonic stage three and conspicuous consumption. The former is based on self-sacrifice for the good of the polity; the latter rarely is. Consequently, the former leads to a sense of triumph over the immaturity of self-centeredness; the latter rarely does. It is this sense of triumph, of accomplishment (or, occasionally, an unforeseen disastrous collapse of one's entire value system), that allows the maturing person to "finish" stage three, and turn his eyes toward higher goals.

There is also a positive side to the possibilities for stage-three maturity in modern society. The combination of social heterogeneity and efficient communication makes it possible for us to join small communities (churches, civic groups, volunteer organizations), or to form our own (movements, self-help support groups), or to follow occupations (teaching, social services, politics) that give us opportunities to achieve honor through selfless devotion to some social good of our own choosing. Occasionally, these efforts reach such proportions that we end up not only with a sense of our own worth but a modest place in the records of our community as well. As with the other stages, there are those among us who have achieved honor. They are not the rich and powerful, most of whom we do not honor, but merely envy. Rather, they are those in public life—politics, religion, the arts, science, industry, sports, education, entertainment—who truly express the deeply held values of a community, however small. They are the people whose work has given us something tangible to aim at with our whole being; who have clarified for us once more what the word *honor* means.

Stage Four: Wisdom

The key role in our modern consciousness of the basic Platonic vision of development can be clearly seen in those recent historical developments of which we in Western civilization are most proud. Our history has been driven by the desire of its architects—both political and technological—to liberate the common man and woman from the insecurity and drudgery that stifle the life of the mind. It has been a history of struggle to democratize the vision of a polis of equal souls, each one free to achieve his or her highest level of development. What I believe has happened instead is that the vision itself has been subtly but profoundly transformed, so that the goal is no longer wisdom, but "adjustment," and the average is seen as a form of disease.

Let me first hastily dispel the suggestion of megalomania in the words that introduce this section. My task is simply to clarify what I think Plato meant by stage four, and to point to some apparent obstacles to its attainment that seem to challenge modern man. In doing this, I plead guilty to the hubris of trying to help people attain something far above my own present abilities. I have two excuses: First, people are often helped to achieve what their helpers cannot do. Granting Plato's superior brilliance, for example, who knows whether he was really enlightened in his own sense; and what difference does it make anyway? Second, I find it more acceptable to try something important even if I fail, than to try something trivial.

In my earlier discussion of the modern transformation of stage four, I pointed out that Plato was talking about the quest for ethical certainty, and that he believed such certainty consisted in union with the actual consciousness of the universe, which is of course infallible and eternal. One's guide in this quest was neither social wisdom nor syllogistic logic, but the inner *feeling* of rightness, philosophy in its original meaning as the *love* of wisdom, or what William James identified as the only valid criterion of truth, the *sentiment* of rationality.

The great obstacle modern society has placed in the way of stage four is the relativizing of truth. The decline of the metaphysical and the spiritual in favor of the empirically demonstrable, the substitution of the religion (science) for the path (personal development), and above all the democratization of learning, have led to a general elevation of practicality and popularity as the goals of knowledge. To be an "expert" commands respect; to be a "seeker of truth" commands scepticism if not suspicion. It amounts to a subtle merging of stage four into stage three, a demotion of the Vita Contemplativa to a form of Vita Activa that is considered genteel by its adherents, effete and snobbish by many of its observers. It is a return to the sophist view of wisdom as an instrument for the achievement of status in the human world.

There is much evidence of this fact. Science is valued to the extent that its results are either practical, like vaccines and electronics, or entertaining, like space travel and nature photography. Although the scientists themselves plead continuously for "pure" research, they are forced to use the argument that what is pure now may be practical tomorrow! "Liberal education" is grudgingly preserved because it produces better-adjusted people, not morally superior people. Throughout my youth I heard this admonition repeated, as I am sure most of us did, by parents and educators: You will enjoy art, music, and literature more. You will be accepted into the "right circles" (a phrase that still makes me shudder). You will be better able to help your children in school, and so on. The fact that there is a clear class distinction based on whether one works with one's head or one's hands simply underlines the stage-three status-seeking utility of learning.

The dilution of the Vita Contemplativa has been speeded by the relative growth of numbers in white-collar over blue-collar occupations and the expansion of leisure time for both groups. The democratic revolutions of the eighteenth and nineteenth centuries, and the movement for public health, education, and welfare of the late nineteenth and early twentieth centuries, were led by middle classes fired by a sense of their privilege and responsibility, their intellectual and moral superiority, and their fitness to lead. In the late twentieth century, middle-classdom is rarely seen as a privilege; it is a mere normality. To be working class is (unless one can prove that the condition is either temporary or the result of free choice) to have failed. It is flagrant evidence of the "psychopathology of the average." By extension, to work with one's mind is no sign of merit, but a mere defense against stigma.

The replacement of the Conscious, Transcendent Universe of antiquity by the Nonconscious, Lawful Universe of modernity, then, has reduced knowledge to its crudely practical dimension. The leveling of social class has eliminated heroism as a stage of development. Together, these processes have revitalized the primitive social definitions of maturity that have always existed alongside more complex definitions: Maturity is normality. The absence of it proves the interference of disease—of natural forces beyond the individual's control.

What, then, of the search for maturity? Must it not be guided by the intuition of ethical superiority, the feeling we have about certain acts and people that their imitation is worthy of our greatest effort? According to positivist psychology (not all psychology) such acts and people inspire us because: (1) they typify what our culture happens to value; and/or (2) they are expressions of widely held aesthetic principles; and/or (3) they contribute to the health and happiness of our species. Are these worth suffering and dying for? Has one achieved integrity if there is nothing one will suffer and die for? We cannot avoid such questions; they are given to us in the deep structure of our consciousness. We cannot seek the answers without a clear view of the questions. To the extent that we lack such a clear view, we are in danger of mistaking the "religious" answers of our institutions (for example, the institutions of science) for the path of wisdom. The need for this kind of awareness strikes me as the most important argument for an historically self-conscious psychology.

14. A Prescription for Irony

The Plight of Maturity

Philosophic thought about maturity since Kant has left us with an absence of secure values. Many still have faith in Christian or other forms of the Conscious, Transcendent Universe, but cannot reconcile this faith easily with the model of the universe that underlies their earthly government, their education, or their material dependence on science. These secular aspects of their lives clash with the very notion of revealed truth, let alone any specific revelation. The dominant view of scientistic society is that man is a creature whose basic nature is determined by biology and physics, and there is no place in these sciences for direct communication with the cosmos.

The rational tradition of the Enlightenment not only leaves us without justification for ethical certainty, it denies us the unique, autonomous existence we require to take responsbility for our souls. The empiricist tradition reduces us to reactive machinery; the idealist elevates us to the expression of universal law. The romantic tradition promises us individuality, but only at the cost of membership in a coherent cosmos. Even Rousseau, who helped to invent the teleology of modern romanticism, immediately retreated to the Greek notion of man as a microcosm, an idea as indigestible in scientistic society as that of divine revelation. Maturity, then, must repudiate both the factual certainty of the prevailing positivist tradition, and the ethical certainty of romanticism.

From such a radically relativistic perspective we must not draw that conclusion, so popular in American academic thought, that the search for truth and goodness are somehow immature (see Bloom 1987). On the contrary, it is of the utmost importance that we find a basis for that search that resonates with our place in history. In my view the ironic position is one of the few—perhaps the only one—that provides such a basis.

The Response of Social Science

The dilemma of relativism has been discussed so thoroughly in the philosophic and psychiatric literature of our age that it needs no further elaboration here. Surely, a science of human development must address it as well. I would like to suggest some features of an attitude that might contribute to such an effort. There is already a promising tendency among some social scientists to cope with this task, but a brief look at the state of social science shows there is still great room for improvement. By "social science," I mean that which social scientists do, and what they recognize amongst themselves as falling within the scope of their profession. This is sometimes the only criterion that distinguishes it from journalism, history, biography, or even realistic fiction.

Seen from the viewpoint of the post-Enlightenment existential dilemma, the philosophy that informs most modern social science is naïve. Being precritical, the mainstream has yet to face the dilemma at all, preferring to act as though positivism were a perfectly adequate method for the study of human maturity. There are three subtypes of this kind of science: First, there is what C. Wright Mills called "abstracted empiricism," the habit of adopting whatever quasiexperimental techniques seem handy, finding a problem suggested by an existing theory, and going after empirical "data" that are thought to bear on the problem. This approach costs a lot of money, and usually produces material that can be cited to credit or discredit various other theories, but whose true relationship with human action, thought, feeling, or potential is impossible to ascertain. A full critique of this and the next type can be found in Mills's *The Sociological Imagination*.

The second type of naive social science is what Mills called "grand theory." A practitioner of this type constructs large-scale models of how patterns of human behavior (societies, personalities, economies, etc.) work, these models purporting to be based on empirical fact, and therefore falsifiable by observation. The models are usually so complex, and the terms used to describe their parts so vague, that it is difficult to be sure whether any particular observation is relevant to the model or not.

The third naive approach is the type I call "rebellion." This type is practiced by scholars who are concerned more about real social problems than about social science as a discipline or a profession. They accept positivism as proper science, and they recognize that it also offers a vocabulary that can legitimize and lend power to their attack on social conditions. The rebels use theory and method eclectically to try to do good; they sometimes achieve admirable results.

When rebellion is practiced by those who are sceptical about the methods they are using, I consider it a form of critical rather than precritical social science; but it is not the only form. Any kind of social science that is consistently and critically aware of its own goals, methods, and limitations falls in this category. Excluded are texts on methods that ignore the last two centuries of philosophy, whatever their conclusions are. Included are works that deliberately avoid the naïve application of positivist methods, and that embody a coherent rationale for doing so.

In contrast to the naïve kind, we now have a growing body of social science that is not only postcritical in the sense that it rejects positivism, but is critical, in the sense that it avoids romantic teleology and achieves awareness of its own limits. Many works of the symbolic interactionist tradition in sociology represent this kind. The interactionists recognize that human behavior is purposeful (as opposed to merely reactive), and understand that in order to understand its purposes, we must understand the meanings it has for the people we study. It is understood that these meanings evolve out of the ongoing interaction between actors, including the observer. In other words, the subjectivity of human truth is taken for granted, and scientific understanding consists in making that subjectivity as conscious as possible. The result is not prediction or control, but increased self-consciousness.

Much of the relativistic or atheoretical school in anthropology, exemplified by the works of Clifford Geertz and Gregory Bateson, also qualifies as critical social science. Followers of this tradition set themselves the task of identifying the meanings that are shared by people as members of a culture—usually deeply unconscious assumptions that are used to make sense out of shared experience. Again, the analyses of these deep patterns do not reveal "real" structures that exist somewhere in an objective world. The patterns emerge out of the relationship between the ethnographer and his or her subject. They are tools for making sense out of otherwise enigmatic experience.

In psychology, many writers of the humanistic movement show critical awareness, especially those who have been influenced by Asian philosophy, like Jacob Needleman and Roger Walsh. Their writing shows a thorough awareness of the limitations of language, both for understanding and for communication, and an appreciation of other ways of knowing things that are nonverbal. Seen from this perspective, social science consists mainly of an attempt to clear away the rubbish of cultural and personal habits, so that the person can begin to appreciate potentials for knowing and feeling that have been obscured by those habits.

Irony: The Essence of Critique

What all these authors' works have in common, and what I wish to see more widespread in social science, is something I call "irony." In the ironic attitude there are three necessary elements: The first is the presence of *absurdity*; the second is *awareness* of the absurdity; and the third is *transcendence* of it. Given the human desire, even weakness, for absolute truth; given that science is supposed to be a search for truth, modernity renders both man and science absurd. Ignorance of this absurdity belongs to an earlier era, and renders one incapable of understanding the real problems of modern society. Failure to transcend the recognized absurdity results either in the rejection of modernity, which is cowardly and dishonest, or in the rejection of all values, which is misanthropic. It is the refusal to do either that constitutes the irony of critique.

How is this kind of irony possible? That is a terribly important question, but it is like asking, How is it possible to ride a bicycle? One can study bicycles, one can watch people riding them, but one must ride in order to know how. I will try to give some examples, and I will try to describe some results.

Example #1: Great Literature

When a great literary artist describes life, he does so ironically. His characters are real, in the sense that they are recognizable from personal experience and stir real emotions in us; but he has *invented* them. He is deliberately manipulating the reader's credulity to his own ends. But what are his ends? Beauty and truth. The lie cannot be cynical and be beautiful. The rapport between artist and reader must be based on loving empathy. The critical, analyzing spirit that looks down on human frailty from its height of literary creativity also mocks itself and idealizes its own antithesis in what Thomas Mann called, "a loving affirmation of all that is *not* intellectuality and art, but is innocent, healthy, decently unproblematical and untouched by spirituality" (quoted in Campbell 1968:328).

Ironic social science is rarely as moving as great literature, but the two forms of understanding do share some features. The self-conscious social scientist is aware that the people, events, and places he describes are fictitious abstractions; no description, however detailed or penetrating, can hope to capture the full experience of another life. Moreover, the attitude of social science as a literary form is intellectual, as opposed to emotional. To the extent that the social scientist tries to render his subject clear to the analytic frame of mind he can expect of his readers, he must translate the passion of his characters into sober language; and he must reveal causes behind his scenes—causes of which his actors know nothing.

Social science, then, is necessarily critical and condescending, and we are correct when we are suspicious of its motives. What saves ironic social science is that its practitioner places himself, and his craft, under the microscope of his analysis as well. He seeks the relevance of his characters' errors to the understanding of his own life. He does not begin, "These people are like such-and-such," but, like the novelist or playwrite, "You and I are like these people." This is the erotic irony Thomas Mann was talking about.

Example #2: Faith

My mother has practised Zen meditation for some twenty-five years. On her living room wall is a beautiful piece of calligraphy, in English, by the great Zen master D. T. Suzuki. In strong, peaceful brush strokes it renders a passage from Thomas Paine:

"To do good is my religion, the world is my home."

The simplicity of these eleven words conceals a complex philosophy. First, as the words "*my* religion" reveal, Paine and Suzuki had in common a deep scepticism of creeds and a deep faith in absolute values. There may be innumerable religions.

The word "do" is also revealing. Paine's religion is not to "think," not to "be"; these have become impossible religions in the modern world. If man is not a microcosm, and does not receive Truth directly from the Universe, his thought can know only itself. "Being" is also metaphysical, as it can be known only by thought. To "do" is the only possible thing!

What about "good"? Again, Paine has chosen the simplest and most general word. It can mean whatever you like it to mean. If you want to know what *he* means, you must watch what he does. Does he know what to do? Well enough to be Thomas Paine.

Finally there is the phrase, "the world is my home." He is not Christ, whose home may or may not be in heaven. He is a human body, free to wander the world, but not free to leave it. He is a seeker. As such he is not an Englishman or a Frenchman or an American (or, in Suzuki's case, a Japanese). He owns nothing, and nothing owns him. One can sum up the attitude of these eleven words:

Creeds, possessions, language, ideas, and identities are unreliable. (Awareness)

But most of us rely on them anyway, because they are all we have. (Absurdity)

But we can still do good. (Transcendence)

Paine's epigram illustrates the moral dilemma of ironic social science in another way. Once we understand the relativity of our beliefs, and the frailty we show by clinging to them, we are tempted to be cynical. Why should we do social science (or anything else), except for personal pleasure or gain? We must intuit the possibility of doing good—absolute good—or our profession is hopelessly without spiritual direction. In our everyday work, we must be constantly seeking this absolute good in what we do. In order to avoid facile rationalizations, we must be self-disciplined. In order to be self-disciplined, we must sustain hope. In order to sustain hope, we must resist the daily pressure our institutions exert to make precritical empiricists of us all.

Example #3: Clowns

Communal rituals in many cultures include comic figures whose dress and behavior contrast sharply with the serious business at hand. They are popular figures in art, folklore, and literature; their presence has excited the curiosity of many anthropologists as well. Clowns' behavior is often, but not always, in polar opposition to norms: foolish, exuberant, and lewd in the face of dignity, reserve, and propriety. Sometimes they combine opposites within their own performance: adroit, feigning clumsiness; brave, feigning fear. Sometimes their play is ambiguous, as when they merge with the spectators to heckle the performance.

The attitude of the clown is ironic. Although he mocks the performance, he is part of it, and his presence would be missed. Although the ordinary performers in a ritual may be "acting," their performance is meant to be taken seriously; but the clown acts the part of an actor, and invites disbelief. In short, he satirizes *himself*, who personifies satire, thereby satirizing satire and turning disbelief back upon itself. In this way, he dramatizes the distinction between fantasy and reality, playing the role of fantasy itself, in contrast to which the rest of the performance is reality. The clown adds majesty both to the performance that he mocks and to its opposite—the attitude of mockery.

I believe ironic social science also embellishes and beautifies the society it mocks when that society is tolerant of scepticism. Obedience and belief are sometimes necessary for the social cohesiveness and stability that can alone make life endurable. but just as all ritual performances use illusion as well as skill and majesty to persuade the onlooker, so all societies use deceit and threat as well as reason and reward. The attitude of mockery is needed as an integral part of a just society in order to keep deceit and threat within bounds, without periodic chaos and painful social disorder. Criticism cannot be mere heckling of the performance, cynical or self-serving of some interest group. It must be aimed at the improved pursuit of shared goals or, like the performance of clowns, at giving vital expression to the society's necessary quotient of disbelief.

Where unself-conscious social science of the "rebellion" variety may detract from social cohesion without suggesting realistic alternatives; where "asbtracted empiricism" tends to serve the unexamined goals of entrenched institutions; and where "grand theory" is simply irrelevant and self-serving, ironic social science refines and legitimizes scepticism, and at the same time legitimizes belief by revealing the beauty and necessity of social forms.

Of course social obedience and belief can serve evil as well as good ends. Given that it can be extremely difficult to know the difference, what paths are open to the ironic social scientist who is faced with a clearly unacceptable use of power? The example of the activist suggests one answer.

Example #4: Activists

In scores of countries around the world, in hundreds of towns, thousands of ordinary people daily devote their time and resources for years at a time, often jeopardizing their safety and livelihood, to correct injustices perpetrated by powerful governments against their fellow man. The chances of any one of these people achieving anything close to the goals for which they tirelessly struggle are ludicrously small. Collectively such people are probably having an effect on human history, but that effect is uncertain, unmeasureable, largely unknown, and possibly reversible by the arbitrary use of force. What motivates these people? Are they so naïve they expect to succeed? Are they expressing private hostility in a socially acceptable way? Are they blindly following their upbringing or the commands of charismatic leaders? Are they simply self-destructive?

All these motives are probably present in some activists some of the time. But I know many of them, either personally or by reputation or written evidence, and I think the majority are neither neurotics nor fools. Many know the odds against success; many are unfettered by metaphysical beliefs. Some do get frightened or discouraged, and quit. But what seems to keep these remarkably happy and well-adjusted people at their sisyphean work is an ironic appreciation of their condition. Faced with the choice between hopeless resignation and absurd rebellion, they have chosen the latter. Having made the choice, they have found what Camus calls the "passion and freedom" of refusing to play someone else's absurd game—which refusal is itself a game, to be sure. They are like novelists writing their own lives; and like novelists their loving action touches the heart—this time a rebellious heart—of humanity at large.

Irony does not necessarily lead to activism, but it is, I believe, the social science philosophy most compatible with the activist's attitude. Precritical positivist philosophy—for example, utilitarianism—tends to be deflected from radical action by the logical absurdity of individual rebellion. The critical position has two advantages. First, it takes into account the absurdity of *not* rebelling. That is the form of its *awareness*. Second, it brackets both the absurdity and the awareness under the intuition of ultimate moral truth. This turns out to be, by the way, a highly practical outlook. If one has such an intuition, one feels much better when one lives according to it.

Hallmarks of Ironic Social Science

These examples should clarify the ironic attitude, and now that I have sketched its place in history and society perhaps I can distinguish it more vividly from its naïve surroundings. Whereas the precritical attitude primarily seeks to achieve greater and greater *certainty*, the ironic seeks to achieve *understandings* that, while remaining uncertain, are more and more *useful*. Of course precritical science aims at usefulness too, but it goes about it differently. The positivist assumption on which it rests locates knowledge in the perceivable world; it holds that the more closely we can predict how that world will behave, the better we have understood it, and the more useful our knowledge is. Since ordinarily there cannot be more than one explanation for our perceptions, science strives to eliminate the ambiguity that leads to competing explanations.

The ironic view rejects the idea that we can know in any final sense what the universe is like; it insists that we must be content with the explanations that serve our culturally and temporally limited human purposes. "Purposes" should be understood in the broadest sense, to include the sheer pleasure of feeling that we understand something important to us—as well as more socially practical ends. Moreover, since there are many purposes in the human world, it is sometimes wise to accept more than one explanation of a thing. Agreement among observers is nice when you can get it, because it enhances the satisfaction attending an understanding, but it is not the main goal of science.

Often the findings of precritical and ironic science agree. But when they do not, the characteristics that distinguish the ironic attitude are:

- It strives to preserve the relevance of its findings to human purposes. As such, it seeks interpretations that allow real actors—not "experts"—to judge better the outcomes of real acts—behaviors-in-context, not abstract categories of action.

- In the interest of such practicality, it tends to preserve the complexity of the phenomena under study.

- This complexity leads to explanations that cannot be subjected to experimental control and verification. "Progress," in the positivist sense of increasing agreement on a growing body of theory, is therefore impossible.

- It takes full account of the variability of human situations, and makes full use of the human ability to appreciate complex patterns. This rarely results in high-level theory-building, except in the sense that general explanations are used heuristically, "as if" they explained a wide range of facts.

- Being tolerant of complexity and variation, it is able to take into account the personal *understandings* that play a key role in all human behavior. The understandings of people under study, and those of the observer become foci of its explanations. It shies away from the study of human aggregates that conceal variations in the understandings of their members.

- Its sensitivity to human understandings usually results in greater acceptance of the diverse purposes of individuals and groups. Ironic social science is less interested in prediction and control than in the promotion of *self*-understanding.

- It accepts paradox and uncertainty. Since there can be many explanations of the world, it is unnecessary to compromise the usefulness of an understanding in search of greater certainty.

- Being aware of its own limitations, it is full of humor.

From this description it should not be inferred that ironic social science is less rigorous or less disciplined than the precritical kind. On the contrary, the search for useful understandings places on the ironic social scientist a heavy intellectual burden: He must know the meaning systems of his subjects, his colleagues, and his clientele; he must have a feeling for the broadest interrelations of the phenomena he studies; and he must have a sense of the relationship among his ideas, the interest groups to which they are relevant, and the power relations of those interest groups. For this reason, ironic social science must study the structures and limitations of all the cultures in which it takes part: nation, social class, profession, and historical era. Historical self-consciousness not only provides the philosophic framework upon which this kind of science is built; it also constitutes an important source of its daily needs for knowledge.

On Teaching Ironic Social Science

Ironic social science is already being taught systematically in schools where relativist/holist anthropology, sociology, or psychology are offered, and there are undoubtedly many productive ways of teaching it. Although it is not within the scope of this book to lay out a curriculum for it, it might help to clarify the idea of such a science if I describe some methods I have found useful in conveying it to students.

One such method is the extensive use of *naturalistic descriptions of behavior*. The complexity of human behavior, its intimate connection with the meanings given it by the actors, and the difficulty of understanding it through reductionist theory or quasiexperimental method, are best conveyed by having students at all levels of training work with relatively unanalyzed narrative descriptions of real or realistic behavior. Depending on the goals of a given course or program, the experience of the students, and the length of the training exercise, a teacher might choose one or more of the following kinds of descriptive material:

1. *Ethnographic, historical, or biographical description:* Case studies of individuals, events, or groups are useful if the analytic hand of the collector is not too heavy. Such materials are easy to use in looking for pattern, because they are always collected for a purpose, and based on some preconceived notions of what is there. The ironic perspective can be clarified by looking at such materials: (a) as an example of a point of view; (b) as source material for answers to a practical question; and (c) as an example of the kinds of things theories are based upon.

2. *Fiction:* Novels, short stories, plays, films, and even poetry can be used to generate explanations and answer questions as well. Again, such materials are easier to use than unanalyzed field notes, because they are much more highly structured and "theory-rich." They are also pleasant to work with. Since students generally accept the idea that creative fiction has a structure, it is very instructive for them to see that it can be analyzed a variety of ways, with a variety of practical outcomes.

3. *Raw Field Notes:* Observational materials collected by students themselves, or by someone else, have the advantage of being relatively unstructured, and useful for teaching the pitfalls of interpretation. Of course it takes time, patience, and skill to learn anything from them. Some students learn the ironic attitude well if they alternate theory-rich readings about a group with raw field materials on that group. This helps them understand: (a) where the sense of understanding comes from; and (b) how the same material can be understood in different ways.

Another useful method is to ask students to think about the *uses of knowledge.* While the use of descriptive material reaches *down* the ladder of generality, and helps show relationships between what is observed and what is inferred, thinking about the uses of inference reaches *up* the ladder, helping to show the positions of ideas in the system of knowledge. A simple example would be to look at Marxism and Weberian historical relativism as ways of explaining history. If the theories are seen in the historical context of the late nineteenth century, and their effects on politics and social science are discussed, the dependence of these *and all other theories* on historical context and on human purposes can be more clearly understood.

Attending to the historical and political contexts of theories is one way of approaching utility. Another is to get students to focus consistently on the uses of their own ideas. Of course, it is important not to be too judgemental about the answers to questions of utility, as long as the answers are honest and make sense. Aesthetic satisfaction and earning a doctorate are perfectly good goals, as long as the ideas fit the uses. The important point is to escape the fallacy of positivism, whereby ideas are held to approximate some abstract truth.

Finally, ironic social science is taught by encouraging students to rely on intuition, feeling, and imagery as well as on logic in developing and evaluating ideas. Whereas intuition itself is not a reliable guide to excellence in science, it is ultimately our only criterion for the measurement of understanding. To have this conclusion seconded, one need not rely on Plato or Erasmus; in the history of science, great figures as diverse as Johannes Kepler, Wilhelm Wundt, August Comte, and Wolfgang Pauli have recognized the foundation of all knowledge in intuition. Wrote Pauli:

> The process of understanding in nature, together with the joy that man feels in understanding, i.e., in becoming acquainted with new knowledge, seems therefore to rest upon a correspondence, a coming into congruence of preexistent internal images of the human psyche with external objects and their behavior. (Heisenberg 1955:65)

In this quote, Pauli seems to say for physics some of the essential things I have been saying for social science: The end of science is understanding, in the service of human purposes (here, joy), and the method is intuition. Pauli needs only add the crucial dimension of historical self-consciousness to arrive at a close approximation of my thesis. In this respect, the next sentence of his remark is not bad:

> This view of natural knowledge goes back, of course, to Plato and was...also plainly adopted by Kepler. (ibid.)

Physics, too, is a form of consciousness, and as such is apparently improved by knowing its place in history.

References

Adler, A. *Understanding Human Nature.* Cleveland: World Publishing, 1927.

Adorno, T. W., E. Frenkel-Brunswik, D. J. Levinson, and R. N. Sanford. *The Authoritarian Personality.* New York: Harper & Row, 1950.

Albright, W. F. *Archaeology and the Religion of Israel.* Garden City: Doubleday & Co., 1969.

Alighieri, D. *The Divine Comedy.* Vol. 20 of *Harvard Classics.* New York: Collier & Son, 1910.

Allport, G. *Pattern and Growth in Personality.* New York: Holt, Rinehart, 1961.

Ames, L. "Arnold Lucius Gesell." *Science* 134, 1961, pp. 266-267.

Ardrey, R. *African Genesis.* New York: Atheneum Publications, 1961.

Arendt, H. *The Human Condition.* Chicago: University of Chicago Press, 1958.

Aries, P. *Centuries of Childhood.* London: Jonathan Cape, 1962.

Aristotle. *Nicomacean Ethics.* Trans. J. A. K. Thompson. London: Penguin Books, 1955.

Augustine. *Confessions.* Vol. 7 of *Harvard Classics.* New York: Collier & Son, 1909.

Balikci, A. *The Netsilik Eskimo.* New York: Natural History Press, 1970.

Barry, H., I. Child, and M. Bacon. "Relation of Child Training to Subsistence Economy." *Amer. Anthropologist* 61 (1) 1959, pp. 51-63.

Barth, F. "Analytical Dimensions in the Comparison of Social Organizations," *Amer. Anthropologist* 74 (1-2) 1972, pp. 207-220.

Bell, D. *The Coming of Post-Industrial Society: A Venture in Social Forecasting.* New York: Basic Books, 1973.

Bellah, R. N. *Beyond Belief.* New York: Harper & Row, 1970.

Bellah, R. N., R. Madsen, W. M. Sullivan, A. Swidler, and S. M. Tipton. *Habits of the Heart: Individualism and Commitment in American Life.* Berkeley: University of California Press, 1985.

Benedict, R. *Patterns of Culture.* New York: Houghton Mifflin, 1934.

Berndt, T., and E. Ziegler. "Developmental Psychology." In *Topics in the History of Psychology,* edited by G. A. Kimble and K. Schlesinger. vol. 2, pp. 115-150. Hillsdale, N.J.: L. Erlbaum, 1985.

Bettelheim, B. "Individual and Mass Behavior in Extreme Situations." *J. Abnorm. Soc. Psych.* 30, 1943, pp. 417-452.

Bishop, M. *The Middle Ages.* New York: McGraw Hill, 1970.

Block, J. *The Q-Sort Method in Personality Assessment and Psychiatric Research.* Springfield, Ill.: Charles C. Thomas, 1961.

———*Lives Through Time.* Berkeley: Bancroft Books, 1971.

Bloom, A. *The Closing of the American Mind.* New York: Simon & Schuster, 1987.

Bloom, B. *Stability and Change in Human Characteristics.* New York: John Wiley & Sons, 1964.

Boring, E. *A History of Experimental Psychology.* New York: Appleton-Century-Crofts, 1957.

Bourguignon, E. *Religion, Altered States of Consciousness, and Social Change.* Columbus, Ohio: State University Press, 1973.

Brennan, Sr. M. R. E. *The Intellectual Virtues According to the Philosophy of St. Thomas Aquinas.* Washington, D.C.: Catholic University of America Press, 1941.

Bronowski, J. *The Common Sense of Science.* Cambridge: Harvard University Press, 1979.

Bühler, C. "Genetic Aspects of the Self." *Annals of the New York Academy of Sciences* 96, 1962, pp. 730-764.

Burton, M., and L. Kirk. "Sex Differences in Maasai Cognition of Personality and Social Identity." *American Antrhopologist* 81, 1979, pp. 841-873.

Butler, J. M., and L. N. Rice. "Adience, Self-Actualization, and Drive Theory." In *Concepts of Personality*, edited by J. M. Wepman and R. W. Hine, pp. 79-110. Chicago: Aldine, 1963.

Campbell, J. *The Masks of God: Occidental Mythology.* New York: Viking Press, 1964.

Cellini, B. *Autobiography.* Vol. 31 of *Harvard Classics.* New York: Collier & Son, 1910.

Charlton, M. "Psychiatry and Ancient Medicine." In *Historic Derivations of Modern Psychiatry*, edited by I. Galdston, pp. 9-18. New York: McGraw Hill, 1967.

Chenu, M. *Toward Understanding St. Thomas.* Chicago: Henry Regnery Co., 1964.

Clark, K. *Civilization.* New York: Harper & Row, 1969.

Clayton, V. and J. Birren. "The Development of Wisdom across the Life Span: A Reexamination of an Ancient Topic." In *Life Span Development and Behavior, Vol. III,* edited by P. Baltes and D. Brim, pp. 104-135. New York: Academic Press, 1980.

Cohen, Y. "Food and Its Vicissitudes: A Cross-cultural Study of Sharing and Nonsharing." In *Social Structure and Personality: A Casebook*, edited by Y. Cohen, pp. 312-350. New York: Holt, Rinehart, 1961.

Copleston, F. *Aquinas.* New York: Penguin, 1955.

———*A History of Philosophy.* Part 1 of Vol. 1, *Greece and Rome.* Garden City: Doubleday & Co. 1962a.

———*A History of Philosophy.* Part 2 of Vol. 2, *Medieval Philosophy.* Garden City: Doubleday & Co. 1962b.

Crabtree, J. M., and K. E. Moyer. *Bibliography of Aggressive Behavior.* New York: Alban R. Liss, Inc., 1977.

Cuffe, H. *The Differences of the Ages of Man's Life.* London, 1626.

Curle, A. *Mystics and Militants*. London: Tavistock, 1972.

D'Andrade, R. G. "Cultural Meaning Systems." In *Culture Theory: Essays in Mind, Self, and Society*, edited by R. Schweder and R. Levine, pp. 88-122. Cambridge: Cambridge University Press, 1984.

Descartes, R. "The Passions of the Soul." 1650. In *Readings in the History of Psychology*, edited by W. Dennis, pp. 25-31. New York: Appleton-Century-Crofts, 1948.

Dreyfus, H., and P. Rabinow. "What is Maturity? Habermas and Foucault on 'What is Enlightenment?'" In *Foucault, a Critical Reader*, edited by D. Hoy, pp. 109-121.

Durant, W., and A. Durant. *The Age of Louis XIV*. New York: Simon & Schuster, 1963.

Eisely, L. *Darwin's Century*. Garden City: Doubleday, Inc., 1961.

Elder, G. H., Jr. *Children of the Great Depression: Social Change in Life Experience*. Chicago: University of Chicago Press, 1974.

Eliade, M. *Cosmos and History: The Myth of the Eternal Return*. New York: Harper & Bros., 1959.

Elias, N. *The Civilizing Process*. Vol. 1, *The History of Manners*. New York: Pantheon, 1978.

——— *The Civilizing Process*. Vol. 2, *Power and Civility*. New York: Pantheon, 1982.

Ellenberger, H. .F. *The Discovery of the Unconscious*. New York: Basic Books, 1970.

Englebert, O. *Saint Francis of Assisi: A Biography*. Ann Arbor: Servant Books, 1965.

Erasmus, D. *The Praise of Folly*. 1509. Trans. L. F. Dean. New York: Hendricks House-Farrar-Strauss, 1946.

Erikson, E. H. *Childhood and Society*. New York: Norton, 1963.

——— *Gandhi's Truth*. New York: Norton, 1969.

Evans-Pritchard, E. E. *The Nuer*. Oxford: Oxford University Press, 1940.

Faris, R. E. L. *Chicago Sociology: 1920-1932*. Chicago: University of Chicago Press, 1967.

Fenichel, O. *The Psychoanalytic Theory of Neurosis.* New York: Norton, 1945.

Folta, J., and L. Schatzman. "Trends in Public Urban Psychiatry in the United States." *Soc. Prob.* 16 (1) 1968, pp. 60-72.

Fortes, M. *Oedipus and Job in West African Religion.* Cambridge: Cambridge University Press, 1959.

——"Age, Generation, and Social Structure." In *Age and Antrhopological Theory,* edited by D. I. Kertzer and J. Keith, pp. 99-122. Ithaca: Cornell University Press, 1984.

Foucault, M. *The History of Sexuality.* Vol. 1, *An Introduction.* New York: Pantheon, 1978.

——"On the Geneology of Ethics: An Overview of Work in Progress." In *The Foucault Reader,* edited by P. Rabinow, pp. 340-372. New York: Pantheon, 1984a.

——"What is Enlightenment?" In *The Foucault Reader,* edited by P. Rabinow, pp. 32-50. New York: Pantheon, 1984b.

Fowler, D. H., L. J. Fowler, and L. Landin. "Old Age in Preindustrial Literature." In *Old Age in Preindustrial Society,* edited by P. N. Stearns, pp. 19-45. New York: Holmes & Meier, 1982.

Frenkel-Brunswik, E. "Psychoanalysis and Personality Research." *Psychological Issues,* 8 (3) Monograph 31, 1974, pp. 36-57.

Freud, A. *The Ego and the Mechanisms of Defense.* New York: International University Press, 1936.

Freud, S. "Infantile Sexuality." 1910. In *The Basic Writings of Sigmund Freud,* edited by A. A. Brill, pp. 580-603. New York: Modern Library, 1938.

——*Totem and Taboo.* New York: Moffat, Yard, 1918.

——*Civlization and Its Discontents.* Standard Edition. Vol. 21. London: Hogarth, 1930.

Fromm, E. *Psychoanalysis and Religion.* New Haven: Yale University Press, 1950.

——*The Sane Society.* New York: Reinert, 1955.

Galdston, I. "Psyche and Soul: Psychiatry in the Middle Ages." In *Historic*

Derivations of Modern Psychiatry, edited by I. Galdston, pp. 19-40. New York: McGraw-Hill, 1967.

Geertz, C. "From the Native's Point of View: On the Nature of Anthropological Understanding." In *Culture Theory: Essays in Mind, Self, & Emotion,* edited by R. Schweder and R. Levine, pp. 123-136. Cambridge: Cambridge University Press, 1984.

Gergen, K. "The Emerging Crisis in Lifespan Developmental Theory." In *Life-Span Development and Behavior,* edited by P. Baltes and O. Brim, vol. 3, pp. 31-63. New York: Academic Press, 1980.

Gesell, A. "Arnold Gesell." In *A History of Psychology in Autobiography,* edited by E. Boring, H. Langfeld, H. Werner and R. Yerkes, vol. 4, pp. 123-142. New York: Russell & Russell, 1952.

Gilligan, C. "In a Different Voice: Women's Conceptions of Self and of Morality." *Harvard Educational Review* 47 (4) Nov. 1977, pp. 481-517.

———*In a Different Voice: Psychological Theory and Women's Development.* Cambridge: Harvard University Press, 1982.

Goethe, J. W. von *Faust.* 1808. Trans. by B. Taylor. New York: Random House, 1950.

Goffman, E. *The Presentation of Self in Everyday Life.* Garden City: Doubleday & Co., 1959.

Goldstein, K. *The Organism.* New York: American Book, 1939.

Gordon, C. *The Ancient Near East.* New York: W. W. Norton, 1965.

Gouldner, A., and R. Peterson. *Notes on Technology and the Moral Order.* Indianapolis: Bobbs-Merrill, 1962.

Gutmann, D. "The Country of Old Men: Cross-cultural Studies in the Psychology of Later Life." In *Culture and Personality: Contemporary Readings,* edited by R. LeVine, pp. 95-124. Chicago: Aldine, 1974.

Haan, N. *Coping and Defending: Processes of Self-Environment Organization.* New York: Academic Press, 1977.

Habermas, J. *Theory and Practice.* Trans. by J. Viertel. Boston: Beacon Press, 1973.

Harris, M. "The Economy Has No Surplus?" *Amer. Anthropologist* 61 (2) 1959, pp. 185-199.

———*Culture, Man and Nature.* New York: Crowell, 1971.

Hartmann, H. *Ego Psychology and the Problem of Adaptation.* New York: International Universities Press, 1939.

Havighurst, R. J. "History of Developmental Psychology: Socialization and Personality Development Through the Life Span." In *Life Span Developmental Psychology: Personality and Socialization,* edited by P. Baltes and W. Schaie, pp. 4-25. New York: Academic Press, 1973.

Heisenberg, W. *The Physicist's Conception of Nature.* New York, Harcourt, Brace, 1955. Quoted in *Quantum Questions,* edited by K. Wilber, pp. 55-68. Boston: Shambhala, 1984.

Hendrick, I. "Instinct and Ego During Infancy." *Psychoan. Quart.* 11, 1942, pp. 33-58.

Henry, J. *Culture Against Man.* New York: Random House, 1963.

Hobbes, T. "Of Man, Being the First Part of the Leviathan." 1651. *Harvard Classics.* Vol. 35 New York: Collier & Son, 1910.

———"Human Nature." 1651. In *Readings in the History of Psychology,* edited by W. Dennis, pp. 32-41. New York: Appleton-Century-Crofts, 1948.

Holborn, H. *A History of Modern Germany, 1648-1840.* Princeton: Princeton University Press, 1964.

Huizinga, J. *Erasmus and the Age of Reformation.* New York: Scribner's, 1924.

———*The Waning of the Middle Ages.* Garden City: Doubleday Inc., 1954.

Ignatius [Saint, of Loyola]. *Autobiography.* 1550. Edited, with introduction and notes, by J. Olin. Trans. by J. O'Callaghan. New York: Harper & Row, 1974.

Jaeger, W. *Paideia: The Ideals of Greek Culture.* Vol. 2. New York: Oxford University Press, 1942.

Jahoda, M. "Toward a Social Psychology of Mental Health." In *Symposium on the Healthy Personality,* edited by M. Senn, pp. 211-230. New York: J. Macy, Jr. Foundation, 1950.

———*Current Concepts of Positive Mental Health.* New York: Basic Books, 1958.

James, W. *The Varieties of Religious Experience.* 1898. New York: New American Library, 1958.

Janik, A., and S. Toulmin. *Vittgenstein's Vienna.* New York: Touchstone Books, 1973.

Jospers, K. "The Axial Age of Human History," *Commentary* 6, 1948, pp. 430-435.

Jones, E. "The Criteria of Success in Treatment." In *Papers on Psychoanalysis,* 5th ed., edited by E. Jones, pp. 379-383. Boston: Beacon Press, 1948.

Jones, M., N. Bayley, J. MacFarlane, and M. Honzik, eds. *The Course of Human Development.* Waltham, Mass.: Xerox Publishing, 1971.

Kagan, J., R. B. Kearsley, and P. R. Zelazo. *Infancy: Its Place in Human Development.* Cambridge: Harvard University Press, 1978.

Kaufman, S. *The Ageless Self.* Madison: University of Wisconsin Press, 1986.

Kaye, K. "Epilogue: Piaget's Forgotten Novel," *Psychology Today* 14 (6) 1980, p. 102.

Kett, J. F. *Adolescence in America, 1890 to the Present.* New York: Basic Books, 1977.

Kluckhohn, C., and H. Murray. "Personality Formation: The Determinants." In *Prsonality in Nature, Society, and Culture,* edited by C. Kluckhohn and H. Murray, pp. 53-67. New York: Knopf. 1959.

Knowles, D. *The Evolution of Medieval Thought.* London: Longmans, Green & Co., 1962.

Kohlberg, L. "The Development of Children's Orientations Toward a Moral Order: A Sequence in the Development of Moral Thought." *Vita Humana,* 6, 1963, pp. 11-33.

———"Continuities in Childhood and Adult Moral Development Revisited." In *Life-span Developmental Psychology: Personality and Socialization,* edited by P. Baltes and W. Schaie, pp. 179-204. New York: Academic Press, 1973.

Kohut, H. *Self Psychology and the Humanities: Reflections on a New Psychoanalytic Approach.* New York: Norton, 1985.

Kretschmer, E. *Physique and Character.* New York: Harcourt, Brace, 1931.

Langness, L. L. *The Study of Culture.* San Francisco: Chandler & Sharp, 1977.

Lasch, C. *The Culture of Narcissism.* New York: Warner Books, 1979.

Lawrence, D. H. *Sons and Lovers.* 1913. New York: Viking Press, 1968.

Leclerq, J., F. Vandenbroucke, L. Cognet, and L. Bouyer. *A History of Christian Spirituality.* Vol. 2, *The Spirituality of the Middle Ages.* New York: Seabury Press, 1982.

Leighton, D., J. Harding, D. Macklin, A. Macmillan, and A. Leighton. *The Character of Danger.* New York: Basic Books, 1963.

Lerner, M. J. and S. C. Lerner, eds. *The Justice Motive in Social Behavior.* New York: Plenum Press, 1981.

Levinson, D. J., C. Darrow, E. Klein, M. Levinson, and B. McKee. *The Seasons of a Man's Life.* New York: Knopf, 1978.

Lindner, R. *Prescription for Rebellion.* Westport: Greenwood Press, 1952.

Locke, J. "Some Thoughts Concerning Education." 1692. In Vol. 37 of *Harvard Classics,* New York: Collier & Son, 1910.

Lynd, R. S., and H. M. Lynd. *Middletown.* New York: Harcourt, Brace, & World, 1929.

Maas, H. S., and J. A. Kuypers. *From Thirty to Seventy,* San Francisco: Jossey-Bass, 1974.

Malinowski, B. *Crime and Custom in Savage Society.* New York: Harcourt, Brace & World, 1926.

Marshall, L. "Sharing, Talking, and Giving: Relief of Social Tensions among the Kung Bushmen." *Africa* 31, 1961, pp. 231-249.

Maslow, A. *Motivation and Personality.* New York: Harper & Row, 1951.

———"A Conversation with Abraham H. Maslow." *Psychology Today* 2 (2) 1968a.

——— *Toward a Psychology of Being,* Second ed. Princeton: van Nostrand, 1968b.

Mead, M. *And Keep Your Powder Dry.* New York: Arno Press, 1942.

Mills, C. W. *The Sociological Imagination,* Oxford: Oxford University Press, 1959.

Menninger, K. *The Vital Balance.* New York: Viking Press, 1963.

Monahan, W. B. *The Psychology of St. Thomas Aquinas and the Divine Revelations.* London: Ebenezer Baylis & Son, n.d.

Montagu, A. *On Being Human.* New York: Hawthorne Books, 1950.

———*The Nature of Human Aggression.* New York: Oxford University Press, 1976.

Moore, S. "Old Age in a Life-term Social Arena: Some Chagga of Kilimanjaro in 1974." In *Life's Career—Aging,* edited by B. Myerhoff and A. Simic, pp. 23-76. Beverly Hills: Sage, 1978.

Mora, G. "From Demonology to Narrenturm." In *Historic Derivations of Modern Psychiatry,* edited by I. Galdston, pp. 41-73. New York: McGraw-Hill, 1967.

Munn, N. "The Translation of Subjects into Objects in Walbiri and Pitjantjara Myth." In *Australian Aboriginal Anthropology,* edited by R. Berndy. Nedlands: University of West Australia Press, 1970.

Murray, H. *Explorations in Personality.* New York: Oxford University Press, 1938.

Myers, F. "Emotions and the Self: A Theory of Personhood and Political Order among the Pintupi Aborigines." *Ethos* 7, (4) 1979, pp. 343-370.

Needleman, J. *A Sense of the Cosmos: The Encounter of Modern Science and Ancient Truth.* Garden City: Doubleday & Co., 1975.

Nietzsche, F. *Thus Spoke Zarathustra.* 1891. Trans. by W. Kaufmann. New York: The Viking Press, 1966.

Norton, D. *Personal Destinies: A Philosophy of Ethical Individualism,* Princeton: Princeton University Press, 1976.

Ochs, E., and B. B. Schieffelin. "Language Acquisition and Socialization: Three Developmental Stories and Their Implications." In *Culture Theory: Essays in Mind, Self, and Emotion,* edited by R. Schweder and R. LeVine, pp. 276-332. Cambridge: Cambridge University Press, 1984.

Onians, R. B., *The Origins of European Thought.* New York: Arno Press, 1951.

Ortega y Gasset, J. *What is Philosophy?* New York: Norton, 1960.

Ortiz, A. *The Tewa World.* Chicago: University of Chicago Press, 1969.

Parkes, H. *Gods and Men: The Origins of Western Culture.* New York: Vintage, 1959.

Pascal, B. "Thoughts on Mind and on Style." 1650. In vol. 48 of *Harvard Classics,* pp. 9-23. New York: Collier & Son, 1910.

Plato. *The Crito.* In *Great Dialogues of Plato,* edited by W. H. D. Warmington and P. G. Rouse, pp. 447-459. New York: New American Library, 1956.

—— *The Republic.* In *Great Dialogues of Plato,* pp. 118-422.

—— *The Symposium.* In *Great Dialogues of Plato,* pp. 69-117.

Polanyi, K. *The Great Transformation.* New York: Rinehart, 1962.

Pope, A. "An Essay on Man." 1734. In *The Selected Poetry of Pope,* edited by M. Price, pp. 123-163. New York: New American Library, 1970.

Quadagno, J. S. *Aging in Early Industrial Society.* New York: Academic Press, 1982.

Radin, P. *Primitive Man as Philosopher.* New York: Dover Publications, 1927.

Redfield, R., and M. Singer. "The Cultural Role of Cities." In *Classic Essays on the Culture of Cities,* edited by R. Sennett, New York: Meredith Corp, 1969 (first published in *Econ. Development & Culture Change,* 3, 1954).

Reich, C. *The Greening of America.* New York: Random House, 1970.

Resta, R. *Dante e la filosofia dell' amore.* Bologna, 1935.

Ricks, C. "Introduction." In *John Milton: Paradise Lost and Paradise Regained,* edited by C. Ricks, pp. vii-xxx. New York: New American Library, 1968.

Rieff, P. *Freud: The Mind of the Moralist.* New York: Viking Press, 1959.

Riegel, K. "Toward a Dialectical Theory of Development." *Hum. Devel.* 18, 1975. pp. 50-64.

Riese, W. "The Neurophysiologic Phase in the History of Psychiatric Thought." In *Historic Derivations of Modern Psychiatry,* edited by I. Galdston, pp. 75-137. New York: McGraw Hill, 1967.

Riesman, D. *The Lonely Crowd.* New Haven: Yale University Press, 1950.

——, R.J. Potter, and J. Watson. "Sociability, Permissiveness, and Equality." *Psychiatry* 23, 1960, pp. 334-336.

Rosaldo, M. "Toward an Anthropology of Self and Feeling." In *Culture Theory: Essays in Mind, Self, & Emotion,* edited by R. Schweder and R. LeVine, pp. 136-157. Cambridge: Cambridge University Press, 1984.

Rudner, R. *Philosophy of Social Science.* Englewood Cliffs, N.J.: Prentice-Hall, 1966.

Sampson, G. *Writing Systems: A Linguistic Introduction.* Stanford: Stanford University Press, 1985.

Saul, L. *Emotional Maturity: The Development and Dynamics of Personality.* Philadelphia: Lippincott, 1960.

Schiamburg, L. B. *Human Development.* 2d ed. New York: Macmillan, 1985.

Schweder, R., and E. Bourne. "Does the Concept of the Person Vary Cross-Culturally?" In *Culture Theory: Essays in Mind, Self, & Emotion,* edited by R. Schweder and R. LeVine, pp. 158-199. Cambridge: Cambridge University Press, 1984.

Scroggs, J. R. *Key Ideas in Personality Theory.* St. Paul: West Publishing Co., 1985.

Searle, J. R. *Speech Acts: An Essay in the Philosophy of Language.* Cambridge: Cambridge University Press, 1969.

Sears, R. "L. M. Terman, Pioneer in Mental Measurement." *Science* 125, (3255) 1957, pp. 978-979.

Sheldon, H. *Varieties of Temperament.* New York: Harper & Row, 1942.

Simmel, G. 1902. "The Metropolis and Mental Life." In *The Sociology of Georg Simmel,* Trans. and edited by K. Wolff, pp. 409-424. New York: The Free Press, 1950.

Skinner, B. F. *Beyond Freedom and Dignity.* New York: Bantam Books, 1971.

Slater, P. *The Pursuit of Loneliness: American Culture at the Breaking Point.* Boston: Beacon Press, 1970.

Smith, M. B. *Social Psychology and Human Values.* Chicago: Aldine, 1969.

————"The Metaphorical Basis of Selfhood." In *Culture and Self: Asian and Western Perspectives,* edited by A. Marsella, G. DeVos and F. L. K. Hsu, pp. 56-88. New York: Tavistock Publications, 1985.

Smith-Rosenberg, C. "Sex as Symbol in Victorian Purity: An Ethnohistorical Analysis of Jacksonian America." In *Turning Points: Historical and Sociological Essays on the Family,* edited by J. Dennis and S. S. Boocock, pp. 212-24. Chicago: University of Chicago Press, 1978.

Smoke, R. *National Security and the Nuclear Dilemma.* New York: Random House, 1984.

Sorokin, P. *The Ways and Power of Love.* Boston: Beacon Press, 1954.

Spengler, O. *The Decline of the West.* Trans. by C. Atkinson. New York: A. Knopf, 1928.

Stevens, W. "Homunculus et La Belle Étoile." In *Harmonium.* New York: Knopf, 1953.

Stevens-Long, J. *Adult Life: Developmental Process.* Palo Alto: Mayfield Publishing, 1979.

Stone, L. *The Family, Sex, and Marriage in England, 1500-1800.* New York: Harper & Row, 1977.

Thomas, L. and P. Cooper. "Measurement and Incidence of Mystical Experiences: An Exploratory Study," *J. for the Scientific Study of Religion* 17 (4) 1978, pp. 433-437.

Thomas, W. I. *The Unadjusted Girl.* Boston: Little, Brown & Co., 1931.

Toffler, A. *Future Shock.* New York: Bantam Books, 1970.

Trilling, L. *Sincerity and Authenticity,* Cambridge: Harvard University Press, 1971.

Vaihinger, H. *The Philosophy of 'As If:' A System of the Theoretical, Practical, and Religious Fictions of Mankind.* 1899. New York: Harcourt, Brace & Co., 1925.

Vernant, J. P. *Myth and Society in Ancient Greece.* Atlantic Highlands, N.J.: Humanities Press, 1980.

Washburn, S. L. "Aggressive Behavior and Human Evolution." In *Social Change and Human Behavior: Mental Health Challenges in the Seventies,* edited by G. V. Coelho and E. A. Rubinstein, pp. 21-39. Rockville, Md.: National Institute of Mental Health, 1971.

Webster, A. M. *Ninth New Collegiate Dictionary.* Springfeld, Mass.: A . Merriam-Webster, 1984.

White, R. W. *Ego and Reality in Psychoanalytic Theory.* New York: International Universities Press, 1963.

———— *The Enterprise of Living.* New York: Holt, Rinehart, 1976.

Whitehead, A. N. *Science and the Modern World.* Cambridge: Cambridge University Press, 1926.

Whyte, W. H. *The Organization Man.* Garden City: Doubleday & Co., 1956.

Wrong, D. "The Oversocialized Conception of Man in Modern Sociology." *Amer. Sociol. Rev.* 26 (2) 1961, pp. 183-192.

Wylie, R. *The Self Concept.* Vol. 1. Lincoln, Neb.: University of Nebraska Press, 1974.

Zilbourg, G. *A History of Medical Psychology.* New York: Norton, 1941.

Zweig, S. *Erasmus of Rotterdam.* New York: Viking Press, 1934.

Index of Names

Abelard, P., 15, 47, 55, 57, 107, 109.
Adler, A., 119, 126, 190.
Albright, W., 33.
Alighieri, D. (Dante), 15, 55-57, 107-108, 157, 158, 189.
Allport, G., 87, 119.
Ames, L., 145.
Anderson, B., 106.
Anthony, Saint, 54.
Aquinas (See Thomas, Saint, Aquinas).
Ardrey, R., 175.
Arendt, H., 42, 49, 158.
Aries, P., 104.
Aristotle: contrast with Plato, 2, 15, 40, 43, 57, 93, 159-164, 193; Freud and, 127; in Enlightenment thought, 73, 134; in medieval thought, 57, 111; in Renaissance thought, 15-16; in scholastic thought, 15-16, 111; Kohlberg and, 159-162; medium of knowledge in, 99, 170; sense experience in, 115; Socrates and, 40; soul in, 100.
Augustine, Saint, 46, 50, 104, 106.
Avebury, Lord J., 19.

Averroes, 58, 74.

Bacon, M., 21.
Balikci, A., 22.
Bandura, A., 146.
Barry, H., 21.
Barth, F., 182.
Bateson, G., 208.
Bellah, R., 15-26, 30, 89, 102, 187.
Benedict, R., 20, 129.
Bentham, J., 73, 134, 160.
Berkeley, G., 128.
Bernard, Saint, of Clairveaux, 15, 47, 55, 84, 107, 108, 157.
Berndt, T., 145.
Bettelheim, B., 35.
Birren, J., 119.
Bishop, M., 46, 60, 61.
Blake, W., 78, 88.
Block, J., 87, 156.
Bloom, A., 3, 207.
Bloom, B., 87, 119, 149.
Boas, F., 138-129.
Bonaventure, Saint, 15, 47, 56, 57, 107.
Boring, E., 120, 121, 134, 138, 141, 143.

Index of Subjects